ABE'S YOUTH

★ ★ ★

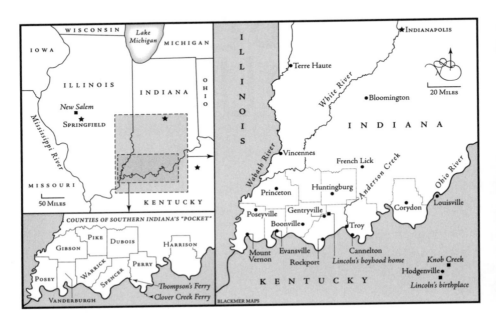

The Indiana Lincoln Inquiry's footprint in southwestern Indiana's eight-county "pocket," the same region where Abraham Lincoln spent his boyhood. New Harmony sits on the Wabash River southwest of Poseyville.

Map by Kate Blackmer. Reprinted from Everybody's History: Indiana's Lincoln Inquiry and the Quest to Reclaim a President's Past. *Copyright © 2012 by the University of Massachusetts Press.*

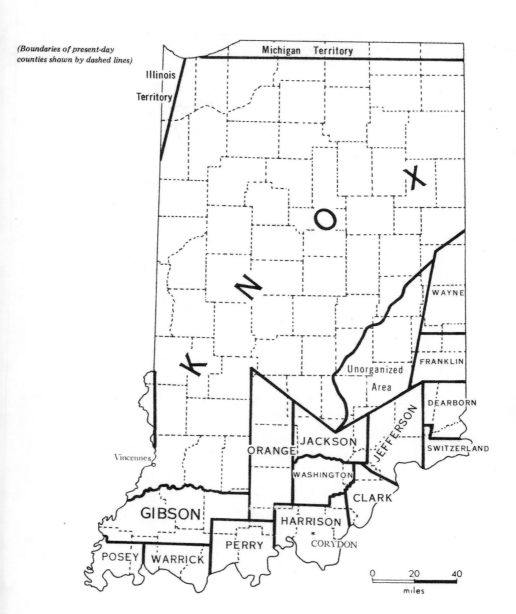

Michigan Territory

Illinois
Territory

K N O X

WAYNE

Unorganized
Area

FRANKLIN

DEARBORN

JACKSON

ORANGE

JEFFERSON

SWITZERLAND

Vincennes

WASHINGTON

CLARK

GIBSON

HARRISON

* CORYDON

PERRY

POSEY   WARRICK

0   20   40
miles

Boundaries of Indiana counties in 1816 with present-day
boundaries denoted by dotted lines.

US National Park Service.

ABE'S YOUTH

SHAPING THE FUTURE PRESIDENT

For Isabel & Camerone

★ ★ ★

With best wishes

EDITED BY
WILLIAM E. BARTELT
AND
JOSHUA A. CLAYBOURN

Enjoy your time with young Abe.

Bill Bartelt

INDIANA UNIVERSITY PRESS

This book is a publication of

Indiana University Press
Office of Scholarly Publishing
Herman B Wells Library 350
1320 East 10th Street
Bloomington, Indiana 47405 USA

iupress.indiana.edu

Manufactured in the United States of America

Library of Congress Cataloging-in-Publication Data

Names: Bartelt, William E., editor. | Claybourn, Joshua A., editor.
Title: Abe's youth : shaping the future president /
    edited by William E. Bartelt and Joshua A. Claybourn.
Description: Bloomington, Indiana : Indiana University Press, 2019. |
    Includes bibliographical references and index.
Identifiers: LCCN 2018049660 (print) | LCCN 2018051362 (ebook) | ISBN
    9780253043924 (e-book) | ISBN 9780253043917 (hc : alk. paper) | ISBN
    9780253043894 (pb : alk. paper)
Subjects: LCSH: Lincoln, Abraham, 1809–1865—Childhood and youth. |
    Presidents—United States—Biography. | Indiana—Biography.
Classification: LCC E457.32 (ebook) | LCC E457.32 .A24 2019 (print) | DDC
    973.7092 [B]—dc23
LC record available at https://lccn.loc.gov/2018049660

1 2 3 4 5   24 23 22 21 20 19

CONTENTS

FOREWORD

IN THE WINTER OF 1860, SHORTLY BEFORE ABRAHAM LINCOLN delivered his memorable speech at New York's Cooper Union, a newspaper there ran a thoughtful assessment of the candidate's early years in Indiana, where he lived between the ages of seven and twenty-one: "Probably six months in all of the rudest sort of schooling comprehends the whole of his technical education. But hard work and plenty of it, the rugged experiences of aspiring poverty, the wild sports and rude games of a newly and thinly populated forest region—the education born of the log cabin, the rifle, the ax, and the plow—made him the man he has since proved himself."[1]

To help tell the story of those formative years in Lincoln's life, during the 1920s intrepid members of the Southwestern Indiana Historical Society performed a great service to Lincoln scholarship by conducting what they termed the Lincoln Inquiry. They could not scour contemporary local newspapers, for none of those published in Lincoln's time survived, nor did they engage in the kind of painstaking work later done by Louis A. Warren in many unpublished records (census returns, tax books, election results, voter rolls, and the like).[2] Rather, they conducted research among people living in "the pocket," the southwest corner of the state where the Lincoln family settled in 1816 and remained until 1830.[3] The society's efforts have been ably chronicled by Keith Erekson in *Everybody's History: Indiana's Lincoln Inquiry and the Quest to Reclaim a President's Past*.[4] But the fruits of their labors have been hard to access, for some of the papers written by society members were unpublished and available only in manuscript form at various repositories, including the Willard and Central Libraries in Evansville and the William Henry Smith Memorial Library in Indianapolis. Moreover, some of their valuable information about Lincoln and his friends is found in the personal correspondence of the society's members, likewise available only in repositories such as the Indiana Historical Society.

The editors of the present volume have judiciously chosen some of the most informative essays and letters, have annotated and indexed them thoroughly, and are now making them available for students, scholars, and general readers interested in Lincoln's youth and adolescence. The most revealing material consists of reminiscences by people who knew Lincoln; but unfortunately by the time the Inquiry got under way few were still alive. Some, however, had shared their recollections of Lincoln with friends and family, who in turn passed them along to the society's investigators. Although that form of testimony is secondhand, it is useful nonetheless. In the following pages, such accounts can be found in contributions by Roscoe Kiper, Thomas Hardy Masterson, Elbert Hayford, and Will Adams.

Some society members had interviewed Lincoln's contemporaries well before the Inquiry was launched, most notably William Fortune and Anna C. O'Flynn. In 1881, Fortune had sought out informants who had known Lincoln. Among them, two were especially noteworthy: Elizabeth Crawford and Nathaniel Gentry. In his paper "Lincoln in Indiana," included in the present volume, Fortune tells how he became such an interviewer. Alas, his notes have not been published.[5]

Anna C. O'Flynn recalls in her paper, "The Environments of Abraham Lincoln in Indiana: The Best Witnesses," how she corresponded with many people who had known Lincoln: "I wrote to nearly everybody in the United States that knew Lincoln when a boy. I think I had over two hundred letters." Along with a friend, she toured Spencer County in 1895 and 1896 and reported that she spoke with "hundreds of good people" and wrote to many others.[6] Few of them had been contacted by earlier Lincoln sleuths. Anna O'Flynn shared her findings with Ida Tarbell, who used them for her book *The Early Life of Abraham Lincoln*[7] and her later full-scale biography.[8] Regrettably, the O'Flynn archive of letters has not been fully preserved; some of those missives, however, can be found in her papers at Vincennes University. (In that repository, researchers will also find useful interview material in the papers of Francis Marion Van Natter, author of *Lincoln's Boyhood: A Chronicle of His Indiana Years*.)[9]

In "The Lincolns in Spencer County," Ida D. Armstrong tells how, in the 1870s, her journalist father pursued his interest in Lincoln by talking with people who had known the future president. She does not reveal much of what he learned, but readers interested to know more about his findings should read his essay, "History of Spencer County," in *An Illustrated Historical Atlas of Spencer County, Indiana*.[10]

In addition to these firsthand and secondhand recollections of Lincoln, many papers in the present volume provide accounts of his friends and neighbors, thus helping to re-create the social, cultural, and intellectual environment of his youth. The picture they paint is rather rosy, for a goal of the society was to describe their region more positively than previous Lincoln authors had done. Readers should be prepared to encounter a fair amount of boosterism in these pages. In contrast, as Jesse N. Weik noted, somewhat harshly, Lincoln's "family were indeed a sorry lot—his father poor, inert, and void of ambition and the other members equally dull, improvident, and shiftless. To spend his days amid such unpalatable surroundings was a proposition from which he recoiled with feelings akin to horror. Therefore not long after reaching Macon county Illinois [in 1830] where the emigrant party from Indiana made their first settlement, he very discreetly left them behind, pushing on to a point in the adjoining county far enough away to escape the burden of their companionship."[11]

Historian Mark E. Neely Jr. reached a similar conclusion, which he put more gently in his noteworthy study, *Escape from the Frontier: Lincoln's Peculiar Relationship with Indiana*. Lincoln's Hoosier years, Neely wrote, "are not to be dismissed merely as an unhappy prelude to greatness. They hold a key to understanding Lincoln's early political career." He became a Henry Clay Whig, not an Andrew Jackson Democrat, because the Whigs "offered a program to change the West, to improve the defects of the environment of Lincoln's youth" through modernization and economic development, facilitated by government-backed banks, infrastructure improvements, and protective tariffs. "Lincoln's first political platform was an attempt to remedy the faults of his Indiana experience—too much wilderness, too little education."[12]

The best source of reminiscent information about Lincoln's time in Indiana is the treasure trove of recollections gathered by Lincoln's third law partner, William H. Herndon, published in a magisterial volume, *Herndon's Informants: Letters, Interviews, and Statements about Abraham Lincoln*.[13] Another good source of such information is a series of articles by J. Edward Murr, "Lincoln in Indiana," which appeared in the *Indiana Magazine of History*.[14] During his days as a minister in southwest Indiana in the late nineteenth century, he interviewed many local residents who either had known Lincoln or whose parents had done so. In addition, some of Murr's unpublished writings, including "The Wilderness Years of Abraham Lincoln," contain important recollections.[15]

The present volume is a worthy companion to those indispensable works.

Michael Burlingame

NOTES

1. *New York Tribune*, 25 February 1860, copied in the *Daily Illinois State Journal* (Springfield), 1 March 1860.

2. Louis A. Warren, *Lincoln's Youth: Indiana Years, Seven to Twenty-one, 1816–1830* (New York: Appleton, Century, Crofts, 1959).

3. The "pocket" consists of Vanderburgh, Dubois, Gibson, Perry, Pike, Posey, Spencer, and Warrick counties.

4. Amherst: University of Massachusetts Press, 2012.

5. Excerpts of those interviews can be found in William E. Bartelt, *There I Grew Up: Remembering Abraham Lincoln's Indiana Youth* (Indianapolis: Indiana Historical Society Press, 2008), 186–187.

6. Among those from whom she collected information were James Veatch, Green B. Taylor, Mrs. Emma Bullock, Mrs. Mary Adams, Mrs. Ruth Huff, Mrs. William Jones, Mrs. David Turnham, Henry Brooner, John W. Lamar, C. T. Doxey, Alfred McCoy, N. S. Roberts, P. A. Bruce, James W. Wartman, F. J. Charlton, George Riley, Roy I. Purcell, Thomas Adams, H. Watson McCoy, Peter L. Studebaker, Schuyler Colfax, William English, William Jones and his son William, Redmond Grigsby, Mrs. James Gentry, Mrs. Nancy Taylor Volke, W. M. Daniel, S. H. Burton, Frank Gahon, and Mary Inco.

7. New York: S. S. McClure, 1896.

8. Ida Tarbell, *The Life of Abraham Lincoln: Drawn from Original Sources and Containing Many Speeches, Letters, and Telegrams Hitherto Unpublished*, 2 vols. (New York: McClure, Phillips, 1900).

9. Washington, DC: Public Affairs Press, 1963.

10.   Philadelphia: D. J. Lake, 1879.

11.   Weik, manuscript of *The Real Lincoln* (Boston: Houghton Mifflin, 1922), Weik Papers, Lincoln Presidential Library, Springfield, Illinois. A toned-down version of this passage appears in the published edition of that volume.

12.   Mark E. Neely, *Escape from the Frontier* (Fort Wayne, IN: The Lincoln National Life Insurance Company, 1983).

13.   Edited by Douglas L. Wilson and Rodney O. Davis and published by the University of Illinois Press in 1998.

14.   *Indiana Magazine of History* 13, no. 4 (December 1917): 307–348; *Indiana Magazine of History* 14, no. 1 (March 1918): 18–74; and *Indiana Magazine of History* 14, no. 2 (June 1918): 148–182.

15.   These writings are located in the John Edward Murr papers at DePauw University in Greencastle, Indiana.

PREFACE

ALTHOUGH FOR NEARLY A CENTURY LINCOLN SCHOLARS HAVE directly or indirectly consulted the Indiana Lincoln Inquiry's work, Keith Erekson's 2012 book, *Everybody's History: Indiana's Lincoln Inquiry and the Quest to Reclaim a President's Past*, stimulated historians to reevaluate the Inquiry's important contributions to the history of Lincoln's life in Indiana. Because Erekson focused primarily on the Inquiry's benefits to public and oral history as a process (rather than feature the Inquiry's actual research), it prompted us to realize no comprehensive collection of the Indiana Lincoln Inquiry's work exists. We thank Mr. Erekson for inspiring us to undertake this project.

Between 1920 and 1939, the Southwestern Indiana Historical Society and the Indiana Lincoln Inquiry featured 369 presentations and produced approximately 217 papers. Although a single-volume collection of the Indiana Lincoln Inquiry's best work necessarily means that hundreds of papers and contributions do not appear here, in our judgment we present the most historically rigorous and significant contributions. To the extent you wish to see a comprehensive list of papers and publications of the Indiana Lincoln Inquiry, Mr. Erekson provides one in appendix B of his book.

Following this book's introduction, we organized each chapter into one of five categories. The various chapters comprise independent papers written at different times by different authors; consequently, each paper may be read as a stand-alone work. Yet, the personalities, places, and events described within these papers often overlap and receive attention in different ways in different articles. As a result, reading the book as a whole provides a far more complete picture of Abraham Lincoln's boyhood in Indiana.

Each chapter includes a brief statement of the paper's background and significance to Abraham Lincoln history. To distinguish between an original author's notes and ours, we place any author's notes in alphabetical endnotes and set our editorial commentary and annotations in numerical footnotes. A note following the author's name in each piece provides information available about the work's original presentation date and location as well as its initial publication and current location (if known).

The papers collected here may include occasional errors; after all, these authors wrote well after the events they describe. The essays may express substantial bias as these authors seek to overcome negative stereotypes about southwestern Indiana and often include family legends undocumented. Although we editors strive to provide comprehensive annotations and appropriate context, some bias and legends nonetheless remain unrefuted and uncorrected. Many manuscripts used in this book were transcribed or typed by the Works Progress Administration after the manuscript's original presentation. In the interest of comprehensibility, we editors made some modern standardization to capitalization, paragraph breaks, and punctuation. On the other hand, we generally retained the spelling exactly as in the manuscript, with inconsistencies and even errors maintained. In the few cases where spelling is corrected or modernized, changes are noted in brackets. By modern standards, some language may be considered racist or derogatory and inappropriate.

This book floats on a sea of friendship and help. First, we acknowledge the work of the Indiana Lincoln Inquiry. Their years of research made this book possible. Although we alone bear responsibility for shortcomings herein, we share credit for achievements with the authors featured here and the Indiana Lincoln Inquiry's leadership.

We also thank Chandler Lighty of the Indiana Historical Bureau, Eva Lindsay of the Spencer County Public Library, Daniel Smith of the Evansville-Vanderburgh Public Library, Steve Sisley and Daryl Lovell of the Spencer County Historical Society, Nancy Kaiser of the Lincoln Pioneer Village, and Patricia Sides and Stan Schmitt of Willard Library for their assistance in our research. Dr. Sherry Darrell provided valuable proofreading and editorial advice.

Finally, we wish to acknowledge our loving, supportive wives, Kathy Bartelt and Allyson Claybourn, for their patience, proofreading, feedback, and understanding as we spent countless hours researching, writing, and compiling this book. None of it would be possible without them.

ABE'S YOUTH

★ ★ ★

★ ★ ★

Introduction

ABRAHAM LINCOLN LIVED A QUARTER OF HIS LIFE, FROM AGE
seven to twenty-one, in southwestern Indiana. Yet for generations after
his death, biographers downplayed his Hoosier years, partly because
of perceptions of this area as backward at the time. Lincoln himself
rarely discussed his Indiana years in detail and once merely described
his youth as "the short and simple annals of the poor."[1] Lincoln's law
partner and biographer, William Herndon, dubbed the area "a stagnant,
putrid pool."[2] Many historians in the first couple of generations after
his death regarded this frontier as inconsequential to Lincoln's life and
career, except perhaps as a negative influence.

Other works contributed to a view of the Indiana frontier as cultur-
ally backward. Edward Eggleston's popular 1871 novel, *The Hoosier
Schoolmaster: A Story of Backwoods Life in Indiana*, associated the state
with ignorance, poverty, hardships, and an odd dialect.[3] Shortly after
the turn of the century, Juliet Strauss, known as a "woman in a tiny
out-of-the-way-town in Indiana," wrote a nationally syndicated column
titled, "The Ideas of a Plain Country Woman."[4] Cartoonist Kin Hubbard
found a national audience during World War I with his character Abe
Martin of Brown County, an unshaved Hoosier rube. Hubbard described
the cartoon's setting as "a rugged, almost mountainous, wooded section
of Indiana without telegraphic or railroad connections—a county whose
natives for the most part subsist by blackberrying, sassafras-mining and
basket making."[5] James Whitcomb Riley rose to fame around the same
time as a poet and best-selling author who frequently relied on rustic
subjects speaking in homely, countrified Indiana dialect. All of these
works influenced popular views of Lincoln's Hoosier youth.

In 1920, a small but determined group of amateur historians in southwestern Indiana determined to shed more proper light on Lincoln's formative years, filling in gaps in the historical record and attempting to reverse negative Indiana stereotypes. John E. Iglehart, a railroad lawyer who read voraciously and studied history, founded the Southwestern Indiana Historical Society (SWIHS) in January 1920. The society naturally attracted educated people with roots in southwestern Indiana and pride in the area's rich history. In a progressive move for its time, the SWIHS opened membership to include women; even more remarkable for the 1920s, women presented papers and held leadership positions. The SWIHS served as an umbrella organization for historical societies in nearby Vanderburgh, Warrick, Spencer, Posey, Perry, Gibson, Pike, Dubois, and occasionally Knox counties.[6] Although these amateurs sought to examine all historical aspects of the region, Lincoln's Hoosier roots formed the focal point of their efforts through what they called the Indiana Lincoln Inquiry: interviews with Lincoln's contemporaries and those who knew them. The SWIHS hoped Indiana's Lincoln Inquiry would improve the state's image by refuting myths and errors and revealing a more balanced account of Lincoln's life on the Indiana frontier. As SWIHS member and regional historian Logan Esarey wrote to Iglehart, "We can hardly blame the world for believing Eggleston so long as we do not furnish better evidence."[7]

Although the Inquiry examined some specific stories about Lincoln's youth, it focused primarily on Lincoln's southern Indiana environment and life between 1816 and 1830. Most notably, contributors to the Inquiry produced extensive biographies on the families in Lincoln's Indiana neighborhood and conducted interviews with their descendants. They excelled at contextualizing Lincoln within the broader framework of his neighborhood and the southwestern Indiana environment. Iglehart admitted that "the witnesses who knew Lincoln and whose memory was of historical value are all dead," but many important secondary sources remained available—and Indiana's Lincoln Inquiry was uniquely positioned to research and interview these secondary sources.[8] The Inquiry conducted much of its work collectively; Iglehart assigned topics for members to research, frequently focusing on interviews and oral history, and they then presented findings and papers at meetings throughout the year. Beginning with its founding in 1920 and lasting through its cessation in 1939, the SWIHS met 46 times, featured 369 presentations, and produced approximately 217 papers, now scattered in libraries and collections throughout the state.[9] This book comprises the Indiana Lincoln Inquiry's most historically rigorous and significant contributions, many of them out of print and unavailable since their first publication.

Iglehart asserted dominant leadership over the SWIHS, and although he was only a trial attorney and not a judge, many referred to him as Judge Iglehart out of respect. As one SWIHS member said of Iglehart's leadership, "He has made us read thousands and thousands of pages of pioneer history. . . . He has cajoled us, he has scolded us, he has even used his corporation methods to win his points. But always and always he has inspired us."[10] In 1923, Iglehart became president emeritus, and Thomas James de la Hunt, a wealthy socialite from Cannelton, became the second president of the SWIHS. The transition was not smooth, however. When Iglehart suspected that de la Hunt had appropriated someone else's research for his weekly newspaper column, "The Pocket Periscope," Iglehart withdrew an offer to publish a collection of those articles; soon thereafter, the two stopped speaking to each other.[11] Some of the division may have resulted from Iglehart's exacting standards for scholarship, but some no doubt arose from Iglehart's reluctance to hand over leadership. As SWIHS archivist Ethel McCollough wrote to de la Hunt during the transition, "Isn't Mr. Iglehart funny? This Society is his very own child and he can not bear to see it wander one inch out of the straight and narrow path."[12] Following de la Hunt as president was Boonville judge and state legislator Roscoe Kiper, who added controversy by prohibiting the publication of Indiana Lincoln Inquiry papers until he could publish his own definitive history of Lincoln in Indiana.[13] The fourth president of SWIHS, Bess V. Ehrmann, assumed leadership in 1926 and sought to mend divisions within the organization. She also carefully collected and archived the Indiana Lincoln Inquiry's papers, ultimately compiling some of them in a book, *The Missing Chapter in the Life of Abraham Lincoln*.[14] Although William Herndon's work remains the crown jewel of source material on Lincoln's Indiana years, Ehrmann's book, relying largely on SWIHS scholarship, has proven an

important supplement for historians wanting to understand Lincoln's
Indiana neighbors.

In addition to working with local residents collecting oral history,
SWIHS members engaged with professional historians and, in some
cases, influenced the broader field of Lincoln history and our knowledge
of Lincoln's Indiana youth. William Barton, one of the early twentieth century's most prominent writers and lecturers on Abraham Lincoln's life, exchanged letters with Iglehart in May 1922 about Indiana's
impact on Lincoln.[15] Later that same year, Iglehart received inquiries
from Ida Tarbell, a well-known journalist and one of the leading Lincoln
biographers of that era. She had written twenty essays on Lincoln for
McClure's Magazine, doubling the magazine's subscriptions, and then,
in 1900, compiled the works into a two-volume *Life of Abraham Lincoln:
Drawn from Original Sources and Containing Many Speeches, Letters, and
Telegraphs Hitherto Unpublished*.[16] The book established Tarbell as a
popular expert on Lincoln, creating a national speaking circuit for her
and leading to the publication of additional articles and books. Unlike
many other historians of the era, Tarbell shared the Indiana Lincoln Inquiry's perspective that Lincoln succeeded in part *because* of his time in
Indiana, not in spite of it. In her 1924 book, *In the Footsteps of the Lincolns*,
Tarbell praised the Inquiry:

> There has been in the last few years a considerable amount of solid work
> done on the character of the men and women who settled this corner of
> the state; particularly important from the Lincoln standpoint, is that of
> Judge John E. Iglehart . . . president of the Southwestern Indiana Historical
> Society. Judge Iglehart's work gives us a better basis for judging the caliber
> of the men under whose indirect influence at least Lincoln certainly came at
> this time, than we have ever had before.[17]

As historian Keith A. Erekson noted, Tarbell's words constituted "a stel-
lar endorsement from the most popular Lincoln biographer of the era."[18]
For many years, Tarbell, Iglehart, and other members of the Indiana
Lincoln Inquiry continued to correspond, interact, and share research.
Christopher Coleman, grandson of Lincoln's second law partner, led
the Indiana Historical Bureau and praised the Indiana Lincoln Inquiry
for "contribut[ing] powerfully to the revision of our interpretation of
Lincoln's personality and its development."[19]

Lincoln scholar Mark E. Neely Jr. summarized the two theories of Lincoln's life in Indiana popular in the 1920s: the "dunghill" thesis emphasized the poor, backward character of the frontier, and the "chin fly" thesis emphasized the positive benefits and wisdom available to Lincoln in the Hoosier state.[20] The dunghill thesis took its name from Ward Lamon and his ghostwriter, Chauncey Black (Lamon purchased the rights to William Herndon's research), who described Lincoln as "the diamond glowing on the dunghill."[21] By contrast, Ida Tarbell's work exhibited the chin fly thesis and helped give it a name when she praised the "horse, the dog, the ox, the chin fly, the plow, the hog" as accompanying Lincoln during his youth and serving as "interpreters of his meaning, solvers of his problems in his great necessity, of making men understand and follow him."[22]

Perhaps the most influential view of Lincoln's frontier youth for both academic historians and the Indiana Lincoln Inquiry was Frederick Jackson Turner's "Frontier Thesis." Turner burst onto the scene with a famous essay presented in 1893 to a special meeting of the American Historical Association at the World's Columbian Exposition in Chicago: "The Significance of the Frontier in American History."[23] In it, Turner argued the frontier shaped American democracy, independence, ingenuity, and optimism. In the process, the frontier also shaped the American story and drove American history. Turner eventually landed a place on the staff at Harvard and shaped the thinking of generations of historians and public intellectuals, both devotees and critics. One notable devotee was the Indiana Lincoln Inquiry's John Iglehart, who cultivated a friendship with Turner throughout the 1920s. In the words of Keith Erekson, Iglehart became Turner's "warm friend, devoted disciple, and enthusiastic supporter while Turner became an authoritative endorser of the Indiana Lincoln Inquiry's work and its mentor in the refinement of the historical record."[24] Members of the Indiana Lincoln Inquiry appreciated how the Frontier Thesis attributed democracy's success to the frontier, emphasized a "transitional zone" in southern Indiana and the Midwest in the 1820s, and used Lincoln as an embodiment of the pioneer spirit. Unlike many writers and intellectuals in the east, Turner refrained from portraying all frontiersmen as backward or ignorant; instead, he recognized the diversity of class and culture that the Indiana Lincoln Inquiry frequently portrayed in its own work.

The Indiana Lincoln Inquiry derived much of its importance from society members' firsthand knowledge of Lincoln's boyhood home. Bess Ehrmann grew up in Spencer County, Ida Tarbell used Anna O'Flynn's Spencer County interviews, and William Fortune interviewed local residents in 1881. In her book, Ehrmann agreed with Iglehart's philosophy that Lincoln's life in Indiana must be written by "the children and grandchildren" of those who knew him and by their descendants, not by "outsiders" who spent little time in Spencer County.[25] She explained that "the people who live near the scenes of Lincoln's early life . . . are best able to interpret its environment. They are intimately acquainted with the descendants of his boyhood friend, have heard the stories of his life as related by their elders and therefore ought to be in a position to write more understandingly of those early days and those pioneer people."[26] In particular, the Indiana Lincoln Inquiry often focused on secondary sources who knew Lincoln's friends and family or those who had interviewed them. Erekson summarized their philosophy: "Because Lincoln's boyhood must be understood in the context of his neighbors, and because the evidence for those neighbors resided in the family stories of then-living grandchildren, and because the information would be lost forever with their deaths, the best witnesses were uniquely positioned to meet the historiographical need with the best available evidence."[27]

Not all of the Indiana Lincoln Inquiry's work gained wider acceptance; indeed, contemporary professional historians viewed oral tradition and public history suspiciously. Shortly after Iglehart died, Lincoln biographer James G. Randall proposed banning amateurs from the Lincoln field.[28] Well-known Lincoln biographer William Barton dismissed the Indiana Lincoln Inquiry's "secondary material" as well as its use of oral tradition.[29] Modern historians generally view oral tradition and public history more favorably. Keith Erekson praised the Indiana Lincoln Inquiry's collective history in his 2012 book, *Everybody's History: Indiana's Lincoln Inquiry and the Quest to Reclaim a President's Past*. Nevertheless, the Indiana Lincoln Inquiry did, in fact, suffer from several deficiencies outlined above: Iglehart and other SWIHS members carried a substantial bias to overcome negative stereotypes about southwestern Indiana; some authors sought to advance a preconceived notion about Lincoln or southwestern Indiana; and some authors reflected family legends and traditions without documentation. Although the works selected here are not immune to these criticisms, they nevertheless provide valuable insight into Lincoln's roots and our approaches to that history. And wherever possible, we strive to present appropriate context for the Inquiry's authors and findings.

Shortly after Abraham Lincoln's death, biographies tended to treat his father, Thomas, as a shiftless ne'er-do-well without ambition. Over time, Thomas was portrayed as a typical pioneer trying to provide for his family. However, historians have recently taken a more critical assessment of the relationship between Thomas and Abraham, concluding the relationship was distant and cold. The Inquiry generally avoided analyzing emotive qualities of their relationship.

By the 1930s, the Indiana Lincoln Inquiry began to wane. In 1933, the SWIHS dropped one of its three yearly meetings. In 1934, its members published their last book. By 1939, the SWIHS ceased to exist altogether. A number of factors likely contributed to the decline, including Iglehart's death in 1934, the Great Depression, and a general ebb of interest in the Civil War. Moreover, the SWIHS faced competition from groups such as the Indiana Lincoln Union, a group formed in 1926 and made up of Indiana's who's who appointed by Indiana governor Ed Jackson, primarily from within Indianapolis political circles, to help secure recognition for Indiana's contributions in the Lincoln story.

The Indiana Lincoln Inquiry's collection of oral and public history can still help us understand the environment of Lincoln's early life. Yet, until now, a judicious collection of the Indiana Lincoln Inquiry's most historically significant work has never been produced. Indeed, the Lincoln story remains encrusted in myth and legend, even in the hands of professional historians. We hope this project preserves and extends the Indiana Lincoln Inquiry's findings and provides greater context for Lincoln's life in Indiana. As the first fully annotated edition of Indiana Lincoln Inquiry papers, this volume offers indispensable reading for anyone hoping to investigate Abraham Lincoln's youth and serves as a gateway for general readers into the environment of Lincoln's early life.

William E. Bartelt and Joshua A. Claybourn

NOTES

1.   John L. Scripps to William H. Herndon, 24 June 1865, in *Herndon's Informants: Letters, Interviews, and Statements about Abraham Lincoln*, ed. Douglas L. Wilson and Rodney O. Davis (Urbana: University of Illinois Press, 1998), 57.

> "Why Scripps" said he, on one occasion, "it is a great piece of folly to attempt to make anything out of my early life. It can all be condensed into a single sentence, and that sentence you will find in Gray's Elegy:
>   'The short and simple annals of the poor'
> That's my life and that's all you or anyone else can make of it."

2.   William H. Herndon and Jesse Weik, *Herndon's Lincoln*, ed. Douglas L. Wilson and Rodney O. Davis (Champaign: University of Illinois Press, 2006), 4.

3.   Edward Eggleston, *The Hoosier Schoolmaster: A Story of Backwoods Life in Indiana* (New York: Grosset & Dunlap, 1871).

4.   *The Rochester Daily Republican*, 2 February 1907, 1.

5.   *The Courier-Journal* (Louisville, KY), 27 December 1930, 2.

6.   "History of Southwestern Indiana Historical Society," SWIHS, accessed 4 October 2017, http://www.swihs.net/?p=45.

7.   Logan Esarey to John E. Iglehart, 31 October 1919, box I, folder 10, John E. Iglehart Papers, 1853–1953, William Henry Smith Memorial Library, Indiana Historical Society, Indianapolis, Indiana.

8.   John E. Iglehart, dictation, 17 November 1925, Southwestern Indiana Historical Society Collection, Willard Library, Evansville, Indiana.

9.   Keith A. Erekson, *Everybody's History: Indiana's Lincoln Inquiry and the Quest to Reclaim a President's Past* (Amherst: University of Massachusetts Press, 2012), 29.

10.   Deidré Duff Johnson in 1928, quoted in Keith A. Erekson, "Alternative Paths to the Past: The 'Lincoln Inquiry' and the Practice of History in America, 1880–1939" (PhD diss., Indiana University, 2008), 71.

11.   Erekson, *Everybody's History*, 37.

12.   Ethel F. McCollough to Thomas James de la Hunt, 14 September 1922, Southwestern Indiana Historical Society Collection, Willard Library, Evansville, Indiana.

13.   Erekson, *Everybody's History*, 121–122.

14.   Bess V. Ehrmann, *The Missing Chapter in the Life of Abraham Lincoln* (Chicago: Walter M. Hill, 1938).

15.   William E. Barton to John E. Iglehart, 26 May 1922, John E. Iglehart Papers, 1853–1953, William Henry Smith Memorial Library, Indiana Historical Society, Indianapolis, Indiana.

16.   Ida M. Tarbell, *Life of Abraham Lincoln: Drawn from Original Sources and Containing Many Speeches, Letters, and Telegraphs Hitherto Unpublished* (New York: Doubleday & McClure, 1900).

17.   Ida M. Tarbell, *In the Footsteps of the Lincolns* (New York: Harper and Brothers, 1924), 150.

18.   Erekson, *Everybody's History*, 52.

19.   Christopher B. Coleman, "Emphasis in the Work of Historical Societies," *Indiana History Bulletin* 6, extra no. 3, *Proceedings of the Southwestern Indiana Historical Society during Its Ninth Year* (August 1929): 16.

20.   Mark E. Neely Jr., *Escape from the Frontier: Lincoln's Peculiar Relationship with Indiana* (Fort Wayne, IN: Lincoln National Life Insurance Company, 1980).

21.   Chauncey Black, quoted in Benjamin Thomas, *Portrait for Posterity: Lincoln and His Biographers* (New Brunswick, NJ: Rutgers University Press, 1947), 36–37.

22.   Tarbell, *In the Footsteps of the Lincolns*, 137.

23.   Frederick Jackson Turner, "The Significance of the Frontier in American History," *Proceedings of the State Historical Society of Wisconsin* (Madison: State Historical Society of Wisconsin, 1894). This essay appeared the year following its presentation to the American Historical Association.

24.   Erekson, *Everybody's History*, 90.

25.   Ehrmann, *The Missing Chapter in the Life of Abraham Lincoln*, vii.

26.   Bess V. Ehrmann, "The Lincoln Inquiry," *Indiana Magazine of History* 21 (March 1925): 3–4.

27.   Erekson, *Everybody's History*, 82.

28.   James G. Randall, "Has the Lincoln Theme Been Exhausted?" *American Historical Review* 41, no. 2 (January 1936): 270.

29.   Erekson, *Everybody's History*, 80, citing Albert J. Beveridge to Bess V. Ehrmann, 2 January 1925, Container 288, Albert Jeremiah Beveridge Papers, Manuscript Division, Library of Congress, Washington, DC; see also Albert J. Beveridge, *Indiana History Bulletin* 2, extra no. (February 1925): 28.

PART 1

LINCOLN'S HOOSIER INFLUENCES

"The Railsplitter" (1909) by Jean Leon Gerome Ferris.

1

★ ★ ★

Lincoln's Boyhood Days in Indiana

ROSCOE KIPER*

Delivered to the Society of Indiana Pioneers in 1922, this paper offers an introductory overview of Lincoln's years in Indiana. Indiana state senator Roscoe Kiper attempts to provide context to help readers understand the people, places, and environment that created the man we know as Abraham Lincoln. Indeed, the Indiana Lincoln Inquiry sought to illustrate how almost fourteen years in Indiana shaped the man.

A number of the persons discussed in this article receive considerable attention elsewhere in this volume. Thus, we keep annotations in this chapter to a minimum, with only a handful of numerical footnotes from us and letter endnotes from Mr. Kiper.

Lincoln
Guy Lee

"Five score and thirteen years ago
The wilderness brought forth a man
To whom life offered little either
In heredity or environment.
From his birth to his death the furies
Waged constant war on the fates
Along his path. When patience and genius
Prevailed against penury and heartache,
With success came malice, treachery, and abuse
To mock his triumph. But, firm of faith,
Steadfast of purpose, and forgiving of heart,
He breasted the storm and marched to martyrdom."

---

* Kiper read this paper at the Society of Indiana Pioneers meeting in Indianapolis in December 1922 and published it in the *Indiana History Bulletin* # 17 in February 1923, pages 50–69.

THOMAS LINCOLN HAD MADE A TRIP FROM KNOB CREEK, HIS
home in Kentucky, to Indiana in search of a new location, and decided
upon a site near the new and promising settlement at Troy, which was
located on the banks of Anderson River at its confluence with the Ohio.
In the fall of 1816 Thomas Lincoln returned with his family, first stopping
at Troy, and within a short time proceeding to the new home previously
selected near Little Pigeon Creek, which at that time constituted the
boundary line between Perry and Warrick counties.

On coming to the top of the line of hills fringing the river course on
the Kentucky side opposite the town of Troy, one is met with the sudden
unrolling of a panorama wonderful to behold, and we can imagine the
lively interest which animated the soul of young Abraham when he first
saw the majestic Ohio flowing against the background made of the hills
covered with the forest trees in beautiful autumnal colors.

This was the first impulse that Indiana gave to the great young heart of
Lincoln which was to be inspired by the scenery of her hills and valleys,
and educated by the influence of her pioneer genius.

When Lincoln arrived at the age of twenty-one years, and had left
Indiana for Illinois, he had much to learn as to the practical application
of the knowledge he had acquired, but an observation of the conditions
surrounding his life, his environment, his opportunities of coming in
contact with and observing some of the strongest minds of the State who
lived in his day, his insatiable desire to appropriate to himself everything
of value and consequence that came his way, together with his frequent
manifestation of certain qualities of mind and character in after life,
drives us to the irresistible conclusion that many of his outstanding characteristics, his uncommon power of observation, his penetrating mind,
his ability to properly appraise individual character, his appreciation of
the problems of those who must struggle and toil, his tenacious adherence to that which he believed to be right, his open mind and freedom of
thought, the ruggedness of the warrior bold, yet possessing the tenderness of a woman's soul, were laid deep in his nature during the nascent
period of his life when living in Indiana.

When the Lincolns arrived at Troy they probably stayed with relatives until a rude open building was constructed on the tract of land
which had been selected as a home. Troy, at that time, was the county

seat of Perry County, and at the January term, 1815, of the Perry Circuit Court, Joseph Hanks, a relative of Nancy Hanks, was drawn as a juror to serve in an important case wherein the United States was plaintiff, and at the November term of said court Austin Lincoln (probably an uncle of Thomas) was drawn as a juror.[a]

When the Lincolns left Troy they traveled westward a short distance on an established highway and then entered the virgin forests where it was necessary to literally cut a way through to the new-found home where Thomas Lincoln had buil[t] his cabin, a distance of about eighteen miles from Troy.[1] Troy had great promise of becoming a shipping point of considerable importance, and was the terminus of the old Fredonia road leading up the Ohio River. On their arrival, neighbors were few, but other emigrants came and within a short time Pigeon Baptist Church was organized, and meetings of the congregation were regularly held. The record of this church which has been religiously preserved by its officials, shows that Thomas Lincoln's was admitted to membership by letter on June 7, 1823, and frequently served as moderator at the meetings of its members.[b]

In this record, which extends over the entire period during which the Lincolns lived in the community, no mention is made of the son Abraham having in any way had connection with the activities of the church.

The Lincolns soon found themselves surrounded by a number of neighbors most of whom were members of the Pigeon Baptist Church, and by the year 1820 the Lincoln's three-sided home had been replaced by the typical pioneer cabin and the organization of the frontier community life was well under way.

But little is now known of the many incidents and experiences in the early childhood of the great Emancipator, except the one great heartrending tragedy of his mother's death. She had endeared herself to the peoples of the countryside by her quiet demeanor, sweet disposition, and nobility of conduct. She was surrounded by the hills and the forest, far removed from the influence of culture and education, yet like the typical mother her heart went out beyond the hills and the forest and she dreamed great dreams for the pride of her heart, and on a November day, with one mighty

1 Abraham Lincoln's immediate family did not arrive in Indiana until 1816.

effort to live for those she loved, the flickering flame of life flared up and then went out, but the memories of her which were burned into the heart of the boy softened and solemnized his life to the end.[2c]

The farm on which the Lincolns settled was entered by Thomas Lincoln from the government on October 15, 1817, but possession had been taken by him a few months prior. Doubtless in choosing a location Lincoln thought the settlement would eventually become of some importance. The public road from Corydon to Newburg in Warrick County had been established and was a means of outlet to the Ohio River and furnished a direct connection with the new State Capitol at Corydon, and while the country surrounding the Lincoln home was uncleared and unimproved, yet the excitement in the making of a new state and the great number of emigrants coming from the South to the Indiana country was proof to Lincoln's mind that within a short time the community would become thickly settled and prosperous.

It should be remembered that about the time of Lincoln's arrival a number of persons came to Southern Indiana from Kentucky, many of whom were relatives and acquaintances of the Lincolns, and a number of whom became prominent in State and National affairs.[d]

Many incidents, unbelievable and otherwise, have been related concerning the boyhood of Lincoln. A great many of these stories are frivolous and of little value in determining what influence had most to do with molding the character of the man. He was the son of a poor carpenter and farmer who had, in hopes of bettering his condition moved to a new country, casting his lot with many others. They endured hardships, had meager but sufficient clothing, had no superior advantages of education, but constant struggle had made the mind alert and receptive. They had brought with them a desire to learn and lost no opportunity to satisfy the desire.

Esarey, in his *History of Indiana* aptly characterizes the pioneer spirit of the times when he says: "One is surprised not at the meager facilities for education but the unusual interest in it and the many ways in which this interest was shown."[3]

---

2 This suggests that Nancy died in November, but in fact she died on 5 October 1818.

3 Logan Esarey, *History of Indiana* (New York: Harcourt, Brace, 1922). The page for this quotation is unknown.

Thomas Lincoln was not lazy and shiftless. No shiftless person could survive the trying conditions under which he lived, much less provide for his family and maintain his standard of respectability as a citizen and churchman.

About the time young Lincoln arrived at sixteen years of age the number of their neighbors had increased materially and the exchange of ideas and information was beginning to arrest his attention. The capitol of the State had been moved to Corydon[e] and a constitution adopted; the legislature had held several sessions and matters concerning State and local government were engaging the attention of the citizens. A school had been established within three miles of the Lincoln home wherein the rudiments of an English education were taught. James Bryant, Crooks and Watson were early teachers of this school. Another schoolhouse was later buil[t] on the same section near the Lincoln home. Dorsey, Bryant, Price and others taught here.[4]

It is well authenticated that Lincoln attended the school taught by Dorsey and Bryant. By the year 1830 two other schools were established within walking distance of the Lincoln home.[f]

On January 10, 1818, Spencer County was created out of the territory comprising Perry and Warrick counties with Little Pigeon Creek constituting the boundary between Warrick and Spencer counties. This placed the Lincoln home in Carter Township, Spencer County, about three miles east of Little Pigeon Creek, whereas, it was originally in Hurricane Township, Perry County.[5]

At an election held in Carter Township in August, 1819, Thomas Lincoln is recorded as casting his vote.

In the year 1819 Pigeon Baptist Church was located about a mile south of the Lincoln home where a log building was erected on land donated by Noah Gordon and Samuel Howell. Owen R. Griffith hewed the hogs [logs]; the lumber was sawed with a whip-saw. Thomas Lincoln made the windows, door casings and pulpit. David Turnham made the bricks which were used in the building. Among the early members of this

---

4 Lincoln remembered his teachers as Andrew Crawford, [James] Sweeney, and Azel Dorsey. See *Autobiography Written for John L. Scripps* circa June 1860, Roy P. Basler et al., eds., *The Collected Works of Abraham Lincoln*. 9 vols. (New Brunswick, NJ: Rutgers University Press, 1953–1955), 4:62.
5 The Lincoln home was one mile south of the creek.

religious organization were William Barker, Jacob Oskins, James Gentry, Jesse Oskins, Reverend John Richardson, Reverend Briscoe and their wives. Among the ministers were Richardson, Briscoe, Lamar, Charles Harper, Stanley Walker, Thomas Sumner, Joseph Price, Henry Hart, and Adam Shoemaker. It is said of Adam Shoemaker that he was one of the outstanding pioneer ministers of Southern Indiana. His sermons were oftentimes prophetic visions of the future greatness of the Republic, and his liberal mind and breadth of vision distinguished him as one of the foremost of his day. He was a strong opponent of slavery, and had a great deal to do with shaping the sentiment of his locality. It has often been said that he is the one character from whom Abraham Lincoln received his first ideas of emancipation.[8]

James Grigsby lived south of the Lincoln home. James Gentry and John Romine were close neighbors. Aaron Grigsby who afterwards married Sarah Lincoln, the only sister of Abraham, lived close by. Sarah died in 1828. She was buried in the cemetery at Pigeon Baptist Church, and friends have recently erected a marble shaft to mark her grave. Masterson Clark, and Edmund Phillips who lived in Warrick County, were neighbors and belonged to the same church as the Lincolns.

The characteristics of these individuals who were neighbors to the Lincolns must have had a great influence on the life of the young Lincoln and instilled in him some of the sterling qualities which manifested themselves in his later life.

The Reverend John Richardson was a native of West Virginia, coming to Kentucky at an early date, and in 1817 in company with a few neighbors, came on a flat-boat to Indiana, disembarking at the site now occupied by the town of Grandview and settled near the Lincoln home. He was a preacher of the Baptist religion, a man of strong conviction.

James Gentry belonged to the North Carolina branch of the Gentry family, and at the age of seventeen went to Barren County, Kentucky. He moved to Spencer County in 1818, and located on a tract of land containing over one thousand acres near the present site of Gentryville. His biographer says that "he was remarkable for his energy and industry and the interest which he took in the welfare of his neighbors and the community in general." His daughter, Agnes, married Benjamin Romine, who in 1827 with Gideon Romine and his father-in-law, James Gentry, began selling goods at the junction of the Corydon and Newburg road with the Rockport and Jasper road where the town of Gentryville is now located, and which afterwards became the center of the community life in that vicinity. Near the homestead of James Gentry was located the home of Allen Gentry who had preceded James Gentry to Spencer County in 1813. Romine and Gentry became the outstanding characters of the community, being large landowners and having established the only store in that surrounding country which became a gathering place for the young and old, where they interchanged ideas and read the newspapers which came to the Gentry store.[6]

Located on the mainly traveled highway leading from the pocket towns of Boonville, Newburg, and Evansville, to the State Capitol at Corydon, the citizens had an opportunity to come in contact with some of the great characters of Southern Indiana. William Jones when a young man began clerking for Romine and Gentry, and afterwards established a small store on his farm about one mile west of Gentryville. This place was given the name of Jonesboro. It was in the store of William Jones that young Lincoln worked as a clerk and assisted in preparing pork and tobacco for the market.[7]

Reuben Grigsby came to the Lincoln settlement in 1820 from Kentucky where he remained for a period of thirty years. The Reverend Allen Brooner came to the Lincoln settlement in 1813, and became a strong character in the community where he resided many years. It is said of him that he was a typical pioneer, a widely known bear hunter, a hardy, resolute man, and a good citizen.

John W. Lamar was a native of Kentucky, and a playmate of Lincoln, and attended the same school where Lincoln received his early education. It is well established that almost every family in the community in which Lincoln lived came from Kentucky, Tennessee or the Carolinas and belonged to that branch of old English stock that has so indelibly impressed itself on the character and customs of Southern Indiana—bringing with them customs and qualities of character which have been manifested by

6 James Gentry Sr. was the first Gentry to come to Spencer County. He sold goods at his home prior to opening a store with Romine at the crossroads.

7 William Jones did not come to Spencer County until the later part of Lincoln's time in Indiana and did not open a store west of Gentryville until after the Lincolns left the area.

so many of their offspring. We wish to emphasize the fact that Abraham Lincoln had the opportunity to come in contact with a great many influences during his life in Indiana which could account for so many traits of character and peculiarities of his personality by which he was so signally distinguished in after life.

Aside from his immediate associates there lived in Southern Indiana a number of distinguished men whose fame and reputation undoubtedly reached to the home and fireside of every family living between Corydon on the east and the struggling village and boat-landing at Evansville, Indiana, on the west. From the age of sixteen to twenty-one years Lincoln had the opportunity of frequently visiting Rockport, the county seat of Spencer County, where lived John Pitcher, one of the great lawyers of Southern Indiana, a member of the legislature in 1830, representing Spencer and Perry counties. He was the first resident attorney of Rockport and was also prosecuting attorney of his district. Pitcher possessed an unusual library and it is said that Lincoln often made visits to the office of Pitcher when he brought pork and other farm products to the boat-landing at Rockport to be shipped to the southland, and that Pitcher formed a great liking for Lincoln, and in after years on a visit to Rockport he inquired of the place where John Pitcher had his office.

When the constitutional convention convened in Corydon in 1816 Daniel Grass appeared as a delegate from Warrick County, which included at that time the present boundaries of Spencer County. Grass had migrated from Kentucky to Indiana and located near the present site of Rockport. A township of Spencer County bears his name. He was a man of unusual ability, a member of the Indiana legislature, and a judge of the county court for a number of years, and on his way to attend the legislature at Corydon he would pass through the little village afterwards known as Gentryville, as did a great many of the other members from the southern part of the State, and they usually remained overnight with the Gentrys or the Joneses. About 1824 political parties in Indiana inaugurated the system of state and county political organizations and sent out literature and posters for campaign purposes, and in this way the voters became familiar with the principles of the political parties and the characters of the candidates. In the Clay-Adams-Jackson contest for presidency in 1824 there were county organizations and platforms with handbills sent out to the voters.[h]

Daniel Grass was a man of unusual judgment and sagacity as a politician and was known in Southern Indiana as a humorist. General Joseph Lane, who was several times a member of the legislature when it met at Corydon, said that Daniel Grass was reputed to be one of the greatest humorists in the territory. Lincoln had the opportunity and no doubt did come in contact with his engaging personality.

General Joseph Lane was elected to the legislature from Vanderburgh and Warrick counties in 1822 and served at intervals in the House and Senate of Indiana from 1822 to 1846. He lived at Sprinklesburg in Warrick County, afterwards known as Newburg, and in order to reach the State capitol at Corydon he had to travel the Corydon-Newburg road which passed the Jones store where Lincoln worked. About 1818 the county seat of Warrick County was moved from Darlington to Boonville.

Boonville was named for Ratliff Boon who came to Indiana from Kentucky in 1814, and settled two miles west of the town which afterwards bore his name.[8] He married Delilah Anderson, daughter of Bailey Anderson, said to be the first man who set foot on Warrick County's soil. Ratliff Boon was an intrepid character, courageous, intelligent, with strong prejudices. He was a hard fighter in political contests and was extremely jealous of his power and influence. He was elected to Congress eight different times from the congressional district in which Spencer and Warrick counties were located, and twice elected Lieutenant Governor and filled out the unexpired term of Governor William Hendricks when he was elected to the United States Senate. He was president of the Senate when the legislature met at Corydon. He moved to Pike County, Missouri, in 1839, and afterwards entered the race for United States Senate, and was defeated by Thomas H. Benton. General Joseph Lane says that Ratliff Boon and Daniel Grass were more than ordinary men in their day, and deserve a place in the history of Indiana.

8 Ratliff Boon (1781–1844) served as the second governor of Indiana from 12 September 1822 to 5 December 1822 and thereafter served as lieutenant governor and congressman. However, the Warrick County seat in Boonville was actually named for Ratliff's father, Jesse. See Linda C. Gugin and James E. St. Clair, eds., *The Governors of Indiana* (Indianapolis: Indiana Historical Society Press, 2006).

It is difficult to believe that young Lincoln did not have an opportunity to come in contact with this great personality in Southern Indiana history, and was not influenced by his life and activities in the community. William L. Barker of Boonville who has devoted a great deal of time to local historical research, and a local historian of unusual ability, relates this incident of Ratliff Boon, which shows his sagacity as a politician: "When out electioneering in the day when joint debates were frequent Boon would propose stopping at a cross-roads blacksmith shop. Here, while his opponent presented his own claims for the blacksmith's support, Boon would cleverly pound out a set of horseshoe nails, some chain links, or other homely device, thus proving that he knew how to handle tools and was not above menial labor. His early apprenticeship to the Kentucky gunsmith made this easy for him."

Boonville was located on a site at the junction of the Yellowbanks Road with the road leading from Corydon to Newburg, and the State road leading from Boonville to Petersburg, at a distance of about thirteen miles from the home of Abraham Lincoln. In 1826 the town possessed less than one hundred inhabitants.

Doctor Reuben C. Matthewson was a physician living in Boonville, and there were two or three general merchandise stores. The town being thus centrally located it was the meeting place for the State Militia on muster days, which was an event of great importance in the life of the local community, at which the citizens of all the surrounding territory met in competitive drills. Ratliff Boon, Daniel Grass, and William Prince were the leading spirits in these drill contests. Boon was commissioned Lieutenant of the Fourth Regiment, and Grass was commissioned an officer in the same regiment. William Prince was commissioned a Captain of the Indiana Militia, and afterwards Boon was commissioned Captain of the First Battalion.

Lincoln came to Boonville first, perhaps, to witness these competitive drills, but it afterwards developed that there were other incentives that prompted the young man to return to Boonville. Here lived John A. Breckenridge [Brackenridge][9] who, perhaps, had more to do with

9 The correct spelling is *Brackenridge*. Kiper misspells the name as *Breckenridge* several times in this article. Several historians question whether Brackenridge lived in Boonville and whether Lincoln witnessed Brackenridge at trial there. See the companion piece in chapter 23 concerning Brackenridge.

directing the attention of Lincoln to the study of law than any other man, and probably influenced his life in that regard the most. John A. Breckenridge came to Warrick County when a young man and married one of the young ladies in that county. He first settled on a farm just west of Boonville, and afterwards moved to the village and conducted a general merchandise store in connection with his law practice. The Breckenridges were eastern people and had had unusual opportunities to acquire an education. John A. Breckenridge became prosecutor of Warrick County, and afterwards became the leading attorney of Southern Indiana. His mind was well-trained, in forensic ability he was unexcelled, and his cogent reasoning was irresistible. Young Lincoln frequently came to Boonville to attend trials, and thereby came in contact with Breckenridge. It is well authenticated that he frequently visited the home of Breckenridge and borrowed law books and other miscellaneous books which he read and returned. The books that were loaned him by Breckenridge and the influence of the character of the man undoubtedly had a great deal to do with shaping the future of young Lincoln.

A portion of the library of John A. Breckenridge fell into the hands of his nephew, Judge John B. Handy, and is now owned by L. A. Folsom, a lawyer at Boonville. Among the volumes of this library are found the following: "*Roman Antiquities,*" published in 1807, containing an account of the manners and customs of the Romans respecting their government and laws. "*Laws of the United States*", containing *Treaties and Proclamations, Spanish Recollections, 1828.* In this volume is a printed book-plate bearing the following inscription: "John A. Breckenridge, No. 457", showing that Breckenridge possessed an unusually large library for that day. Also the following books: "*An Abridgement of Coke's Library, 1813,*" "*Speeches of Charles Phillips, Esq., Delivered at the Bar in Ireland and England, Dedicated to William Roscoe, 1817,*" containing speeches on civil and religious liberty and the character of Napoleon. "*Law Miscellanies,*" containing *Introductions to Study of Blackstone, 1814.* "*Reminiscences of Charles Butler, Esquire, of Lincoln Inn,*" containing classical studies of Modern English poets, Jurisprudence, letters on Junius, 1822. "*Notes on Grecian, Roman, Feudal, and Canon Law*" by Charles Butler, Esquire, of Lincoln's Inn, 1808.

The identification of these books with the library of John A. Breckenridge is unquestioned. There is no positive evidence that Lincoln actually
read these books, but it is reasonably presumed that owing to his inquiring mind and his desire for an education if he had the opportunity which
he undoubtedly did, he became familiar with their contents.

There were other lawyers practicing at the Warrick County Bar at this
time who were able and influential and occupied prominent positions.
Richard Daniels at one time presiding judge, William Prince, prosecuting attorney, John Pitcher, James R. E. Goodlett, who for many years was
the presiding judge of the circuit court, and many of the ablest lawyers of
the southern portion of the State, came to Boonville to attend court. No
doubt young Lincoln journeyed to Boonville to attend these sessions of
court and hear the arguments of these lawyers. There were also a number
of influential laymen living in and near Boonville who were identified
with the progress of the community, among whom was Zachariah Skelton, commonly known as Judge Skelton, who lived in Warrick County,
a short distance from the home of Lincoln, and Levi Iglehart, both of
whom were members of the Board of Justices and took a prominent part
in the financial and prudential affairs of the county, the latter being the
grandfather of Judge John E. Iglehart, now of Evansville, Indiana.

A tradition has been handed down from the oldest settlers in the vicinity of Boonville, some of whom knew Lincoln, that at an important
trial in the old courthouse in Boonville, John A. Breckenridge made a
masterly argument for the defense, and when he had finished a number
of the by-standers rushed to him to congratulate him, among whom was
young Lincoln, who for some reason did not get an opportunity to tell
Breckenridge how much he appreciated his argument. Years afterwards
when Lincoln became President Mr. Breckenridge had an occasion to
appear before him in the White House in the interest of some applicant
for a federal position, and on his presence being announced Mr. Lincoln
arose and rushed to him with extended hand and said: "Mr. Breckenridge, I have always wanted to congratulate you and tell you what a great
speech you made in that trial at Boonville." The Breckenridges became
staunch abolitionists, and after Lincoln left for Illinois John A. Breckenridge moved to Texas. Some of his relatives are now living in and near
Boonville.

Thomas James de la Hunt in his excellent history of Perry County details the circumstances relative to Lincoln being in the employment of James Taylor, who lived at the mouth of Anderson Creek near Troy, and was a large shipper of pork, hay, and grain, to the southern market. Through this connection Lincoln made his trip to New Orleans and return, and while in this employment had the opportunity to secure the eastern newspapers as they were brought down the river on the boats, and thereby acquaint himself with current events and public affairs.[10]

In this same volume is given an account in detail of the incident of the wrecking of the boat on which General Lafayette was traveling in 1825 near what is now the site of the city of Cannelton. General Lafayette was cast ashore and remained for some time at a house located near the large spring that now bears the name of Lafayette Spring, and during the period of his stay the presence of the distinguished officer became widely known to the citizens, and pioneers from all portions of the country came to pay their respects.[i] It is highly probable that the news reached as far as Troy where Lincoln could have been employed, or even as far as his home in Spencer County, which at that time had been connected with Troy by a fairly well-established road. The fact that Lafayette was making the trip down the river, his speeches, and the incidents of his journey to the western country were widely published in the local papers. He had been tendered a banquet at Jeffersonville on April 16, 1825, which fact had been published in the Corydon *Gazette*, and in the Louisville Papers. These publications unquestionably reached the Lincoln settlement and were read at the Gentry and Jones stores. As early as 1819 President Monroe and Andrew Jackson had stopped at Jeffersonville and were escorted by the State militia to Corydon where a barbecue was tendered.

On February 11, 1825, commissioners who had been appointed to lay out a State road from Harmony, Posey County, to Polk Patch in Warrick County, so as to intersect a State road leading from Princeton to Corydon, reported the establishment of the road to the Dubois County line, and in 1826 a road from Fredonia to Wabash, that part running through Warrick County beginning at the east line of the county, thence north to Pigeon Creek, thence to the west line of the county, was reported.

10 Lincoln's flatboat trip was made in connection with James Gentry, not James Taylor.

The road from Boonville to Princeton had long been established, and the line of communication between Boonville and New Harmony was established by well traveled roads. There was also a line of passenger boats running down the Ohio River passing Troy and stopping at Newburg, Evansville, and Mt. Vernon, and boats running from Mt. Vernon up the Wabash River to New Harmony.

When Robert Owen purchased the New Harmony settlement from the Rappites an impetus was given to educational ideas in the southern part of the State. The Harmony community under the regime of the Rappites from 1815 to 1817 established factories and schools, and their factories produced broadcloth, tinware, shoes, saddles, flour, beer, and other commodities. A market was established in the surrounding towns and the reputation of the community extended over the southern part of the State. In 1824 Rapp sold to Robert Owen the holdings, and the Owens took possession of the property and under their management soon attracted to their community a select circle of scholars, artists, and educators, which made the place famous throughout the country. For a few years it was the most noted place in the state.

Many noted men came to this community and the story of this adventure is universally known. In 1825 Robert Dale Owen, the son of Robert Owen, the elder, brought with him a number of educators to New Harmony, and he began the publication of a newspaper called *The New Harmony Gazette*. This paper attained a wide circulation in the southern part of the state, and in the east, and the publication was continued for a number of years. On December 9, 1825, forty-six paper exchanges were received by the *New Harmony Gazette*. Agents were appointed in numerous towns and localities in the southern part of the state where the paper could be had. Thomas Say, the naturalist, William Maclure, and other prominent educators naturally attracted a great deal of attention from those who were interested in the development of educational ideas.

Robert Dale Owen was a man of strong personality and had revolutionary ideas relative to social and political conditions, which he exploited in his paper. Religious liberty and freedom of will were the outstanding ideas of the New Harmony movement. These principles received a great deal of attention from those who considered the New Harmony movement a harmful innovation on the social conditions existing at that time.

One traveler observed that Owen's idea was to "allow each person liberty to believe in what he considers to be good."

It is not an extravagant presumption to say that this influence reached to the home of Lincoln, and the New Harmony settlement, together with its ideas, were subjects of discussion at the Jones and Gentry stores. Lincoln, if he so desired, since it is well established that he went as far as Princeton to a woolen mill, could have gone to New Harmony and become acquainted with the institution and its teachings. Also, he could have come under the influence of the prominent educators connected with the Owen movement. The distance from the Lincoln home to New Harmony overland is about thirty-nine miles.

In 1820 publication of the *Corydon Gazette* was begun and continued for many years, it being a paper published at the State Capitol would naturally go into the homes of those who lived in the surrounding territory, and Corydon was connected with the Lincoln settlement by a well established highway. The publication of the *Louisville Advertiser* was begun at an early date, and it was a much read paper during the period of the young manhood of Lincoln.

In the year 1815 Huffman's Mill was erected on Anderson River and has been operated continuously to this day. At an early date the Board of Justices of Perry County ordered a road established from Huffman's Mill to the north line of the county, and in 1826 the same board established a road leading from Troy to Hindostan in Perry County. This mill was the largest known in Spencer County at that date, and the people came from a distance of forty miles to have their corn ground into meal. The Lincolns lived within a distance of eighteen or twenty miles from this mill. In 1825 Peter Whittinghill operated a small "corn cracker" just west of the present site of Gentryville, and James Gentry started a cotton gin in 1824 which he operated for several years, receiving patronage from a radius of thirty miles. Considerable cotton was then raised in that community. At an early date another small mill was located on Little Pigeon Creek by John Phillips a few miles west of the Lincoln settlement. One of the burrs used in this mill is still in possession of a member of the Phillips family. In 1820 George, Nicholas and John Taylor operated a grist mill on Polkberry Creek between the present sites of Dale and Gentryville about six miles north of the Lincoln home.

Little Pigeon Creek between Spencer and Warrick counties, and Anderson River from its mouth at Troy to Hurricane Fork were declared navigable streams by an act of the legislature in 1820, and in 1829 Moses Matthew was granted a license by the County Board of Warrick County to ferry across Little Pigeon Creek. While waiting their "turn" at these mills the people of the countryside would discuss all matters of local, State, and National importance, and these gatherings constituted the pioneer symposium wherein all questions, however weighty, were given careful consideration. It was at these gatherings that young Lincoln buil[t] his reputation as being the best educated young man in the community.

Pigeon Baptist Church was one of a number of Baptist churches in Spencer and adjoining counties which constituted Little Zion Baptist Association.[11] Little Zion Baptist Church was located in the eastern part of Warrick County near Little Pigeon Creek on the Corydon and Newburg road. The membership of the several churches would travel many miles to attend these yearly sessions of the association to which came the leading ministers from Kentucky and southern Indiana. This is the association to which Thomas Lincoln belonged, and having frequently held office in his local church, he no doubt attended these associations. These meetings furnished an opportunity for the discussion of religious, moral, and social questions, the influence of which no doubt made an impression on the mind of young Lincoln.

William Jones, in a verified statement says: "That he is the son of Colonel William Jones who was killed in the battle of Atlanta, July 22, 1864; that his father stated to him at many different times that he (Colonel Jones) and Abraham Lincoln were intimate friends and he worked in his store at Jonesboro, located three-fourths of a mile west of where Gentryville is now located, and during the last winter of his employment cut pork. Jonesboro was the post office and was named for me. The main roads at that time were the Corydon and Newburg road passing the Jones store and running west to Boonville and one running south to Rockport; when the Lincolns left for Illinois they had ox teams and came to the

---

11 The name should be Little Pigeon Church. The Baptist Association's name was the Little Pigeon Association of United Baptists. See Louis A. Warren, *Lincoln's Youth, Indiana Years, Seven to Twenty-One, 1816–1830* (New York: Apple-Century-Crofts, 1959), 114.

store for supplies, and young Abraham bought thirty-six dollars' worth of goods including knives and forks, to peddle on the way to Illinois, and several months thereafter I received a letter from Abraham saying that he doubled his money on these articles. The morning they started a crowd gathered at the store to bid the Lincolns good-bye. A remark was made by someone that they were late and young Lincoln explained that one of the oxen had strayed away during the previous night and he had to hunt him and found him about two and one-half miles from there at David Turnham's; that the wheels of their wagons had truck wheels, i.e., solid without spokes, and were sawed from the ends of large logs; that in 1844 Abraham Lincoln made a visit to Spencer County, coming first to Rockport where I was engaged in some court proceedings, and when court adjourned I went to Lincoln and shook hands with him, and then before the crowd dispersed I called the people to order and announced that the Honorable Abraham Lincoln, candidate for elector-at-large in Illinois would address the people of Rockport that night on the political issues of the day, and when asked by Lincoln by what authority I made this announcement my father struck his own breast and said 'by this authority.' After this meeting Lincoln came the next day with my father to Jonesboro and stayed overnight with him, and while there I sat on his lap, and the next day he made a speech a short distance east of the old Lincoln home where Lincoln City now stands. In 1860 my father campaigned for Lincoln in Spencer and adjoining counties."ʲ

Sarah Gray in a sworn statement made in her eighty-sixth year, says: "Her father, Henry Hart, came to Indiana in 1815 and settled near the Lincoln home. He was one of the pioneer preachers of the Baptist Church and was a preacher for Pigeon Baptist Church at the time Lincoln was a member, and has told me a great many instances that occurred in the boyhood days of Lincoln. He told me that Thomas Lincoln was elected a deacon in the church and often acted as moderator in the absence of the pastor; that he visited the home of the Lincolns frequently; that the Corydon road ran through the neighborhood near Pigeon and Little Zion Baptist Church and was the road leading from one church to another, and Thomas Lincoln often attended Little Zion Baptist Church located near my father's home; that on one occasion when father was preaching at Pigeon Baptist Church Abe Lincoln got up on a stump a short distance from the church and made a speech, and soon had as large a crowd of listeners as my father had in the church; neighbors were few and would go a great distance to attend log-rollings, house-raisings, and look after the sick."

James Stevens in a verified statement says that he knew James Romine and William Oskins who lived just south of the Lincoln home, and knew the Lincoln family well, and they talked with me frequently about the Lincolns. John Romine said that Abraham Lincoln never hurried about anything; that they started to Illinois in a wagon drawn by oxen and the roads were very bad; that Thomas Lincoln owned a certain tract of land of eighty acres which he wanted to sell or trade for a good horse, and after they had started he (Romine) followed them and traded a young horse for the eighty acres of land. (Record shows the conveyance of this land to Romine by Lincoln.)k12

No attempt has been made to record all of the established incidents in the life of Abraham Lincoln which occurred while he resided in southern Indiana. It has been our intention, so far as we could from reliable sources, to create the home life and circumstances surrounding young Lincoln while living in Indiana. The story of his early life belongs to the stage of civilization which even the older people of our day have almost forgotten and which the younger never knew. It was a life of toil, of hardship, of poverty, but it was the independent poverty of the western wilderness, and it made men of those who fought their way out of it.

Little can we know or understand of the struggles of the toiling men and women; of the utter destitution of their surroundings; of their desolate loneliness in the rude and isolated backwoods of the frontier; of the mental starvation; of the physical suffering; and the pitiful striving to make a home and secure shelter against the rigors of the climate.

The romance of the life of this greatest American of Americans, and the struggle from mediocrity to empyrean heights of human fame will always inspire the lovers of genius and true character. For out of these humble conditions in the fertile field of American opportunity he arose to the highest pinnacle of human fame. And now America, yea, the

12 For the complete affidavits mentioned here, see William L. Barker, "History of the Lincoln Route," *Indiana History Bulletin* 4, extra no. 1, *Proceedings of the Southwestern Indiana Historical Society during Its Seventh year* (December 1926): 43–70.

civilized world, bows in humble reverence at the tomb of the "mightiest of the mighty dead."

I shall conclude by reading portions from an article entitled, "At the Shrine of Motherhood," written by me some years ago:

It is a general rule that all superior men inherit the elements of superiority from their mothers. The mother, in her office, holds the key of the soul; and she it is who stamps the coin of character and by her gentle care, she transforms the vital forces of life. She is crowned queen of the world. Whether her realm embraces the title heads and kings of earth, or the lowly of men, the power and beauty, the sweetness and gentleness, the heroism and majesty of a mother's love remains the same.

It was a company of distinguished men who bared their heads and stood in reverential silence at the tomb of the mother of the great emancipator in the Lincoln Park located a few miles from Boonville.

Here, in an unpretentious place, rests the ashes of one of nature's sweetest daughters who gave to the world a life that was so profoundly to affect the future of human-kind.

On this beautiful June day, nature had clothed the little city of distinguished dead in her finest robes of beauty and when the line of pilgrims halted at the hill-top and stood encircled about the tomb, the sunlight struggling through the branches of the trees shot athwart the granite shaft and threw a spell of sublime reverence over those who stood about.

Her tomb is not marked by a mausoleum, stately and grand, but a granite monument of simple design, the gift of loving friends of her distinguished son marks her resting place.

Here then, amid the heaven-kissing hills of southern Indiana rests the mother of Lincoln. Here, within these peaceful valleys she lived her life of love and peace and sacrifice. Here, she met the simple folks of the country-side and won their love by her womanly bearing and sweet demeanor. Here, she toiled and wrought and planned and dreamed, perhaps of future greatness for those she loved, and while her life was circumscribed by weary toil and uneventful days, within her soul was a kingdom of love and truth, a heritage to transmit to the illustrious off-spring of her heart.

Here, when life was dreary and her pathway led through life's adversity, with faith and hope she looked beyond the density of hill and forest and saw, for him, the dream come true.

And here, the shadows darkened, the evening star began to set, the parting day of life began to wane and here the flickering flame of life flared up in one last mighty effort to burn for those she loved, and then died out.

Here, beside a new made mound at eventide of an October day, stood the boy of ten, who in after years was to shape the destiny of millions of men and wear the martyr's wreath of glory. Here, at this very spot, his childish tears made wet the earth that enfolded in its close embrace, his hope and stay.

With sobbing heart he turned and went away, leaving behind the greatest treasure of childhood, and carried with him only the memory of her sweet voice, her gentle touch and sympathetic smile.

And in after years when life was full with deeds achieved and duty well performed, he paid immortal tribute to the memory of his love by saying, "All that I am, or hope to be, I owe to my angel mother."

—*At the Shrine of Mothers, Roscoe Kiper*

KIPER'S NOTES

a.   *Record Book*, Perry Circuit Court, page 8.

b.   Little Pigeon Baptist Church *Minute Book.*

c.   *Nicolas [Nicolay] and Hay*, Vol. I, p. 31, gives the date of death of Nancy Hanks Lincoln as October 5, 1818.

d.   Judge John E. Iglehart, "The Coming of the English to Indiana," *Indiana Magazine of History*, June 1, 1919, page 139.

e.   The state capital was moved to Indianapolis in 182[5].

f.   *History of Spencer County*, page 4.

g.   *History of Spencer County.*

h.   Esarey, *History of Indiana*, p. 297. As early as 1810 Jonathan Jennings had inaugurated the practice of sending out handbills to voters. See Dunn's *Indiana*, p. 408.

i.   De la Hunt, *History of Perry County*, 1916, p. 63.

j.   William Jones, who made this affidavit, was a reputable citizen of Spencer and Warrick counties, and has lived in the locality of the Lincoln home all his life. He was a captain in the Union Army in the Civil War and has in his possession a gold ornamented sword and scabbard which was presented to his father by the citizens of that community. He died a few years ago.

k.   A number of affidavits of early settlers of their recollection of the Lincoln family is carefully preserved in numerous issues of the Boonville *Standard*, of which Thomas E. Downs, now Secretary of the Warrick County Historical Society, is the editor.

ROSCOE KIPER (1874–1937) was an attorney in Boonville, Indiana; a circuit court judge; and a two-term state senator representing Vanderburgh, Warrick, and Posey Counties. He was a student of Lincoln lore, a well-known speaker, and president of the Southwestern Indiana Historical Society.

2

★ ★ ★

Lincoln's Environment in Indiana

ROSCOE KIPER*

Judge and state senator Roscoe Kiper contends that Lincoln's Indiana years significantly shaped the man Abraham Lincoln.

IT IS DIFFICULT TO MEASURE JUST HOW MUCH OF INHERITED quality and how much of environment enter into the make-up of a personality, but it is evident that environment has much to do in opening the door of opportunity for inherited characteristics to manifest themselves in the life of an individual.

Circumstances of environment are the vehicles by which the born and bred characteristics may be transported from obscurity to the light of day. Thus, while environment may not be everything in shaping character, it is a very important factor in enabling us to interpret character.

A view of the character and personality of Lincoln associated with finance, captains of industry, theologians, or scientists, would take away everything that has contributed to our conception of the man, his life and destiny. Therefore, Lincoln is Lincoln, and no one else, because of his personal qualities, both inherited and acquired through environmental influences. Of course, we are unable to say just how much of Lincoln's greatness can be attributed to his associations while living in Indiana, and if measured by the meagre emphasis placed upon the period of his

* Presented to the Southwestern Indiana Historical Society on 27 May 1925 and published in *Indiana History Bulletin* 3, extra no. 1, *Proceedings of the Southwestern Indiana Historical Society: Papers Read before the Society at Various Meetings, 1920–1925* (December 1925): 94–96.

sojourn upon Hoosier soil by all the historians and his biographers, it did not amount to very much. It is pertinent to ask if there were any personal traits of character, peculiarities of disposition, or manifestations of qualities of power and influences shown by him in future years, which had their counterpart in, or could have been the result of, his environment and associations while living in Indiana. Lincoln was probably seven years of age when he came to Indiana with his parents, and he remained on Hoosier soil until he was twenty-one years of age. From reliable information we gather the fact that during this time he was out of the state on only one occasion—when he made a trip to New Orleans—and with this exception fourteen years of his life were spent among the hills, streams and valleys of Indiana, and in social life and environment that has Lincoln, the man, to speak for its power and influence in character building.

It would be contrary to human experience and all established laws of individual development to say that all the elements in Lincoln's character were acquired and his personal traits were entirely developed after leaving Indiana for Illinois. When Lincoln moved from Indiana it is no doubt true that he had much to learn as to the practical application of the knowledge he had acquired, but an observation of his environment, his opportunities of coming in contact with and observing some of the strongest minds of the state who lived in his day, his insatiable desire to appropriate to himself everything of value and consequence that came his way, together with his frequent manifestation of certain qualities of mind and character in after life, drives us to the irresistible conclusion that many of his outstanding characteristics, his uncommon power of observation, his penetrating mind, his ability to properly appraise individual character, his appreciation of the problems of those who must struggle and toil, his tenacious adherence to that which he believed to be right, his open mind and freedom of thought, his ruggedness of mind and tenderness of soul, were laid deep in his nature during the nascent period of his life when living in Indiana.

Lincoln had a rugged physical frame built on great proportions; his sinews of iron and powers of endurance, which came to him through the struggles incident to pioneer life in Indiana, built for him a strong body which became a fit dwelling place for his fruitful mind and great soul—a physical structure that in after years could not be broken by fatigue nor shaken by storms that raged like Furies. Incessant physical toil, simple but nourishing food, a life lived close to mother earth, and a being surcharged with forces coming from a free and open existence, all in the forests of Indiana, gave Lincoln a power of endurance that attracted the attention of all who knew him.

Among the great things that were said about Lincoln was this, that "he carried his homely virtues throughout his life to his death."[1] There is a world of meaning in the words "homely virtues." One who possesses homely virtues is incapable of cant and hypocrisy. Lincoln had acquired the ability to appraise men and things at their real value. His sense of moral proportion was developed to a high degree and this characteristic was manifested in many of his boyhood circumstances. He felt it right and proper to pay for damages to a borrowed book when the damages were caused by his own thoughtlessness. And in after years he maintained that the laborer was worthy of his hire and involuntary servitude was the greatest iniquity of man.

The simple folk who were Lincoln's neighbors in Indiana and in whose social atmosphere he lived and grew were men and women possessed of homely virtues. Call the roll of the men and women who were associates of Lincoln and we find that they were law-abiding people. The records do not show a single instance where they violated the laws of the land. Their ancestors were clean and pure. Their helping hands went forth to neighbors in distress, their ideals of justice and fair dealing were high and character, rather than wealth, was the medium of exchange. Their wants were few but temperate and wholesome. Theirs were lives of toil, of hardship, of poverty, but it was the independent poverty of the western wilderness and it made men of those who fought their way out of it.

Lincoln was religious. Pigeon Church, located a short distance from his home, was the religious and social center of the community. Here came the pioneer preachers of his day. They were men whose moral and

---

1 We cannot discern who Kiper quotes here because the specific quotation does not appear in any available academic searches, but "homely virtues" does seem to be a phrase applied to Lincoln and other leaders during the early twentieth century. See, for example, *Lincoln Centennial Addresses Delivered at the Memorial Exercises Held at Springfield, Illinois, on 12 February 1909 Commemorating the One Hundredth Birthday of Abraham Lincoln* (Springfield: Illinois Centennial Commission, 1909).

religious ideas could not be subsidized. Men, devoted and sincere, whose utterances came from souls on fire with a holy zeal. They stood on the outposts of the wilderness implanting in eager minds and souls the high ideals of a pure and righteous life. Under this influence religion became to Lincoln the way of life, a materialized influence for good, a life of loving deeds, an influence that followed him to his grave.

Lincoln believed in the sanctity of womanhood. This high respect for womankind was characteristic of the pioneer. Although her life was a hard and uneventful one, as the queen of the household and mother of the race, the pioneer father and husband threw about her the magic circle of reverence and high respect, and woe be to the charlatan who violated this sanctity of womanly virtue. The affection and tenderness of Lincoln for womankind which he manifested in after years were implanted in his being in his boyhood days when mother love was the only ray of light that cheered his humble existence. Many and varied were the influences of his Indiana home that were planted and grew in his great soul.

ROSCOE KIPER (1874–1937) was an attorney in Boonville, Indiana; a circuit court judge; and a two-term state senator representing Vanderburgh, Warrick, and Posey Counties. He was a student of Lincoln lore, a well-known speaker, and president of the Southwestern Indiana Historical Society.

3

★ ★ ★

Lincoln in Indiana

WILLIAM FORTUNE*

William Fortune (1863–1942) was born in Boonville, Indiana. Although he later moved to Indianapolis as a successful businessman, he retained a lifelong interest in Lincoln and their shared roots in southwestern Indiana. Fortune published several essays about Abraham Lincoln and the area and interviewed persons who knew Lincoln during his Indiana years. In this paper, Fortune defends Indiana's influence on Lincoln and highlights the impressive background of those living in the region.

I COME BACK ALWAYS TO THIS REGION WITH FEELINGS THAT are almost inexpressible. There is something of emotion, not only because of the associations of my own early days, but also because of the thoughts that come regarding the life of the man who lived here in the formative days of his great life. It impresses me profoundly to think that Abraham Lincoln in his boyhood days roamed through these woods and over these fields. There were even then growing within him the mind and soul that afterwards made him not only the greatest man of this country, but, I think, one of the greatest men that ever lived on earth. As time goes on that judgment, I think, is growing in the minds of the people. The last years of Abraham Lincoln's life seem to have been lived with his head above earthly things, under an influence that can only be considered as divine. I believe that as time goes on Abraham Lincoln's position in the

---

* Fortune originally presented this paper on 14 October 1925 and published it in Indiana History Bulletin 3, extra no. 1, Proceedings of the Southwestern Indiana Historical Society during Its Sixth Year: Papers Read before the Society at Various Meetings, 1920–1925 (December 1925): 60–64.

world and in the minds of the people will be surpassed by only one other life. Those last years of his have in them the evidence of inspiration and almost of divinity.

When we trace back through the life of Abraham Lincoln and the experiences that made the man we are brought here to this region where he lived from his seventh to his twenty-first year. Out of this humble life in the woods and amid these associations with the plain people of this part of the world there was gathered by him that sort of understanding of human nature, there was developed in him that greatness of soul that made the man he finally became. I have long had the feeling that there has yet never been any estimate of the man produced that sufficiently traces out the influences of this home in the forest where he grew up. The usual historical sketch does not sufficiently illuminate the subject. It is usually treated rather perfunctorily. I am hoping that there will yet be written a history of the life of Lincoln that will show fairly and sufficiently the part that this region had in his making.

This part of Indiana, in the days when the Lincoln family came here, was one of the most important parts of the State. It was more of a political center than is realized by most of us, for here within ten or twelve miles of where Lincoln grew up as a boy lived a man who was at that time one of the leading political figures in Indiana. I refer to Ratliff Boon, one of the early governors of Indiana, who afterwards became the representative of Indiana in Congress, which was regarded in those days as an honor comparable in importance and influence to a Senatorship.[1] It was a position that commanded much power; Ratliff Boon was a person to whom people came from over the State. It is significant that when the first contract was made for a mail route through Indiana, it was made to embrace the place of residence of Ratliff Boon. It was from New Harmony to Louisville via Boonville, and this part of the State was therefore traversed by many travelers; not a few of them were visitors to Ratliff Boon to seek his influence and help in their political aspirations.

Gentryville, I believe, is not much more than twelve miles from where Ratliff Boon lived. In Gentryville there was a store where the people of

1 Ratliff Boon (1781–1844) served as the second governor of Indiana from 12 September 1822 to 5 December 1822 and thereafter served as lieutenant governor and congressman. Also, Boon was instrumental in forming the Indiana Democratic Party.

this neighborhood gathered to talk, to gossip perhaps, and to hold their discussions of public questions. Abraham Lincoln was an important figure in all that. The boy's great desire for knowledge and his limited opportunities were such that he took advantage of every chance to get information. They tell us, you know, that he used to sit on the roadside waiting for some traveler to come by, merely to get the opportunity to ask questions and to learn more about the world. The talk in a locality of this kind, with such an important political figure as the founder of Boonville so near, naturally had an important influence upon Lincoln. His education was only such as he could gather for himself from others and from a few books in the neighborhood, only a half dozen, I believe. Not very far from here, at New Harmony, was one of the very best libraries in the Western country, but it was not available to Abraham Lincoln.[2] There were only a few books that he could borrow.[3]

Not only Ratliff Boon, but Joe Lane, even then a popular aspirant for political honors, lived only a few miles from here. In 1860 on one of the Democratic tickets in opposition to Lincoln were Breckenridge and Lane; the latter was the Joe Lane who had lived in this neighborhood in the days when Abraham Lincoln was here. There were still others that might be mentioned, who were figures of great interest in this locality. Yet in most of the lives of Abraham Lincoln you find no reference to the surroundings and the circumstances here that undoubtedly had a very great influence upon his life. I am hopeful that we shall yet have a proper treatment of that subject.

It was back in 1881 that I first became interested in what you now call the "Lincoln Inquiry," though at that time there was no thought of characterizing it in that way. General James C. Veatch of Rockport came down to Boonville where I lived, and proposed to me that I go with him to visit this region of Spencer County and talk with the survivors who had known Lincoln when he lived among them. We came here together and spent three or four days talking with such survivors as there were and getting their stories. General Veatch knew Lincoln personally and

2 In 1814, New Harmony was established in far southwestern Indiana by Lutheran separatists, but they sold it about 1824 to a group of intellectuals seeking to form a utopian society. The town became a center of learning and research and boasted an extensive library.

3 There is no conclusive evidence that Lincoln interacted with the community of scientists and educators at New Harmony.

was his friend. He was the man chosen to represent Indiana in meeting Lincoln at the western border line of the state when he passed through Indiana on his way to Washington to become President of the United States. General Veatch told me that his greeting from Lincoln was most cordial and that Lincoln immediately began asking questions about people in Spencer County whom he had known when he lived there. It seemed that he remembered them all and he sent many messages.

I am mentioning General Veatch for another reason. He was a grand man, an outstanding figure in his locality, an outstanding man in his state.[4] He rendered great service in the Civil War, and he is one of the men, who, if I might suggest it to you, I think your Historical Society should find some way to properly honor. I think it will be found, if it is thoroughly investigated, that General Veatch left some important data relating to Lincoln's life in this region. I remember his telling me at that time that he had written some things himself. I have appealed to Mrs. Rabb, who is here today, a native of this county, and a great honor to it, and who is doing a great work in stimulating interest in historical matters in Indiana. I have appealed to her to endeavor to get a worthy story of the life of General Veatch, as one of the things that ought to be preserved, and I think that she has taken some steps in that direction.

I wonder if there is sufficient appreciation of the importance of Lincoln to this locality. It seems to me that there is an opportunity to do a thing here which will not only be fine for your locality, but stand out before the whole world. Over at Hodgenville, Kentucky, there has been erected a memorial that has given great distinction to that locality, and has probably brought more visitors to the State of Kentucky than anything else. I refer to that wonderful memorial building that stands over the log cabin in which Abraham Lincoln was born. The nation voluntarily contributed that structure to mark the place of his birth; but the place of his birth is not more worthy of honored recognition than the place where he grew up and where there came into his life those impressions and influences and thoughts that helped to make him great.

4 James Veatch (1819–1895) served as auditor of Spencer County, Indiana, state legislator, and prominent officer during the Civil War. In Daniel Hayford's piece in this volume titled, "Early Days in Spencer County," Hayford asserts that Veatch played a notable role in securing Lincoln's nomination for president in 1860.

This hill over here in which the Lincoln home stood is properly the site for a great memorial structure of some kind. What could be done by the people of this part of the state that would bring to them greater distinction and greater honor, and if you want to think of it in that way, greater financial returns, than the development of this site into one of the outstanding historic spots of this country? There ought to be something there worthy of the life of Abraham Lincoln, and if there were no better way of getting it, it ought to be and would be worth every penny that could possibly be raised by taxation among your own people to put it there, not merely as a glorification of that which is most distinctive in your history, but as a means of bringing the world to Spencer County. I know of no greater opportunity than you have right here.[5]

These undertakings have to start in some way. Usually they begin with a mere expression of an idea. One of the most interesting things in life is to see an idea grow into a great concrete achievement. If in Spencer County you should start a movement for a great memorial located where Lincoln's home stood, would it not obtain the co-operation of the rest of Indiana, which would like to have its share in a proper memorial to Abraham Lincoln? It is something to think about.

WILLIAM FORTUNE (1863–1942) became interested in Lincoln's Indiana period while growing up in Warrick County. Although he later moved to Indianapolis (and was integral to that city's development), Fortune always retained a lifelong interest in Lincoln and their shared roots in southwestern Indiana. In 1881, Fortune published a history of Warrick County. Later that year, he joined General James L. Veatch in interviewing Spencer County residents who remembered Lincoln. Fortune wrote several papers about Lincoln's Indiana boyhood and corresponded with Lincoln biographers, notably Ida M. Tarbell and Albert J. Beveridge. In Indianapolis, Fortune worked as a newspaper editor and successful businessman.

5 Today, this site is part of Lincoln Boyhood National Memorial.

The belated funeral of Nancy Hanks Lincoln.

Originally appeared in Wayne Whipple, The Story-Life
of Lincoln *(Philadelphia: J. C. Winston, 1908).*

Facing, Artist John Rowbotham made this sketch of Nancy Hanks
Lincoln's grave in 1865. The cemetery was no longer used by pioneers
after the Little Pigeon Baptist Church Cemetery was laid out in 1825.

Indiana Historical Society, from Joseph H. Barrett, Life of Abraham
Lincoln *(Cincinnati: Moore, Wilstach, and Baldwin, 1865).*

The grave of Nancy Hanks Lincoln was permanently marked with this marble stone placed at the site on 27 November 1879. Peter Studebaker of South Bend, Indiana, sent $50.00 to the postmaster of Rockport, Indiana, to cover the expense. The grave is now located in Lincoln Boyhood National Memorial.

Lincoln Boyhood National Memorial Historic Photo No. 251.

In the 1920s, visitors to Lincoln Park (Nancy Hanks Lincoln's gravesite) entered from the Lincoln City side through gates guarded by lions on stone posts. In 1925, the area became part of the Indiana State Department of Conservation. This park served as a favorite location for Civil War veteran reunions.

Indiana Historical Society. From *Joseph H. Barrett,* Life of Abraham Lincoln *(Cincinnati: Moore, Wilstach, and Baldwin, 1865).*

Facing top, Indiana Lincoln Inquiry authors make frequent comments about photographs or sketches of the Indiana Lincoln cabin. This is one of the earliest made by John Rowbotham in 1865. All images depict the cabin being built when the Lincolns decided to move to Illinois and thus not having been lived in by them. This cabin is generally referred to as the 1829 cabin.

Indiana Historical Society, from Joseph H. Barrett, Life of Abraham Lincoln *(Cincinnati: Moore, Wilstach, and Baldwin, 1865).*

Facing bottom, In the first attempt to mark the location of the Indiana Lincoln cabin, this stone was placed on 28 April 1917. It is known as the Spencer County Memorial Stone. The memorial probably marks the site of the 1829 cabin the Lincolns were building when they decided to move to Illinois.

Lincoln Boyhood National Memorial.

Above, The Spencer County Memorial Stone was moved to another location in the park, and in 1935 a bronze casting of sill logs and a hearth, designed by Indiana native Thomas Hibben, was erected on the site. A stone wall enclosed the cabin-site memorial. This memorial remains in Lincoln Boyhood National Memorial today surrounded by a living historical farm.

O. V. Brown Collection. Photo courtesy of Daryl Lovell.

Thomas Lincoln oversaw construction of the Little Pigeon Baptist Church in 1821, depicted in this sketch by John Rowbotham in 1865. Lincoln's father, stepmother, and sister were members but not Abraham. The church is now surrounded by Lincoln State Park.

Indiana Historical Society. From Joseph H. Barrett, Life of Abraham Lincoln *(Cincinnati: Moore, Wilstach, and Baldwin, 1865).*

Above, This large monument replaced a simple stone on
Sarah Lincoln Grigsby's grave in 1916. She died in 1828 as
a result of childbirth. The baby was buried with her.

O. V. Brown Collection, courtesy of Daryl Lovell.

Facing, Sarah Lincoln Grigsby (Abraham's sister) was buried in the Little
Pigeon Church Cemetery. This cemetery is less than one mile south of
where her mother was buried. In this early view, Sarah's stone is the
simple one to the right of her husband's, Aaron Grigsby's, tall stone.

Originally appeared in Ida Tarbell, ed., "Abraham Lincoln,"
McClure's Magazine 5, no. 6 (November 1895).

Reportedly an image
of Thomas Lincoln
(1778–1851),
Abraham's father.

*Courtesy of the Abraham
Lincoln Library and
Museum, Lincoln
Memorial University.*

THE CRAWFORD PLACE. [See Pages 25 & 26.]

The Josiah and Elizabeth Crawford house where Lincoln frequently
worked and visited.

*Indiana Historical Society. From Joseph H. Barrett, Life of Abraham Lincoln
(Cincinnati: Moore, Wilstach, and Baldwin, 1865).*

ANDERSON CREEK FERRY,
Where Mr. Lincoln was Ferryman for Nine Months.

A mid-1800s view of the Anderson River site where Abraham Lincoln operated a ferry for James Taylor in 1825. Lincoln talked with passengers of the Ohio River steamboats and read newspapers from cities up and down the river.

Indiana Historical Society. From Joseph H. Barrett, Life of Abraham Lincoln *(Cincinnati: Moore, Wilstach, and Baldwin, 1865).*

After Abraham ferried two men with their baggage from the shore out to a steamboat in the Ohio River, they dropped two silver half-dollars into the boat. Thrilled, Abraham later remarked, "I could scarcely believe my eyes as I picked up the money."

Originally appeared in Clifton M. Nichols, Life of Abraham Lincoln *(New York: Mast, Crowell & Kirkpatrick, 1896).*

"The Boyhood of Abraham Lincoln" by Eastman Johnson.

*Eastman Johnson, Chromolithograph by L. Prang & Co., Boston.
Image is available from the United States Library of Congress's
Prints and Photographs division under the digital ID ppmsca.18446.*

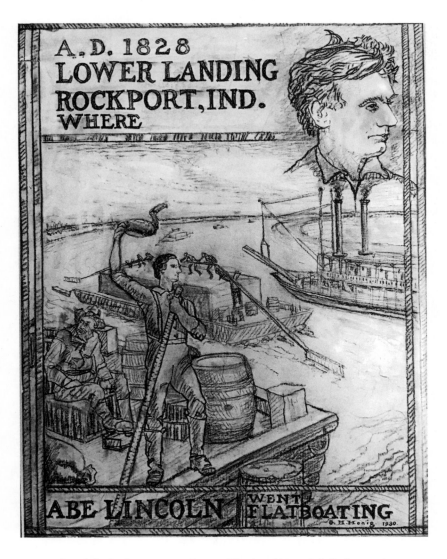

A 1930 sketch by Indiana artist George Honig of Lincoln's flatboat trip.

Drawing made by George Honig; original owned by William E. Bartelt.

In her presentation to the Southwestern Indiana Historical Society, Anna O'Flynn referenced a cedar tree planted by James Gentry in remembrance of the Lincoln family when they moved to Illinois in 1830. This sketch was made from a photograph taken for O'Flynn at the time.

Originally appeared in Ida Tarbell, ed., "Abraham Lincoln," McClure's Magazine 5, no. 6 (November 1895).

Judge John Pitcher, who lent law books to Abraham
Lincoln and helped inspire his legal career.

Originally appeared in Jesse W. Weik, The Real Lincoln
(Boston: Houghton Mifflin, 1922).

John E. Iglehart, founder of the Southwestern Indiana
Historical Society and the Indiana Lincoln Inquiry.

Willard Library.

Bess Ehrmann, former president of the Southwestern Indiana Historical Society and curator of the Spencer County Historical Society.

Spencer County Public Library.

PART 2

LINCOLN'S NEIGHBORS AND INFLUENCES

4

★ ★ ★

Lincoln's Indiana Neighbors

BESS V. EHRMANN*

Bess V. Ehrmann summarizes the Indiana Lincoln Inquiry's purpose when she writes here, "I hope to prove that the environment of Lincoln was such as to inspire him and cause him to yearn for better things in life, and to give him opportunities of social and intellectual life generally among a good class of people." She introduces us to prominent citizens of the time who perhaps inspired the young Abraham Lincoln.

MANY WRITERS HAVE WRITTEN BOOKS ABOUT ABRAHAM Lincoln, his ancestry, childhood, manhood, and political career, but little thought has been given to the environment of his youth or to those neighbors and boyhood friends of his in Indiana and the influence they undoubtedly had on his life and character.

Almost eight years ago John E. Iglehart, of Evansville, founded the Southwestern Indiana Historical Society and started the "Lincoln Inquiry" which aroused the state to the realization that neither the site of the Lincoln home nor the grave of Lincoln's mother had been properly marked. Also there was the fact of over two thousand histories written about Lincoln, but none on the fourteen years of his life spent in Indiana. Historians had passed over that period as if it counted for little in the making of the man, yet they were the formative years from seven to twenty-one.

* Ehrmann delivered this paper on 17 November 1925 and later published it in the *Indiana History Bulletin*, Vol. 5, extra no. 2, *Proceedings of the Ninth Annual Indiana History Conference* (April 1928): 65–75.

Several years ago I wrote a paper on the "Lincoln Inquiry" in which I mentioned a list of pioneer families whose descendants are still living in Spencer County, and made the statement that Lincoln could have known and been influenced by any of these early settlers—all of them upright, honorable men, some of them highly educated and of aristocratic lineage, many of them holding public office. It is of those pioneer neighbors that I wish to write to portray the type of the early settler in southwestern Indiana where Lincoln lived from the age of seven to twenty-one. I hope to prove that the environment of Lincoln was such as to inspire him and cause him to yearn for better things in life, and to give him opportunities of social and intellectual life generally among a good class of people.

Historians have given southern Indiana a black eye, claiming that there was great illiteracy and unusually low standards of life, and that few desirable people lived in Spencer County at that early date. This has resulted from an absence of historical data available to persons out of the state and to historians generally and the fact that no history of the people and institutions of southwestern Indiana has been attempted outside of local histories until the Southwestern Indiana Historical Society was organized among the descendants of pioneers themselves and carried on under Mr. Iglehart's direction and untiring efforts. In the short time we have been working, a field so rich in Lincoln data relating to the character of these people in Lincoln's time has been developed by us that investigators like Miss Ida Tarbell freely recognize a revolution which supersedes the view taken by many historians, some of them recent, who still insist on the Kentucky and Illinois view of Lincoln's history.

To live in a community one's entire life and to have heard of the early people from those who have lived there before you causes you to know such a community and its many families well. You know their social and economic status and those of their ancestors far better than an outsider. We who have spent most of our lives in Spencer County and know those early families, claim that those pioneer men and women were in many cases the most highly educated (for that time) and aristocratic people ever living in southern Indiana. To stamp out the blot of this supposed illiteracy of southern Indiana's early settlers and to describe fairly the better class of people whom the early travelers seldom saw and did not know is the desire of many people living in Indiana. People who have lived here, and their ancestors before them, for several generations know such statements to be false. In a late and splendid history of the *Literature of the Middle Western Frontier* previous to 1840 by Dr. Ralph Leslie Rusk of the history department of Columbia University, which applies the Turner doctrine[1] of the frontier in American history in its political and social phases to the creation of new literature west of the mountains, a book that will be used for several generations as a reference book, this assertion, and for the reasons I have stated, is again made. How impossible it is to always judge people's ancestry, breeding and mental qualities by mere physical appearance or manner of dress! It is small wonder that people from a distance coming to a small country town and seeing its inhabitants for a few hours more or less are unable to speak correctly of the people.

Abraham Lincoln's boyhood and young manhood was spent in what is now the little village of Lincoln City, a part of Spencer County, where the land is not the best for agricultural wealth. This being true during the days of Lincoln's living there, as well as now, the people were plain, hard-working men and women, but some of them had the best blood of our country in their veins.

I remember reading one of Elbert Hubbard's *Little Journeys* to Lincoln City to visit the grave of Lincoln's mother. He spoke of the drab, washed out and hopeless looking people who came to the train to meet them and of his thinking that Lincoln could have found no inspiration either from the country or people when he lived there.[2] Sometimes one fails to judge correctly. I know just such looking people in our county today who, if known well, with their background of ancestry and tradition compare favorably with people of a higher education and culture. The lifelong struggle with the soil often takes all the pride, vanity, and affectation

1 Typically referred to as the Turner Thesis, the idea originates in an influential essay by Frederick Jackson Turner presented in 1893 (and published a year later) titled, *The Significance of the Frontier in American History*. Turner argued the frontier shaped American democracy, independence, ingenuity, and optimism. In the process, he says, the frontier also shaped the American story and drove American history.

2 For an account of Hubbard's visit to Lincoln City, Indiana, see Elbert Hubbard, *Abe Lincoln and Nancy Hanks* (East Aurora, NY: The Roycrofters, 1920). Hubbard sounds more complimentary of the locals in this account, published five years after his death on the *Lusitania*.

from people's character, leaving them plain and simple in manner, looks, and speech.

I have in mind one Spencer County man, a wealthy farmer of today, who to a stranger might seem crude, almost illiterate, on a mere acquaintance, and yet the bluest of blood flows in this man's veins. He is well educated, his family tree goes back to royalty, and his grandfather and father were among Spencer County's early men, educated and cultured, the grandfather a man whom Lincoln undoubtedly knew when he lived here. This is just one illustration of how one can only judge men by having lived long enough among them.

The Lincolns did not come to a county of illiterates when they came to Spencer County, but settled within a few miles of some of the most brilliant minds that Indiana ever produced. No doubt there were at that time among many of the backwoodsmen of the Alleghenies, men who could not read and write well, some not at all, as Roosevelt describes them in his *Winning of the West*, but Roosevelt fairly, impartially, and sympathetically described this class of people as a different class from those referred to by some travelers and a few well-known novelists, who from ignorance, bias, or some special reason have pictured the lowest class of low life (found everywhere), leaving the impression that these were all of the people here to be found.

Being the third generation of my family on my grandfather's side and the fourth on my grandmother's to live in Spencer County, I have known these old families here most intimately. Some of my grandfather's and grandmother's friends of that early day I knew also, as a goodly number of them lived to a ripe old age.

Among this number was Mrs. Margaret Wright,[3] granddaughter of Daniel Grass, the first white settler in Spencer County. Mrs. Wright talked to me many times of those early days and early people, as did my grandmother and mother, and you had only to know Mrs. Wright and talk to her to realize that Daniel Grass and his people were persons of culture and refinement. Indians had killed the parents of Daniel Grass and he was reared by the family of Colonel Andrew Hynes, of Elizabethtown, Kentucky. William P. Duvall married a daughter of Colonel Andrew

3 Margaret Elizabeth Wright lived from 1831 to 1922.

Hynes. These men were not only friends of Daniel Grass but they financed his land operations in the Indiana Territory around Rockport, in Spencer County. Daniel Grass was such a prominent man in Spencer County, being Lay Judge in the early courts, elected by the people of the county, and county agent in 1818, and for some years later, that the Lincolns undoubtedly knew him. Judge Grass was also in the Constitutional Convention of 1816, and then in the legislature and was known far and wide. On his way to attend the legislature at Corydon, he would pass through the little village of Jonesboro, afterwards known as Gentryville although one-half mile from the present site of Gentryville.[4] Travelers often spent the night with the Gentrys and the Joneses. Lincoln had the opportunity to see and know such persons as they traveled back and forth. Judge Kiper, of Boonville, in a short history of Lincoln expresses the opinion that Daniel Grass no doubt had a great influence on the young Lincoln.

Then there was General Joseph Lane who lived but a few miles from the home of the Lincolns. He served in the state legislature as a representative or senator from 1822 to 1846, and in order to reach the state capital at Corydon, he traveled the road which passed the Joneses' store where Lincoln worked.[5] Ratliff Boon[6] lived near the Lincolns and was an unusual man in many ways, intelligent and with a wonderful personality, eight times elected to Congress and twice elected lieutenant-governor.

John Morgan,[7] who was the first clerk of Spencer County, from 1818 to 1825, was an educated man who came from Pennsylvania about 1816. He was well educated, although a self-made man, and his county records have seldom been equalled for neatness and accuracy. He was also the first postmaster in Rockport from June 6, 1[8]18, to May 9, 1823. I have

4 Ehrmann provides an incorrect account of Jonesboro. William Jones (1803–1864) did not come to Spencer County until the latter part of Lincoln's time there. Jones probably worked for Gentry and Romine in stores at the current location of Gentryville. Lincoln certainly knew Jones well and probably worked for Jones at this time. Jones opened his first store in that location shortly after the Lincolns left, and Jones did not own land in the Jonesboro area until the mid-1830s.

5 Joseph Lane (1801–1881) lived on the Ohio River near the boundary of Warrick and Vanderburgh Counties, some twenty-five miles from the Lincolns. Another road along the Ohio River provided him a more direct route to Corydon.

6 Ratliff Boon (1781–1844) also served as second governor of Indiana from 12 September to 5 December 1822 upon the resignation of Governor Jonathan Jennings.

7 John Morgan lived from 1785 to 1825.

known many of John Morgan's descendants, all of whom show their good blood and breeding, several in this family being unusually gifted in an intellectual way. I have seen their heirlooms of furniture, linen, silver, and pictures which tend to prove their ancestry. The Lincolns were almost sure to have known John Morgan. At the time Morgan became postmaster, Rockport was known as Mt. Duvall, having been named in honor of Honorable William Duvall, friend of Daniel Grass.[a] Duvall lived at Beardstown and so did W. R. Hynes and Daniel Grass. These men were promoting their land investments and brought to the attention of their Kentucky neighbors the wonderful county in Indiana. Duvall was born in Virginia in 1784, and received much of his education there. He had studied law under Judge Brodnax, one of the early judges near Hartford, Kentucky. The Lincolns could have known Duvall and W. R. Hynes and Grass in Kentucky and may have been influenced by them to come to the new county in Indiana.

Abe Lincoln was of an inquiring mind—we have his own words, addressed to Leonard Swett, that he (Lincoln) had read through every book he had ever heard of in that county for a radius of fifty miles from the farm upon which he lived; he must have availed himself of every opportunity to talk to people as well as read their books.[8] As Rockport is only a little over seventeen miles from where Lincoln lived, and Boonville is almost as near, Lincoln did not have far to go to come in contact with some of those well-known public men.

Stephen P. Cissna[9] was the first doctor in Rockport and perhaps visited the Lincolns in a professional way as he rode horseback for miles over the county. I knew some of his descendants, good, intelligent people, some of whom are still living in Spencer County today.

John Pitcher[10] was the first resident attorney in Rockport. He was one of Indiana's most intellectual men and a wonderful orator. He was a member of the legislature in 1830 representing Spencer and Perry counties. He had a splendid library and it has been proved that he loaned Lincoln books. Pitcher was postmaster in Rockport from 1827 to 1832.

8 Although Lincoln did like to read, this statement seems a hyperbole.
9 Stephen P. Cissna lived from 1784 to 1841.
10 John Pitcher lived from 1795 to 1892.

There is no evidence I have seen of any post office nearer the Lincoln farm than Rockport.[11] Thomas Lincoln paid his taxes there and probably the farmers generally knew the postmaster at Rockport, and I think Lincoln knew all of the leading men of the village. He is shown to have known Pitcher well and to have been intimate and confidential with him.

John W. Graham,[12] a man of education and culture, was elected Lay Judge in 1825. His descendants have all been worthwhile people, showing the inheritance of mental gifts and good breeding. There is little doubt that he and young Lincoln were acquainted, for Graham was a candidate for Lay Judge to succeed himself and continued as judge till long after Lincoln left Indiana. Lincoln is known to have frequented the courthouse at Rockport, where he must have seen Judge Graham frequently.

The Crooks family were people of splendid education and were leaders in public affairs during the later years of Lincoln's residence here.

Thomas and Alexander Britton were brothers who came from Virginia to Indiana in 1827. They were both men of culture and education. Alexander Britton's home was the center of church and social activities in those early days, and before any church was built in Rockport, services were held in his house.

Thomas P. Britton[13] was my grandfather. He spoke several languages and his handwriting in the county record books is so beautiful that the county officers of today delight in showing it to visitors. I have often heard my mother and aunt tell how many foreigners were brought to their home on their arrival in Spencer County because my grandfather could speak their language. Often at night there would be so many guests that my grandmother had to make beds on the floor. Many of the older people in Rockport have told me that they spent their first night in Rockport in my grandfather's home. Being clerk and recorder of the county for a number of years, he helped the foreigners to get settled and looked after their land. My mother told me much concerning the social affairs of that early day, the schools and their teachers, and she said my grandfather was often so depressed over the fact that his children could not have the

11 Gentry's Store, less than two miles from the Lincoln cabin, became a post office on 15 June 1825.

12 John W. Graham lived from 1791 to 1855.

13 Thomas Britton lived from 1806 to 1853.

education he wished for them because they only had school at intervals when a teacher could be secured. My grandfather had the first frame residence built in Rockport and the first brick residence, both of which are still standing and in excellent condition. He owned much land in and around Rockport. Azel Dorsey[14] was one of the first school teachers in the county and a man who played rather an important part in affairs of the county. It was in his home, a few miles west of Rockport, that the first court was held. He was one of Abraham Lincoln's teachers.

The very earliest newspapers in Spencer County were destroyed by fire, but I have read and reread several volumes of *The Planter*, a newspaper published in 1848, by Thomas Langdon, who lived here in Lincoln's time. He was a lawyer and had practiced at the bar in New York. He had a college education and was a brilliant man. His grandson and great grandsons are living in Rockport and are engaged in newspaper work today. These early newspapers that are filed in our library tell much of the social, literary, and business affairs of the county, and although published eighteen years after the Lincolns left Indiana, they show the kind of people (for they were the same) who lived near the Lincolns all those formative years of Abe's life. In these papers are mentioned banquets, balls, dinner parties, musical affairs, etc. There was a philosophical society with members such as General J. C. Veatch, W. W. Cotton, James DeBruler, and many others. They studied astronomy, literature, phrenology, magnetism, mesmerism, etc. All young men who desired to improve their minds were urged to belong. In the papers were long lists of books that could be ordered by mail and magazines advertised for sale. News from all over the world was printed, and readers of those early papers would have a general fund of information, if they read nothing else. A phonetic alphabet was edited weekly by General J. C. Veatch and John Crawford.

Such was the type of newspapers in Rockport a few years after the Lincolns moved to Illinois, and we have the proof of Abe Lincoln's going on Saturdays to Gentryville to read the *Louisville Journal*, which was taken by William Jones (Colonel Jones), of Gentryville. Judging from what I

14 Lincoln lists Azel W. Dorsey (1784–1858) as one of his teachers in his autobiographical statement for John L. Scripps.

have read in those early Rockport papers, the *Louisville Journal* would be a still greater source of education to a constant reader.

The Gentry family in Spencer County has always been considered one of the most substantial and respected of any family ever in the county, and we know how much time Lincoln spent with the Gentry boys. I have often talked with different members of the family concerning Lincoln's working for them. They are people of such standards of honesty, right living, and intelligence that they would influence anyone who lived with them as Abe did. Their home life and manner of living was such as to attract and hold the attention of a boy like Lincoln.

It was with Allen Gentry[15] that Lincoln took his first flatboat trip to New Orleans. James Gentry, the father of Allen, owned property in and near Rockport. In 1826 Allen came to live in the house near the river and a short distance from the boat landing where their produce was loaded on the flatboats for southern markets. Mr. and Mrs. Roby and their two daughters came from Gentryville with Allen to keep house for him, and on March 19, 1828, just a short time before Gentry and Lincoln started on their trip, Allen and Ann Roby were married. Lincoln stayed two weeks in Rockport helping to prepare and load the boat for its long trip. The flatboats were made from hewn logs as the trees were chopped down. They were "pegged" together and calked as best they could with the material that they had.[16]

We Spencer County people feel that this first trip of Lincoln's had much influence on him in later years because there is a tradition that on this trip he saw slaves whipped and sold, and vowed to his friend Gentry that if ever he had a chance to hit this evil he would hit it hard.

The Greathouse family was a notable one. John Greathouse[17] had one of the earliest home libraries in Spencer County. He and his family had a good education for that day and time.

John Proctor was one of the county's brilliant men in that early day. He graduated from Harvard in 1813, and came to Spencer County in

15 Allen Gentry lived from 1806 to 1862.

16 For a complete account of the flatboat trip, see Richard Campanella, *Lincoln in New Orleans: The 1828–1831 Flatboat Voyages and Their Place in History* (Lafayette: University of Louisiana at Lafayette Press, 2010).

17 John Greathouse lived from 1791 to about 1857.

1818. His family then and his descendants who live in Rockport today, are some of Spencer County's most cultured and progressive people. I have been told many interesting stories concerning John Proctor, and his culture and refinement by his granddaughter, Mrs. Carrie V. Halbruge.

The Rays and Lamars were the very earliest settlers, educated and of fine family. They did much for Spencer County and are today Spencer County's leading families. They show a background of breeding and culture. The Lincoln family could not have lived fourteen years in Spencer County without knowing the Ray and Lamar families and being impressed by their manner of living and their influence in the county.

The Huffmans came in 1812, and their children and grandchildren have "carried on" in Spencer County and are among its most honored and educated families.

Isaac Veatch[18] was an early settler in Spencer County, coming from Harrison County to Spencer in 1825. He was a Baptist minister and no doubt preached a number of times at Old Pigeon Baptist Church where Thomas Lincoln was a member. He was in the Indiana legislature in 1827, representing Spencer and Perry Counties. He had seven children, the youngest of whom was James, born December 19, 1819, in Harrison County. He was later to become an outstanding figure in Spencer County and Indiana. He became a major general in the Civil War. Although he was a small boy when the Lincolns lived in Spencer County, he was a type of that western frontier life, showing the culture, intellect, and training of his ancestors. He studied and taught in the fields of both botany and history. He has children and grandchildren that I have known all my life.

I cannot mention every separate family in those pioneer days and tell their ancestry and their opportunity for education; I have taken a few from my original list to prove that Lincoln found within less than one-half of his own mentioned radius of fifty miles, many cultured and educated people whose lives could have inspired him, all of whom lived in the same county with him, and during his years spent here there was full opportunity for Lincoln to know them.

18 Isaac Veatch lived from 1786 to 1833; his son, General James Clifford Veatch, lived from 1819 to 1895.

It would have been impossible for anyone with average intelligence to have lived where Lincoln did in those early days in Spencer County and not have come in contact with many of the public men of that time. John A. Breckenridge,[19] who lived in Boonville, perhaps did more than any other man in attracting Lincoln to the study of law. Lincoln frequently went to Boonville to attend trials and hear the lawyers argue their cases and thereby came in contact with Breckenridge. Breckenridge came from the east where he was well educated in an outstanding college. He is one of the prominent men of pioneer days in Indiana.

The DeBruler family, who produced such brilliant men, lived in Jasper. It was a notable family, first in Pike County in 1818, then in Dubois, and later in Spencer County. The twin brothers, Lemuel Quincy and James Pressbury DeBruler, were the two who came to Rockport in the forties. The DeBruler family were such outstanding people in southern Indiana at the time the Lincolns lived here that Abraham must have had knowledge of them. During the Civil War, Judge L. Q. DeBruler was sent to Washington to see Lincoln on some business matter. After the conference was over and DeBruler started to leave, Lincoln brought his great hand down on DeBruler's shoulder and said, "Sit down and tell me about the folks back home." This showed the continued interest of Lincoln for his boyhood friends in Spencer County.

The Crawford family, who employed both Abe and his father, loaned Abe books. I know the grandson and great grandchildren of the Crawfords and have heard the grandson tell of the Crawford home life and Lincoln's connection with his grandfather's home, etc. The Hyland family were early aristocrats in Spencer County, also the Mattinglys and Browns. The Hackleman family came in 1819, and there have been four generations of them. They were foremost men of the county. The Roberts, Brooners, Berrys, Cottons, Wilkinsons, Grigsbys, Richardsons, Wrights, Huffs, Romines, Medcalfs, Basyes, and many more families could be named whose genealogies are familiar to me.

Lincoln's social affiliations were not alone in Spencer County, but in Dubois County around the neighborhood of Enlow Hill, as

---

19 The correct spelling is John Brackenridge. He lived from 1800 until 1862 and is described further in a chapter in this book titled, "John A. Brackenridge."

George R. Wilson has described it.[20] Could any pioneer community be started with more blue blood and education than were those early settlements in southern Indiana, with New Harmony leading them all?

We must not forget that the stepmother of Lincoln, Sarah Bush Lincoln, did much to mold the character of the boy Lincoln and to arouse his ambitions. She loved the motherless boy and he gave her a son's devotion. Although Sarah Lincoln had little education, she encouraged Abraham in his desire to learn.

Here in this new, free state, the boy Abraham Lincoln grew to young manhood. His neighbors were largely clear-minded, unpretending men of common sense, whose patriotism was unquestionable. He was undoubtedly molded by their influence and inspired by their intellect and so became the first true type of American citizen with sterling qualities of heart, humane sympathies, purity of life, the emancipator of a race.

EHRMANN'S NOTE

a.   When Edwin Moore, the second postmaster, took office May 9, 1825, the name had been changed from Mt. Duvall to Rockport. I have in my Spencer County historical archives a letter written to John Morgan while he was postmaster and addressed to him at Mt. Duvall or Rockport. The letter was written January 22, 1821, by his brother, William. This letter is now one hundred and six years old.

BESS V. EHRMANN (1879–1963) was a Rockport, Indiana, native who dreamed that Spencer County would receive deserved recognition in the Lincoln story. She wrote a number of books including *Missing Chapter in the Life of Abraham Lincoln*. Ehrmann was instrumental in creating Lincoln Pioneer Village in Rockport, served as president of the Southwestern Indiana Historical Society, and was curator of the Spencer County Historical Society.

---

20 George R. Wilson (1863–1941) was a well-known historian of Dubois County, Indiana.

5

★ ★ ★

Life of James Gentry Jr.

J. HELEN RHOADES*

In this article, Gentry family member J. Helen Rhoades relates a few well-known Gentry and Lincoln family stories. Unfortunately, she confuses the names in a couple of the stories. For instance, Allen Gentry, not his brother Joseph, accompanied Lincoln on the New Orleans flatboat trip. Allen's wife, Anna Roby Gentry, received assistance in the spelling match, not Hannah Gentry.

Perhaps the most significant revelation in the article is the Gentry family's loyalty to the Democratic Party. No Gentry voted for Lincoln, which may explain why Lincoln historian William Herndon did not try to talk with the family—he interviewed only Anna Roby, a Gentry by marriage.

Matthew Gentry attacked his mother, Elizabeth Hornbeck Gentry, in about 1825. Lincoln wrote about this incident concerning Matthew in 1846: "At the age of nineteen he unaccountably became furiously mad, from which condition he gradually settled down into harmless insanity." In 1844, Lincoln saw Matthew while campaigning for Henry Clay and wrote a poem about Gentry's ordeal:

> Poor Matthew! I have ne'er forgot,
> When first, with maddened will,
> Yourself you maimed, your father fought,
> And mother strove to kill. . . .[1]

Elizabeth Hornbeck Gentry died in 1825, about the time of the attack, although no account relates her death to such an event.

---

* Rhoades first delivered this paper on 24 June 1926. A copy is part of the *Southwestern Indiana Historical Society Annuals* 4: 126–130, at Evansville-Vanderburgh Public Library.

1 Abraham Lincoln to Andrew Johnston, 6 September 1846, in Roy P. Basler et al., eds., *The Collected Works of Abraham Lincoln*, 9 vols. (New Brunswick, NJ: Rutgers University Press, 1953–1955), 1:384–386.

THE FIRST GENTRY TO SETTLE IN INDIANA WAS JAMES GENTRY
Sr. who came from North Carolina and located first in Davis County,
Kentucky. He married Elizabeth Homback[2] and afterward became a
slave holder, but later sold out his land and slaves, and in April 1818 came
to Indiana settling in Spencer County between what is now Gentryville
and Lincoln City. Gentryville was named for him, for it was here he
entered land and afterward accumulated to about five thousand acres.
He proved to be a great stock raiser, marketing his cattle in Cincinnati
and after returning with a flat boat loaded with dry goods and groceries
landing at Grandview hauling his goods from there to Gentryville and
Winslow. This merchandise was transferred by means of oxen. In those
days there were neither bridges nor roads, often times waiting on the
bank of a swollen stream for a week at a time before crossing. Often in
the fall of the year, he would slaughter enough wild hogs out of the woods
and load the same flat boat for southern markets, coasting either side of
the Mississippi to New Orleans. He kept this up for several years. His
family consisted of four boys and four girls, Mathew [sic], Allen, Agnes,
Hannah, Joseph, Sarah, James Jr., and Elizabeth. All the children living
to old ages and rearing large families.

The son James Jr, my great grandfather is the subject of this biography. He was born near the village of Gentryville Feb 24, 1819. Although
his educational advantages were limited he succeeded in gaining a fair
English education. Receiving the little education in schools that the
meager facilities of those early days afforded. And this he was only able
to supplement in educational institutions with one year at school at
Owensboro, Kentucky, where he was a classmate of the late Senator
Thomas McCreary[3] and other noted Kentuckians. His youth was spent
on his father's farm, engaged in the duties of farming and stock raising. In
1839 he married Eliza Montgomery. He accumulated quite a fortune and
was a leader in the community, donating land to churches, the graveyard,
flour mill and the land on which Gentryville now stands, dividing it into
lots and selling it out to the people.

---

2 Elizabeth Hornbeck lived from 1787 to 1825.

3 Thomas McCreary lived from 1816 to 1890 and served as a United States senator from
Owensboro, Kentucky.

At this time young Abraham Lincoln an awkward boy of about twenty years, was employed on my great grandfather's farm, his father Thomas Lincoln having settled on an adjoining farm to my great grandfather in 1816.

My great uncle Joseph worked with Abraham splitting rails, but great uncle Joseph said, "that Abe was lazy and always preferred a book instead of an ax." Great grandfather told there two stories about Lincoln: One Friday afternoon during a spelling match, the teacher gave out a word that none of the scholars were able to spell correctly. After Lincoln had missed like the rest, he remembered that, where they had spelled the word with an "e" it should have been an "i", Lincoln said nothing but watched his chance and slipped out the back door, when the teacher's eyes were turned. He walked quietly to one of the side windows where my great aunt Hannah was standing. When the word came to her, she was about to give up, when her attention was suddenly drawn to the window. There stood Lincoln madly jabbing his finger in his eyes. She caught the meaning of the gesture spelled the word correctly and received the praise of the teacher.[4]

When Lincoln was a young man he started down the river on a flat boat with great Uncle Joseph. At some point on the Mississippi, while the boat was morred [sic] a gang of negroes attacked the boat.[5] Lincoln fought like a Tiger. In the fight one of the negroes hit him over the head with a heavy tobacco stick. The wound left a scar that Lincoln carried to his grave.

When the Lincolns left Indiana great grandfather accompanied them as far as Pigeon Creek, on that creek the last goodbyes were said. As they were leaving grandfather placed a small whip in the hands of Abraham, as a remembrance. Great grandfather had used the whip in driving cattle to Cincinnati. The families kept in touch with one another by frequent communications. One point on which the two families could not agree, that was politics. Although the Gentrys were overjoyed to hear of

4 For a more accurate account, see William H. Herndon's interview with Anna Caroline Roby Gentry, 17 September 1865, in Douglas L. Wilson and Rodney O. Davis, eds., *Herndon's Informants: Letters, Interviews, and Statements about Abraham Lincoln* (Urbana: University of Illinois Press, 1998), 131–132.

5 Allen, not Joseph, accompanied Lincoln on this trip. For a complete account, see Richard Campanella, *Lincoln in New Orleans: The 1828–1831 Flatboat Voyages and Their Place in History* (Lafayette: University of Louisiana at Lafayette Press, 2010).

Lincoln's election, there was not a member of the family that cast a vote for him. After Lincoln had taken his office, several of his Spencer County friends visited him, after he had shaken hands all around, he asked about the Gentrys. He was told of there [sic] joy for his success. Lincoln laughed and said, "yes, I know it, but they were too good Democrats to vote for me, I bet on it."

Great grandfather was considered a man of his word, and as a businessman he was honorable, straight-forward and esteemed in the community. He was a reader and thinker and added to his scholastic education by his own efforts in later life. His reading and chief interest was in matters of government and history, national, state and local. He was familiar with the works of Benton, of Gladstone, of Gobden and our national history and was authority on the history and principles of political parties. It will not be deemed a violation of propriety or feeling to allude to his devotion to his political principles and in fact it would be unjust to his memory to fail to do so. He was an ardent adherent to the principles of a democracy and devotee at the shrine of that political faith to the extent that it was almost a religion with him. Modest and unaware of his own capability, he never sought personal preferment and only once was he ever induced to accept office. He represented his county once in the legislature from 1870 to 1873, in which he was member of important committees. Even afterwards it was a pleasure to him to remember that it was his vote and influence that served to defeat a proposed measure of his party attacking the later amendment to the constitution. His tocsin in that battle was that Democrats should be supporters of the constitution and not destroyers of it. This spoke in trumpet tones his loyalty to principles and his earnest good faith and fairness.

While he avoided his own personal advantages, unselfish, and unenvious as he was, the welfare of his party in what he deemed the right, always intensely interested him, and his safe counsels were always sought by his party friends, as a leader and a wise counselor and were never sought in vain. During all his manhood his home was a veritable Mecca for members of his party visiting this part of the state, where he has enjoyed meeting and entertaining many of national fame. Vice president Hendericks, Gov Willard, Senators McDonald, Voochies, and Turpie, Representatives Loolhart [Lockhart], Niblack and many others have found and appreciated the warmth of his welcome, the ardor of his fealty to principle, and the wisdom of his counsels.[6] Judge Curan DeBruler in speaking of him once said, "Mr Gentry is one of the best posted well on the tariff and all political questions I ever met." He was one of the men that helped make possible the present Traction line from Evansville to Grandview. And it was he among others who was instrumental in getting the Southern R. R. to build a branch road from Lincoln City to Rockport.

In 1864 he removed to a farm on the river three miles from Rockport, then in 1877 he removed to the home one mile west of Rockport on what is now known as the Gentry home. Here he died May 3rd, 1905. He had a family of six children, Mrs Eliza Gentry Bullock, Wayne, Allen, Mrs Lizzie Gentry Wright, Malissia wife of Dr. Hackelman, and Robert, who is my grandfather. Great grandfather had ten grandchildren, eight whom are now living and eight great grandchildren, of whom the writer J. Helen Rhoades is one.

J. HELEN RHOADES (Trobaugh) (1902–1990) was the great-great-granddaughter of James Gentry Sr., the most prominent member of the Little Pigeon Creek community during Abraham Lincoln's youth. She lived in Rockport, Indiana.

6 Their full names are Thomas A. Hendricks, Ashbel P. Willard, Joseph E. McDonald, Daniel W. Voorhees, David Turpie, James Lockhart, and William E. Niblack; all were Hoosier Democrats.

6

★ ★ ★

The Grigsbys

BESS V. EHRMANN*

Of all the Little Pigeon Creek community neighbors, the Lincolns and Grigsbys maintained the most intimate, but complicated, relationship. Lincoln grew up with the Grigsby children. One of them, Aaron, married Lincoln's sister; and another, Nathaniel, probably became his best friend. Nevertheless, Lincoln held the family responsible for his sister's death and wrote one of his most satirical compositions, the *Chronicles of Reuben*, about this family.[1]

In this presentation, Bess Ehrmann relates the Grigsby family history as provided by Nancy Grigsby Inco, the daughter of James Grigsby, another of the Grigsby brothers.

The Nathaniel Grigsby letter published here is one of at least three extant letters written by Lincoln to his Spencer County acquaintances in 1860. The 20 September 1860 Grigsby letter is owned by Lincoln Boyhood National Memorial; a 23 October 1860 letter to David Turnham is at the Evansville Museum of Arts, History, and Science; and an 18 June 1860 letter to William Jones sold at auction in 2013 after appearing on *Antiques Roadshow*.

NOW THAT THE SEARCH-LIGHT OF INVESTIGATION AND publicity has been turned on the people with whom Abraham Lincoln came in contact, during his residence in Spencer County, it is well to consider the Grigsby family.

---

* Ehrmann presented this notice and letter on 28 February 1923, and published it in *Indiana Historical Commissions Bulletin* 18, *Proceedings of the Southwestern Indiana Historical Society* (October 1923): 89–91.

1 William E. Bartelt, *There I Grew Up: Remembering Abraham Lincoln's Indiana Youth* (Indianapolis: Indiana Historical Society, 2008), 166–169.

The formative years of his life were lived in Spencer County and the people who were his friends had an influence on his life. There was no other family, except the Gentrys, with whom Lincoln was so intimately associated as he was with the Grigsby family.

There has lived in Rockport, Spencer County, for many years, Mrs. Nancy Grigsby Inco, daughter of James Grigsby. She was born in 1846 on the Grigsby farm near Lincoln's old home and is now seventy-seven years of age. Her mind is clear and active and to her I owe this history of the Grigsby family.

Reuben Grigsby, Sr., came from North Carolina to Bowling Green, Kentucky, about 1805. In 1819 (three years after the Lincolns had come to Indiana) he with his wife and children immigrated to Indiana, settling about two miles from what is now the town of Lincoln City.

There were twelve children in the Grigsby family, five girls—Millie Goble, Elizabeth, Mary, Liddie and Nancy, and seven boys—Aaron, Charles, Reuben, James, William, Nathaniel, and Redman.

Aaron Grigsby was the oldest son and after moving to Indiana, he went some place in the northern part of the state to read law, expecting then to be a lawyer.[2] The younger children attended a school which was near Gentryville and this only for short periods. When the weather was bad, the pupils had to remain at home.

It was this same school that Abe Lincoln attended and the Grigsby boys in later life delighted to tell how Lincoln would sit on a log at recess time and with a piece of charcoal and a board, cipher and write his letters, instead of joining in the games of his comrades. The Grigsby farm was not far from the Lincoln home and there was much visiting back and forth.

When Aaron returned from where he had been studying law he brought with him a couple of law books, which interested Abe greatly. It was always said in the Grigsby family that Abe's first knowledge of law was gained through reading and studying these books of Aaron's.

Aaron later married Sarah Lincoln and the ties of friendship were further strengthened.[3]

2 This letter may contain the first and only Grigsby assertion that Aaron studied law and provided law books to Lincoln. There is no documentation to support this story.

3 Aaron Grigsby married Lincoln's older sister Sarah on 2 August 1826. She died in childbirth on 20 January 1828.

Lincoln spent many a day with the Grigsby boys at their home. In winter when the Grigsby boys visited at the Lincoln cabin they would usually find Abe seated on the end of a huge log whose other end would be burning in the fireplace.

James Grigsby, the father of Nancy Grigsby Inco, was born in 1813 and was six years old when the family moved to Indiana. He was four years younger than Lincoln and was the fifth child in his father's family.

Nathaniel was the ninth child in the family and Mrs. Inco has given me a photographic copy of a letter written by Lincoln to Nathaniel in 1860. I will read this letter and then a paper written by Mrs. Inco at the time of the dedication of the Sarah Grigsby monument.

I have the photograph of James Grigsby which she has given to our County Museum.

Springfield, Ill., September 20, 1860.
Nathaniel Grigsby, Esq.,

My dear Sir:

Your letter of July 19th was received only a few days ago, having been mailed by your brother at Gentryville, Ind., on the 12th of the month.

A few days ago Gov. Wood of Quincy told me he saw you and that you said you had written me. I had not then received your letter.

Of our three families who removed from Indiana together, my father, Squire Hall and John D. Johnston are dead, and all the rest of us are yet living. Of course the younger ones are grown up, marriages contracted, and new ones born. I have three boys now, the oldest of which is seventeen years of age.

There is now a Republican electoral ticket in Missouri so that you can vote for me, if your neighbors will let you. I would advise you not to get into any trouble about it.

Give my kindest regards to your brother Charles.

Within the present year I have had two letters from John Gorden who is living somewhere in Missouri, I forget exactly where, and he says his father and mother are both still living near him.

Yours very truly,
A. LINCOLN

BESS V. EHRMANN (1879–1963) was a Rockport, Indiana, native who dreamed that Spencer County would receive deserved recognition in the Lincoln story. She wrote a number of books including *The Missing Chapter in the Life of Abraham Lincoln*. Ehrmann was instrumental in creating Lincoln Pioneer Village in Rockport, served as president of the Southwestern Indiana Historical Society, and was curator of the Spencer County Historical Society.

7

★ ★ ★

More Lincoln Memories

NANCY GRIGSBY INCO*

Nancy Grigsby Inco relates family memories in this essay. Her source was her father, James Grigsby (1813-1889), the younger brother of Lincoln's brother-in-law, Aaron (1801-1831), and Lincoln's good friend Nathaniel (1811-1890). Originally, Inco delivered this paper on 20 June 1916 at the dedication of Sarah Lincoln Grigsby's monument.

LADIES AND GENTLEMEN: AS I HAVE BEEN ASKED TO MAKE A few remarks in regard to the Lincoln and Grigsby families, I will endeavor to do so. However, I do not know that I can add anything of interest to what most of you know, since there has been such a great interest created in the Lincoln family in this county, and so many of our pioneer residents have brought to light the many interesting things and facts relative to the earlier history of our county.

What I know of the Lincolns I have heard from my father who was a school mate of Abraham Lincoln and who lived near the Lincoln family. It is useless to go into details of that early school life as you have all heard about it many times.

Aaron Grigsby, my father's oldest brother married Sallie Lincoln, but she lived only a short time after the marriage and her husband died about three years later. They had a very bright future before them for the people

* Inco published this paper in *Indiana Historical Commissions Bulletin 18, Proceedings of the Southwestern Indiana Historical Society* (October 1923): 91–92.

of that day, and Sallie Grigsby was much thought of and loved by all her husband's people. She was given the best kind of burial that could be given and my father erected a sandstone marker to the graves of both she and her husband, and always looked after these graves as well as others of our family as long as he lived.[1]

My father also attended the funeral of Nancy Hanks Lincoln, and has often told me how poor the family was and how they took Nancy Hanks Lincoln to her grave on a rude homemade sled. Her grave was always a place of great interest to me and my brother and sisters when we were children, and I have often gone to the grave which was enclosed by a rail pen in those days.

I might mention that the father of Aaron Grigsby lived with the Indians for about eight years. While his father was out looking for game, the Indians came to the house, and after killing three of the older children took Reuben, his mother, and a small baby away with them. They soon discovered that the mother could not walk fast enough so they killed her and knocked the baby's brains out against a tree. For some reason they liked the small boy, and so they carried him on their backs. They grew very fond of him and used to take him on their hunting trips with them. He said he always wanted to go, and to tease him if they did not want him to go with them, they would insist on his drinking a quantity of bear oil before they would let him go along.

There are many things I have heard from my father that I do not remember well enough to tell here. However, it has been a great pleasure to me to bring these things of the past to light and it is needless to say that we Grigsbys are all very proud of the fact that Sallie Lincoln married into the Grigsby family, and are also proud of the prominent part they played in the early settlement of this county. It is also very gratifying to know that the younger people of this county are becoming more interested in knowing something of these good folk who have gone before and endured such hardships in order that their children and their children's children might enjoy the best of the earth.

1 This simple marker was replaced with a granite one in 1916. The Indiana Lincoln Route Commission initiated the effort. The stone lies in Little Pigeon Cemetery in Lincoln State Park.

I only hope this interest will continue and I am sure that Spencer County has as much or more to be proud of in an historical way as any county in our good state.

I thank you for your indulgence.

NANCY GRIGSBY INCO (1846–1927) was the granddaughter of Reuben and Nancy Grigsby and the niece of Aaron Grigsby, the man who married Lincoln's sister, Sarah. Inco was a schoolteacher and active in the Daughters of the American Revolution.

8

★ ★ ★

Biographical Sketch of Josiah and Elizabeth (Anderson) Crawford

WILLIAM FRANKLIN ADAMS*

As close neighbors of the Lincolns, Josiah and Elizabeth Crawford often interacted with the family. Abraham Lincoln and his father helped work on the Crawford farm and home. According to one famous tale, Abraham borrowed a biography of George Washington from Josiah, but, after reading a portion of the book, left it overnight in the chinking of the cabin wall where a rainstorm ruined it. Poor and without money, Lincoln paid for the damage in work. Subsequently, Lincoln often worked for the Crawfords, sometimes staying overnight and studying their books by the fireside.[1] Mrs. Crawford is often considered one of William H. Herndon's and later interviewers' best informants. This essay from the Crawfords' grandson provides valuable insight into the family's background and outlook.

THE EARLY SETTLERS OF SOUTHERN INDIANA WERE MAINLY emigrants from Kentucky, and the immediate progenitors of these emigrants had come from the older states of Pennsylvania, Virginia and the Carolinas. Spencer County was settled almost exclusively by people from Kentucky. My maternal grandparents came from Bardstown, or as it was sometimes called, Beardstown, Nelson County, Kentucky.

---

* Adams first presented this paper to the Southwestern Indiana Historical Society on 17 November 1925. A copy can be found in the *Southwestern Indiana Historical Society Annuals* 3: 1–9, at the Evansville-Vanderburgh Public Library.

1 Rodney O. Davis, "William Herndon's Indiana Oral History Project, 1865," *Indiana Magazine of History* 89, no. 2 (1993): 136–146.

Josiah Crawford, Jr., my grandfather, was of Welsch [sic] and Scotch ancestry. His father, Josiah Crawford, Sr., was born near Philadelphia, Pennsylvania, May 6, 1767. His wife, whose maiden name was Ruth Ricks, was born near the same place December 19, 1773. They were of the Quaker or Friends sect, and their ancestors had come over with William Penn. They were married about the year 1790 and came at once to what is now Nelson County, Kentucky, where they lived until their deaths.

They raised a family of eight children, four boys and four girls. The names of these children indicate the religious character of the parents. The boys were Abel, Ephraim, Josiah, and Elijah. The girls were named Ruth, Sarah, Leah and Rachel.

Grandfather was born near Bardstown, Kentucky, September 23, 1802.

My maternal Grandmother was of English stock, whose ancestors had also settled in Pennsylvania. Her father, Samuel Anderson, was born in April 1780, in Westmoreland County, Virginia. His wife, whose maiden name was Polly Summers, was born in the same locality in August, 1784. After their marriage they also came to Nelson County where they lived until their deaths, the wife in 1837 and Grandfather Anderson in 1864. They raised a family of six girls and one boy. The girls were Elizabeth, my grandmother, Mary who married Silas Richardson; Sarah who married Benedict Hagan; Martha who married Vincent Shields; Sophia who married Smith Hubbard; and Susan who married Wesley McDaniel. The boy's name was William.

All of these children, after their marriage, emigrated to Indiana, except Martha. William, settled at Corydon, Indiana. The five girls settled in Spencer County in what is now Clay Township.

Grandmother was born in Bardstown, Kentucky, November 14, 1806. She and Grandfather were married at that place March 27, 1823. Grandfather was in his 21st and Grandmother in her 17th year. The first three years of their married life was spent in Nelson County, where their first two children were born. In 1826, they emigrated to Spencer County and settled about 1¼ miles west of the present village of Buffaloville.[2] Two years previous, in 1824, Grandfather's elder sister Sarah, who had

2 The Crawfords purchased about eighty acres of land southeast of the Lincolns' Indiana farm. See Vincennes Land Office Book 8, p. 2022, Bureau of Land Management, Springfield, Virginia.

married William Barker, had come with her husband to Spencer County and settled about one-half mile southwest of where Grandfather later settled. In 1836, the Barkers moved to where the village of Buffaloville now stands and built their homes one-fourth mile north of where this village is now. The village was platted by William Barker and his sons and was first known as Barkertown. [The] Barkers raised a family of ten children, eight boys and two girls. The boys were Silas, Hardin, Elijah, Isaac, William, Thomas, Hamilton and Abel. The girls were Mildred who married John Wesley Lamar, and Sarah who married Jacob Varner, and after his death she married Thomas Littlepage. They all raised large families some of whose descendants still reside in Spencer County.

When my grandparents arrived they immediately began the erection of a rude cabin in which to live until better quarters could be provided. Their nearest neighbors were the Barkers about one-half mile to the southwest; the Grigsbys about two miles to the west, and the Lincolns about two and one-half miles to the north. There were no neighbors nearer than four miles to the east or south.

I well remember the wagon in which they came. It was still in use in the late fifties. The running gears were very heavy with large hickory axels [sic] with wood spindles, the wheels held on the spindles by linchpins. The wheels were very heavy, the rear wheels being much higher than the front ones. The bed or body was of a type never seen in these days and was the only one of the kind I ever saw. It was constructed of a frame-work, boxed on the inside of the frame. The bed was large and instead of being rectangular in shape the bottom curved upward from the center to the rear and front ends, the sides curving upward to conform to the bottom and also flaring outward, being wider in the center than at the ends. The bed was about two feet in depth. On the trip from Kentucky, this wagon was drawn by two stout horses. Grandfather was a farrier of that day and was a great lover of horses. In this wagon and another which Grandfather had hired for the trip, they brought their household goods, and farming and mechanical tools. Grandfather was possessed of some means in money in addition to his personal effects. The Lincolns were the nearest neighbors that worked for hire. Young Abe was then 17 years old, a strapping, raw boned youth who could wield an ax and a maul as few men could. Abe and his father were employed to help

build the first cabin which was soon constructed. They were then employed to clear and fence land and assist in planting and cultivating the
crops.

Game was plentiful. Deer, wild turkeys and many kinds of smaller
game was to be had in abundance, and there were also some black bear.
Panthers, catamounts, wild-cats and wolves roamed the forests. I have
heard Grandmother say that when they were living in their first rude log
cabin, with unchinked open spaces between the logs, the wolves would
come so close at night that they could see their eyes by the reflection of
the light from the fire in the fireplace. It was necessary to protect the pigs,
lambs and poultry at night by penning them up. Grandfather employed
young Abe to make rails for pens. These rails were longer than the ordinary ten foot fence rails and larger. Abe notched the rails at the ends
to make them fit close together. After they were no longer needed for
protecting pens they were used about the place to repair fences. When
Lincoln, in 1860, became a candidate for president, there were a number
of these rails scattered about the farm in the fences. When it became
known that they were there and that they could be identified as rails
made by Lincoln "The Rail Splitter", there was such a demand for them
to be made into canes that the supply soon exhausted.[3] I well remember,
as a boy of eight, going about over the farm with Grandfather searching
for these rails. They were easily identified by their length and size and the
notches at the ends. There were many rails of the usual size that Lincoln
had made, but they could not be identified from others of like size and
length.[4]

As soon as land had been cleared to raise crops for actual needs, Grandfather began the construction of a more commodious and comfortable
home. He built a hewed log house some twenty-six feet in length and

3 During the Civil War, some rails were sold at "Sanitary Fairs" to raise funds to improve
hygiene in Union Army camps. A piece of rail now in the Smithsonian National Museum of
History, with a letter signed by John Hanks, reads, "This is to certify that this is one of the genuine
rails split by A. Lincoln and myself in 1829 and 30." See Owen Edwards, "The Legend of Lincoln's
Fence Rail," *Smithsonian Magazine*, February 2011, https://www.smithsonianmag.com/history
/the-legend-of-lincolns-fence-rail-35283/.

4 Elizabeth Crawford told William Herndon someone stole *her* cane; yet, she gave Herndon
a cane. William E. Bartelt, *There I Grew Up: Remembering Abraham Lincoln's Indiana Youth*
(Indianapolis: Indiana Historical Society, 2008), 166.

eighteen feet in width, and one and one-half stories in height. Young Abe helped to cut and hew all these logs. As there was no sawmill near, the boards for the floors were whipsawed on the place. Young Abe and Grandfather whipsawed these boards. I was born in the room in which this floor was laid, and spent the first fourteen years of my life in that home. I can well remember that old oak floor grown slick and dark with age and use.[5]

In time Grandfather built an addition to this house in the form of another hewed log building of the same length and height and eighteen feet in width. This was joined to the other building and all roofed with joint shingles of oak made by Grandfather. A huge brick chimney was built between the two rooms with a fireplace in each. This entire building was afterward weather-boarded on the outside and [sealed] on the inside with dressed poplar material, the dressing all being done by hand. A porch or veranda eight feet in width was built along the entire west front, and a frame room and porch along the entire east front. The outside of the entire house was painted with white lead and oil and made a very comfortable and respectable home for that time and place. This was the condition of the home as I first remember it. The building burned about 1890, but the cherished memories of the happy hours of childhood spent in and about it, of the dear faces that once glowed in the firelight of evening around those hearths still linger fresh and vivid and awaken a longing and homesickness that nothing can appease, and that shall endure while memory abides.

"The glamour of a fairy wand is over all the past of mankind, but on nothing else does it cast so potent a spell as on the personal reminiscences of our own youthful years."

After the construction of the first rude home it was necessary to provide for a supply of water. Young Abe was employed to dig a well and get out stone to wall it. He, with Grandfather's assistance, walled the well. It has been more than twenty years since I have been on this farm, but the last time I was there the well was still in use.

---

5 The Crawfords' house was built after the Lincolns left Indiana, and some of the flooring was reportedly prepared by the Lincolns for use in the new house they were building when they decided to move to Illinois. William E. Bartelt, *There I Grew Up: Remembering Abraham Lincoln's Indiana Youth* (Indianapolis: Indiana Historical Society, 2008), 161.

Grandfather was a cooper and wheelwright by trade, having learned the trade while a young man in Kentucky. As the surrounding country began to fill up with emigrants and the marriage of the children of the settlers, he devoted the greater part of his time to his trade, making barrels, casks, buckets, spinning wheels, both large ones for spinning wool and the small or tread wheel for spinning flax or tow, looms for weaving, reels, winding blades etc.

Grandmother was a woman above the ordinary in intelligence, possessing a wonderful memory that remained clear and unclouded until her death at the age of 83, when she succumbed to an attack of pneumonia. She possessed a good English education for the time and was a great reader. She knew her Bible as few people know it today. She was a midwife by profession and had several medical works in which she was well read. She practiced not only in accouchments [sic] but also in general practice. She was frequently called in consultation by neighboring physicians. She went wherever and whenever called in all seasons and in all kinds of weather, until she quit practice at the age of about sixty years. She was a woman of robust health and strong constitution. She always rode horseback in her practice; had her own horse, her physician's saddle bags of "pill bags", which was stocked with the prevailing remedies of the time. She was often called for [a] distance of twelve or fifteen miles to treat the sick or minister in childbirth.

She bore and raised five children, three boys, Abel, Samuel and Joseph, and two girls, Ruth and Mary. The latter, the youngest, was my mother, and was born when Grandmother was two and one-half months less than twenty-five years of age. These five children all married and had large families of children, but few of them are now living. It was a coincidence that the three sons each married a woman whose first name was Nancy Ann.

While the parents of both Grandfather and Grandmother were owners of slaves, they were both abolitionists, and while it meant some financial loss to them, no one rejoiced more than they when the slaves were freed. I have often heard them relate the particular incidents which embittered them against slavery. Grandfather's elder brother, unlike his father, was a stern and severe man with his family and slaves. He owned a negress who was the cook for the family. Grandfather once saw his brother Abel punish this woman severely for an act that Grandfather did not regard as even a trivial offense. While he had never believed slavery to be right, this act of cruelty and injustice made him an uncompromising foe of the institution.

Grandmother's parents owned a slave woman named Leah, who had been with them ever since their marriage. She had been the trusted housekeeper and the mamma of the seven children. In 1837, Grandmother Anderson died, and not long afterward Grandfather Anderson remarried. This new wife took a bitter and unreasoning dislike to Leah, and insisted that she be sold. To keep peace in the family, or at least with his wife, against the prayers and protests of his children, he sold Leah to a southern planter, taking her away from the home in which she had been a true and trusted servant, and separating her forever from her own husband and children. Is it a matter for wonder that Grandmother was an abolitionist? I have often heard them say that their chief reason for coming to Indiana was that they might live and raise their children on free soil away from the curse and blight of slavery.

When Lincoln had entered public life and began his fight against the institution of slavery, Grandfather and Grandmother looked to him as a prophet of the Most High. They took an interest in the campaign of 1860. They looked upon Lincoln as a second Moses and the savior of the Nation, and when he issued the emancipation proclamation, they almost deified him. They knew, as did Lincoln, when the Civil War began, that it meant a divided union or the death of slavery. They never lost confidence that the North would prevail. Two of their sons and their son-in-law, my father, enlisted at the beginning of the war. One son never came back.

When all loyal hearts were rejoicing that the long bitter struggle was drawing to a triumphant close, the nation was suddenly shocked and cast in deep sorrow and gloom by the tragic death of their beloved and revered leader. It was I who broke the news to Grandfather and Grandmother. I shall never forget that scene. I had been sent on an errand on the morning of the 15th of April, to a country store kept by another Lincoln Worshiper, Grandfather Alexander. There I heard the news and hastened home to tell the folks. When I told Grandfather, he slumped down and sat for some time as one stunned. He seemed to feel that all was lost. He had always been a strong, robust man, but from that day he began to fail, and on May 12th, 1865, in his 63rd year, he entered the eternal rest, three days less than a month after the death of his idol.

WILLIAM FRANKLIN ADAMS (1852–1933) was the grandson of Elizabeth and Josiah Crawford whose house Abraham Lincoln and his father helped build. Born in Spencer County, Indiana, he served as commissioner of education in Kansas and was a principal in Dale, Grandview, and Troy.

9

★ ★ ★

Daniel Grass

LAURA MERCY WRIGHT*[a]

Daniel Grass (1774–c. 1836) was among the first settlers and landowners in Rockport and Spencer County, Indiana. Many subsequent early settlers and distinguished visitors gathered at his home. Grass held many civic positions, including delegate to the 1816 Indiana constitutional convention at Corydon; first Indiana state senator from Warrick, Perry, and Posey Counties (1816–1818 and 1821–1827); and state representative (1819–1821). As a well-known community leader, Grass doubtless influenced the young and ambitious Lincoln. In 1828, while helping Allen Gentry construct a flatboat to travel to New Orleans, Lincoln stayed for weeks with the Daniel Grass family in Rockport. This paper by Grass's great-granddaughter provides a succinct history of Grass and his life.

LIKE MANY FAMILIES IN THE PIONEER DAYS OF OUR COUNTRY, the Grass family suffered much at the hands of the American Indian. The father of Daniel Grass, with his wife and two daughters, were surprised one morning by nine Indians while hoeing corn outside of the fort at what is now Bardstown, Kentucky. The father was killed; the mother and two daughters were taken captive. Later in the day the Indians, after much contention over the captives, separated into three groups; each group took one of the women.

* Wright first presented this paper in Poseyville, Indiana, on 28 September 1920 and later published it in the *Indiana History Bulletin* 3, extra no. 1, *Proceedings of the Southwestern Indiana Historical Society during Its Sixth Year: Papers Read before the Society at Various Meetings, 1920–1925* (December 1925): 7–11.

After five years of captivity, the daughter Julia took sick, was taken to Detroit and there exchanged for whiskey and blankets. There was much excitement in the fort over the recovery and the arrival of the white girl. A mother in that fort, who had herself been a captive, and exchanged for whiskey and blankets, wondered if the white girl could be her daughter. When the Indian garments were put aside, the mother of Daniel Grass greeted her long-lost daughter Julia. Nothing was ever heard of the other daughter; she probably died in an Indian wigwam, or by the tomahawk.

This account was made known in part to Daniel Grass by Julia herself, who visited her brother, probably in the year 1834. She had married a man by the name of Grant. Searching for her brother and not finding him in Bardstown, she journeyed to Rockport, Spencer County. Here she stayed a year. I heard an uncle of mine, Daniel Greathouse, say she acted so much like an Indian that he himself was afraid of her. Daniel Grass and probably another brother, still younger, were in the fort at the time the father was killed and the mother and sisters were taken captives. My mother, a granddaughter of Daniel Grass, now in her ninetieth year, told me her brother, Daniel Greathouse, and uncle, James Grass, visited a cousin near New Albany, Indiana, when they were young men.

Daniel Grass was two and a half years old at the time of his father's death. Dr. William R. Hynes, a wealthy man of Nelson County, Kentucky, who owned much land in Daviess and Henderson Counties, Kentucky, and in what is now Spencer County, Indiana, took the child and educated him as his own son.

Daniel Grass first came to Hanging Rock, now Rockport, in Spencer County, probably in 1803.[b] Before coming here, he went to Yellow Banks, now Owensboro, Daviess County, Kentucky. Here he married Jane Smithers, the daughter of William Smithers, the first settler of that place. On May 9, 1807, Daniel Grass entered land in Section 26, southwest of Rockport. This was the first land entered by an actual settler in what is now Spencer County. In the same year Daniel Grass and his wife moved to Rockport, then called Hanging Rock. He built his home on one of the bluffs in south Rockport.[c] He was evidently a man of refined taste, for a more beautiful spot in Rockport could not be found. On the east flowed the beautiful Ohio, while beyond, the green hills of Kentucky lent an added charm to the landscape. On the south could be seen the graceful windings of the river through the rich bottom lands. On the west and north stood the primeval forests. After he built his home, he journeyed back to Bardstown, Kentucky, and induced his friends and their families to follow him into the wilderness—what is now Spencer County. The Wrights, Morgans, Barnetts, and Greathouses, with others, whose descendants now live in Spencer County, came here through the influence of Judge Grass in 1808.

Daniel Grass took part in Harrison's march against the Indians at the Prophet's town [sic], and was wounded in the battle of Tippecanoe, November 7, 1811. He walked on crutches the remainder of his days.[1]

Judge Grass's political life began in 1812, as justice of the peace. In 1813, he was an associate judge for Warrick County—more than half of what is now Spencer County was then in Warrick County. About this time a political rivalry sprang up with Ratliff Boon, the man for whom Boon-ville was named.[2] Grass, Boon, Berry and others had been instrumental in having Warrick County organized and in making the county seat at Darlington, a place several miles west of Yankeetown, Warrick County. Nothing is left of the site of this first county seat of Warrick County, except Darlington station on the Rockport traction line. Here they sank a salt well and manufactured salt for a year or two.

A memorial asking for the admission of Indiana into the Union as a state was adopted by the General Assembly of the territory, December 11, 1815. The same was presented in Congress to the House of Representatives by the delegate Jonathan Jennings, on the 28th of the same month and was referred by that body to a committee of which Mr. Jennings was chairman.[3] On the 5th of January, 1816, he reported a bill to the House of Representatives enabling the people of Indiana Territory to form a

1 The Battle of Tippecanoe involved about 1,100 American forces under the leadership of future president William Henry Harrison (1773–1841) against about 500 to 700 Native American warriors associated with the Shawnee leader Tecumseh and his brother Tenskwatawa (commonly known as "the Prophet"). See Adam Jortner, *The Gods of Prophetstown: The Battle of Tippecanoe and the Holy War for the American Frontier* (New York: Oxford University Press, 2011).

2 Ratliff Boon (1781–1844) was the second governor of Indiana from 12 September to 5 December 1822. However, the Warrick County seat in Boonville was actually named for Ratliff's father, Jesse. See Linda C. Gugin and James E. St. Clair, eds., *The Governors of Indiana* (Indianapolis: Indiana Historical Society Press, 2006).

3 Jonathan Jennings (1784–1834) was the first governor of Indiana and a nine-term congressman from Indiana.

constitution upon which they should be admitted to the Union on equal terms with the original states. The election was held on Monday, May 13, 1816. Daniel Grass was elected a delegate to this Constitutional Convention at Corydon, the capital, to represent Warrick County. He served on three of its most important committees and took an active part in its deliberations. On June 12, 1816, Daniel Grass was appointed by the president to the committee on the legislative department of the government; other members of the committee were Messrs. Noble, Ferris, Milroy and Benefiel. On the first Monday in August, 1816, Daniel Grass was elected a senator in the first Indiana State Legislature from Warrick, Perry and Posey Counties. Shortly after his election as senator, he was appointed on the committee on prisons, along with Carr, Pennington, Milroy, Hunt, Graham and McCarty.

Spencer County was organized by an act of the legislature in the session of 1817–18 through the influence of Daniel Grass, who was at that time a representative from Warrick County. He had a bitter political fight with Ratliff Boon of Warrick County over its organization, but Grass won out.[4]

Colonel Hugh McGary, the Kentucky pioneer who founded Evansville, had a bitter controversy over Darlington being the county-seat of Warrick County. Colonel McGary had a scheme—carried out several years later—to sell 130 acres of land in what is now Evansville to General Robert M. Evans and James W. Jones, of Gibson County. These three men laid plans for the town of Evansville instead of Darlington to become the county-seat. Colonel Ratliff Boon, who had settled in Warrick County about 1809 (he later became the lieutenant-governor of the state and governor from September 12 to December 5, 1822) opposed this plan.

At that time General Joseph Lane, who later became a man of national repute, was rafting logs near Darlington, and floating them down the Ohio River to Red Bank (now Henderson, Kentucky) where J. J. Audubon, later the famous American ornithologist, had a sawmill. While rowing

---

4 In 1813, the large area south of the Wabash River was divided into two new counties, Gibson and Warrick. Spencer County was formed in 1818 from parts of Warrick County and Perry County. See *History of Warrick, Spencer and Perry Counties* (Chicago: Goodspeed Publishing, 1885), 35–51. As a result of the separation of Vanderburgh, Warrick, and Spencer Counties, several powerful personalities—Hugh McGary and Robert Evans (Vanderburgh), Ratliff Boon (Warrick), and Daniel Grass (Spencer)—were each left with their own domains.

back, General Lane stopped overnight with Colonel McGary, who acquainted him with the facts concerning the county-seat. Lane suggested to Colonel Boon that Warrick be divided into two counties, and McGary's town became the county-seat of the new county.[5]

Through General Lane's suggestion, a meeting was held. Those present were Colonel McGary, General Lane, Colonel Boon, General Evans, and Judge Daniel Grass. Warrick County was divided, and although the courthouse had been erected in Darlington, the county-seat was moved to Boonville. Then through the influence of Judge Grass, Spencer County was organized by an act (approved January 10, 1818) of the legislature in the session of 1817–18. Judge Grass in this session sat in the senate from Perry, Posey and Warrick Counties. He lived in what is now Ohio Township, and caused Spencer County to be formed between Anderson Creek on the east and Pigeon Creek on the west, and extend north to Dubois County, then also in the making. Spencer and Dubois Counties were organized February 1, 1818. Judge Grass had a bitter political fight with Ratliff Boone [sic] of Warrick County over the organization of Spencer, but Judge Grass won out. It was Judge Grass who had the county named Spencer, in honor of Captain Spier Spencer, his very warm friend, who was killed at Tippecanoe on November 7, 1811, in the battle in which Judge Grass had been wounded. He also caused the county seat to be located at Rockport.

In 1819 and again in 1820, Judge Grass was elected representative from Spencer County. In 1821, he was again elected to the state senate from Spencer, Perry, Dubois and part of Warrick; he was re-elected for every session and he served until 1827. In 1826 the district was changed and Judge Grass sat from Crawford, Perry and Spencer Counties.

Dr. William R. Hynes, the foster parent of Daniel Grass, Mr. Wright and Mr. Griffith were the original owners of the land where the city of Rockport is now located. This is shown by the titles to the land and the surveys of the lots. Daniel Grass was appointed treasurer of Spencer

5 By some accounts, because Joseph Lane's growing popularity threatened Ratliff Boon, Boon was more than willing to accommodate a new county for Lane. Lane's farm in Vanderburgh County's southeast region accounts for the offset line of the county's eastern boundary. *Indiana History Bulletin 16, Proceedings of the Southwestern Indiana Historical Society during Its Sixth Year: Papers Read before the Society at Various Meetings, 1920–1925* (October 1922): 76.

County in 1818, but he never served. In the same year he was appointed
county agent (a pioneer official whose duties are now those of a county
auditor) to take charge of these lots. All the early deeds were signed by
Judge Grass as agent of Spencer County. Judge Grass was one of only four
men who held the office of county agent, which was abolished in 1835. He
was sheriff of Spencer County from 1833 to 1836.

Judge Grass died in 1837 of a stroke of apoplexy.[6] He was found in his
chair by his wife. Judge Grass had been unable to lie down for some time
and a chair was made for him in which he rested at night. His remains
were laid to rest on the hillside of what is known as the Old Grave Yard,
not far from the hill on which he first settled. Sad but nevertheless true,
this grave is unknown. No one can mark the spot. We blush to admit
that these heroes and pioneers, men of fortitude, of thought and action,
and their wives of kindred spirit, who loved their families, have been forgotten by their children and grandchildren, until now, only the memory
of what they have done lives. Thanks to the historical society for preserving their deeds. May it teach the present and future generations to revere
the resting places of our heroic dead.

WRIGHT'S NOTES

a.   Laura Mercy Wright is a great-granddaughter of Daniel Grass.
b.   I quote from D. L. Morgan, now of Pittsburg, Kansas, and a relative of
my mother, familiarly known throughout Spencer County as Uncle Billy Stateler.
Mr. Stateler was a man of unusual intellect and memory, and a man interested in all
public affairs. Mr. Morgan, also formerly a resident of Spencer County, and likewise
interested in county history, verifies the fact that Daniel Grass first came here in
1803 to look after entering land for Dr. William R. Hynes, previously mentioned.
c.   J. A. Gentry now lives on the identical spot where the original house
stood.

LAURA MERCY WRIGHT (1871–1947) was a Rockport, Indiana, resident
who was a great-granddaughter of Daniel Grass. She was the organizing
regent of the Spier Spencer Chapter of the Daughters of the American
Revolution and an officer in the Southwestern Indiana Historical Society.

---

6 Grass's headstone (a replacement military marker set in the 1980s) in Olde Rockport Pioneer
Cemetery (Spencer County, Indiana) provides a death date of 25 May 1836.

10

★ ★ ★

The Athe Meeks Sr. Tragedy

AARON MEEKS*

In spring 1811 or 1812, a group of Shawnee Native Americans attacked Athe (sometimes spelled Atha) Meeks Sr. (1750–1812) and his family, killing Meeks and wounding his teenage son. According to tradition, Meeks was the last Caucasian killed by Native Americans in Indiana territory. The Shawnee were pursued and one, possibly a chief, was captured and brought to the home of a justice of the peace but killed in an apparent conspiracy designed to leave no witnesses. Thereafter, remaining Shawnee left the area, and new settlers soon arrived.[1] Although the Meeks tragedy occurred five and a half years before the Lincolns reached Indiana, the story loomed large in the consciousness of the community and surely young Lincoln heard it.

Abraham Lincoln's father, Thomas, witnessed the murder of his own father, also named Abraham. In spring 1786, while Abraham Lincoln the elder worked in his Kentucky field with his three sons, a Native American attacked and shot him dead. Afterward, Native Americans were one of Thomas Lincoln's favorite subjects; according to one historian, "Thomas's multiple stories reveal that the family did not view this relationship with Native Americans as an isolated incident. Rather, the stories functioned in the context of the ongoing struggle for security along the frontier and propagated the broad social divisions between white people and natives. As Lincoln matured, this environment of insecurity would manifest itself in a view of Native Americans as foreign, dangerous, and intriguing."[2]

---

* Meeks first presented this paper to the Southwest Indiana Historical Society on 11 October 1921. It is now part of the SWIHS Collection at Willard Library in Evansville, Indiana.

1 *History of Warrick, Spencer, and Perry Counties, Indiana* (Chicago: Goodspeed Brothers, 1885), 251–254; Louis A. Warren, *Lincoln's Youth: Indiana Years, Seven to Twenty-One, 1816–1830* (New York: Appleton-Century-Crofts, 1959), 35; William Fortune, ed., *Warrick and Its Prominent People* (Evansville, IN: Courier Company, 1881), 10–13.

2 Christopher W. Anderson, "Native Americans and the Origin of Abraham Lincoln's Views on Race," *Journal of the Abraham Lincoln Association* 37, no. 1 (Winter 2016): 11–29.

ATHE MEEKS, OR THE SKETCH OF THIS STORY, WAS BORN IN the State of Virginia and served his country in the Revolutionary War for the Independence of his country. After the war closed he came home and married, and then moved to Charleston, South Carolina, where he and his wife reared a family of ten children. His oldest son, William Meeks, had grown to manhood and was a man of a family. Now Athe Meeks, Sr., his ambition having been aroused to seek a new country to build a home in, prepared himself for the journey by taking with him one horse, a flintlock rifle gun, and salt, and a chopping axe, and five dogs, and plenty of ammunition. This completed his outfit for the journey of his northwestern trip through a dense forest, almost untrodden by white-man, and he started in March 1804 to make his all summer's journey.

After he started from Charleston, South Carolina, the first white men he met was at Nashville, Tennessee. From there he followed down the Cumberland River to its mouth where it empties into the Ohio River; there he constructed a raft of logs to cross the Ohio River on, and when he crossed over the river he went up the Ohio River about thirty miles to what was known as Cave-in-Rock, on the banks of the Ohio River, in the State of Illinois, and there was the first white men he had met since leaving Nashville, Tennessee. Only a few men were there. From there he continued northwest until he reached the Mississippi River at where St. Louis, Missouri, now stands. There was quite a number of French merchants, traders as they were called, and who sold beads and cheap jewelry, and powder and lead, to the Indians, and in return received all kinds of furs from the Indians for their goods. These white men were the second lot he had met since leaving Nashville, Tennessee.

From St. Louis he directed his course eastward to Vincennes, Indiana, and there he met some white men, French traders, who lived in a wild Indian country in the Territory of Indiana; from there he traveled east of south until he arrived in Warrick County, Indiana, about six miles north of Boonville, and there he found a small creek running east of south. He followed down this creek about twelve miles to where it emptied into Pigeon Creek, which was much larger than the creek he was fol-lowing. He named this small creek Otter Creek owing to the amount of otter that lived along this creek. He crossed Pigeon Creek and camped at what is known as Lake Drain, where it empties into Pigeon Creek. He camped there several days and reconnoitered over the country and concluded that was the place he was looking for. Then he went to Yellow-banks, now Owensboro, Kentucky, and crossed the Ohio River there. A few white settlers lived there at that time, and from there he went south to Nashville, Tennessee, and from there he retraced his course back to Charleston, South Carolina, arriving there in the latter part of October 1804, and in March 1805, he and his family and his son William Meeks started to move to an unknown wilderness.

There were no public highways in this country at that time. They had to use pack horses to carry every article they brought with them, and when they had the[ir] horses securely packed then the journey commenced and continued until they reached their destination, about the middle of April 1805, on the banks of Pigeon Creek, in Spencer County, Indiana, in Luce Township, on section number 21, and then the work of building a couple of log cabins commenced. Next was ground to clear, to raise corn for bread and hominy, then as winter approached the beaver and otter traps were brought from their places in the packs where they had lain all summer.

Time passed by and nothing happened to mar the peace and quietude of the Meeks family, not until an Indian chief began to complain, his name was Settedown, he claimed that the Meeks[es] were intruding on his hunting ground, but the Meeks[es] did not think that the chief would do them any harm.[3] All of the Indians had been ordered by the United States Indian Agent at Vincennes to report to the Agency at once,[4] but

3 Although the real name was probably Set-te-tah, it became corrupted over the years to Set-te-down. Terminations of Shawnee and most other Native American languages involve vowel sounds, typically with an *a* sound. The Shawnee have no words terminating with the *down* sound. *History of Warrick, Spencer, and Perry Counties, Indiana: From the Earliest Time to the Present; Together with Interesting Biographical Sketches, Reminiscences, Notes, Etc.* (Chicago: Goodspeed Bros., 1885), 251.

4 Residents of the Indiana Territory and Kentucky, fearing a union of northwest tribes into a great confederation, joined William Henry Harrison and the regular US Army in defeating the confederation at the Battle of Tippecanoe on 7 November 1811. The county created in 1818, now remembered as the Indiana home of Lincoln, was named for Spier Spencer, a casualty at Tippecanoe. *History of Warrick, Spencer, and Perry Counties, Indiana: From the Earliest Time to the Present; Together with Interesting Biographical Sketches, Reminiscences, Notes, Etc.* (Chicago: Goodspeed Bros., 1885), 251.

Chief Settedown was determined for revenge before leaving his old hunting grounds,[5] so on the morning he and his tribe was to leave their old home and hunting ground, which was near Richland Lake post office in Spencer County, Indiana, Settedown and two other[s] came to the Meeks home just at daylight, and made a noise at the door, and Athe Meeks, Sr., opened the door and one of the Indians shot him dead as he stood in the door of his house.[6] The shooting aroused the family and Athe Meeks, Jr., then a boy of nineteen years ran out of the house unarmed, and one of the Indians seized hold of him and commenced to strike him with a tomahawk or hatchet,[7] and by this time William Meeks, the married son, who lived about one hundred and fifty yards distant from his father's house, hearing the shot fired, jumped out of bed and saw the Indian striking his brother Athe Meeks, Jr., with the tomahawk, and another Indian was standing nearby slapping himself on his thighs as though bullying up the fight, so William Meeks took aim and killed this Indian dead, and the Indian who was fighting with Athe Meeks, Jr., let go of him, and he and the other Indian picked up the dead Indian and ran off with him, leaving one rifle gun laying in the yard. William Meeks followed after these two Indians hoping to get a shot at them, but whenever he came any way near them they would lay down the dead Indian, and one would go right and one to the left so as to get Meeks between two fires, then Meeks would have to retreat, and finally he gave up the chase and returned to the house. After Meeks gave up the pursuit the Indians hid their dead comrade where a tree had fallen against another tree and

5 Different sources cite different motivations for the "revenge." Some surviving relatives—Susan Meeks Tucker and Peggy Meeks Carter, both daughters of Athe Meeks Sr.— allege nearby neighbors with a grudge against the Meeks family induced the Native Americans to attack. Others argue that Shawnee warrior chief Tecumseh had recently encouraged Native American violence against white settlers. *History of Warrick, Spencer, and Perry Counties, Indiana,* 251–252.

6 The daughters of Athe Meeks Sr. indicate that a Native American named Big Bones pulled the trigger. They also say that, after killing the patriarch, Big Bones started to scalp him and enter the cabin; however, Mrs. Meeks quickly dragged her husband inside, barred the door, and sustained a severe tomahawk cut to her ankle as a result. *History of Warrick, Spencer, and Perry Counties, Indiana,* 252.

7 Goodspeed gives Athe Meeks Jr.'s age as seventeen years old. The same source states that he received several severe cuts to the shoulders. According to one account, a musket ball struck his knee and another hit his wrist. *History of Warrick, Spencer, and Perry Counties, Indiana,* 252.

had the forks split apart—they piled leaves and chunks of wood on him and left him there.

When Meeks reached his father's home, his brother, Athe Jr., whom the Indian had cut with a tomahawk, had nearly bled to death, as the women had barred the doors, for they were afraid to go out to see what had become of Athe Meeks, Jr., and he had hid in the weeds and was afraid to call for help, and afterwards was wounded in the knee at the battle of Tippecanoe in Indiana. As soon as William Meeks got his brother in the house, he, William Meeks, then started for help to pursue the Indians. There were four families living at French Island Landing on the Ohio River, on the Indiana side.

Twelve miles from the Meeks home they were the nearest white people to them. He told them what had happened, and then he went up to the Yellow Banks, now Owensboro, in Kentucky. Then someone went up to the mouth of Blackford Creek in Kentucky—a few families lived there. It is just above Grandview, Indiana on the Kentucky side of the Ohio River. A few families lived in the fort, which was about one hundred and fifty yards southwest of Cadicks flour mill at Grandview, Indiana. A few families lived a few miles from the fort in the country. Next morning after the tragedy fifty men were at the Meeks home all ready to pursue Settedown and his tribe. These fifty men followed Settedown's trail by where they had went through the wild pea vines. After following the Indians about twenty miles over in Warrick County, Indiana, they found them camped in about two acres of polk stalks. Wild pigeons had roosted there and polk stalks had come up. Many years ago there was a small village near there called Polk Patch—it is now called Selvin. These Indians were brought back to Spencer County in Hammond Township, near Grandview, Indiana, to a Mr. Uriah Lamar's, who was a Justice of the Peace. He was the only officer here in southern Indiana, now composing the counties of Knox, Gibson, Posey, Vanderburgh, Pike, Warrick, Dubois and Spencer. It was Justice Lamar's duty at that time to see that these Indians were sent to the Reservation, which was situated six miles from Vincennes in Knox County, Indiana. After the men arrived at Mr. Lamar's, the Indians as prisoners, the rifle gun that the Indians left lying in the Meeks yard was at Mr. Lamar's, and a son of Settedown aged about nineteen years, would put his hand on the gun and point to his father, the same as to say, "It's my father's gun," but the old Chief would shake his head disowning his own gun.

There was a man named William Smithers who lived in Kentucky, whose parents and brothers and sisters had all been murdered by the Indians. He himself, a boy of ten years, had escaped by being sent for neighbors to come to their rescue, but before their arrival the Indians had murdered all the family and set fire to the house and were gone. It was claimed that Smithers liked to kill every Indian he could get to see, so when night came, before going to leave on the next morning for the Reservation, it had been arranged among most of the men on guard for William Meeks to kill Chief Settedown that night, but there was one man among the guards that all of the other men were afraid would tell who done the killing of Chief Settedown. One of the guards threw out the drinking water so as to have an excuse to get this man away from the house. All the men except this one understood why the water was gone. One man said he was quite thirsty and must have water but said he was afraid to go alone to the spring and everyone said they were afraid to go. Finally the man they wanted out of doors when the killing came off said he would go with him. William Meeks' gun failed to fire, the man with the water spilled the water and had to go back to the spring for more water, Chief Settedown raised himself up in his bed and said whiteman kill me this night, and laid down again. This time it fired and Chief Settedown's earthly career was blotted out, and the people all said it was Bill Smithers who killed Chief Settedown. It is human nature to lay your own misdeeds on someone else, and William Smithers was not here to deny the charge.

There were six Indians left after Chief Settedown's death, his wife and five males. When they started on their way to the Reservation, William Meeks followed up in the rear, and every time one of the Indians got in the rear William Meeks would kill him. The last one killed was between Vincennes and the Reservation. Only the wife of Chief Settedown reached the reservation alive, his wife would come back here every year and visit the grave of her husband, Chief Settedown, I suppose as long as she lived. The house that Chief Settedown was killed in was destroyed but a few years ago, but the old spring is still in use.

Athe Meeks, Sr., of the within sketch, was my great grandfather, and Athe Meeks, Jr., was my grandfather, and I am a Civil War veteran, and was 75 years old the 29th day of October, 1920, the above sketch was written by me in my own handwriting.

AARON MEEKS (1845–1927) served as a private in the 42nd Indiana Volunteer Infantry Regiment during the Civil War. He lived in both Indiana and Utah.

11

★ ★ ★

The Mystery of Lincoln's Melancholy

LOUIS A. WARREN *

Unlike most of the authors who contributed to the Lincoln Inquiry, Louis A. Warren was a professional Lincoln scholar. Presented in Lincoln City in 1924, this paper could be titled, "The Five Women Lincoln Loved." It reminds us that three of those women lived in Spencer County and two lie buried there.

THE TITLE OF THIS PAPER DOES NOT IMPLY A NEW DISCOVERY nor the solution of a current biographical problem. It is used merely because many biographers have insisted that the source of Lincoln's melancholy spirit was the presence of a family skeleton.

William Herndon was the first to champion this theory; in the preface to his three volume work on Lincoln he presents this query: "In drawing the portrait tell the world what the skeleton was with Lincoln. What gave him that peculiar melancholy? What cancer had he inside?" Herndon then proceeded in the subsequent pages to lead out for exhibition, a skeleton which had been created as late as the political campaign of 1860. With the assistance of some aspirants to a place in the Lincoln family tree, he essayed to advise the world why the president was possessed of a dejected spirit. He also tried to describe the alleged cancerous growth of his patient without ever making an incision to determine whether or not such a growth really existed.

* Warren delivered this paper on 14 October 1924 and published it in *Indiana History Bulletin* 3, extra no. 1, *Proceedings of the Southwestern Indiana Historical Society: Papers Read before the Society at Various Meetings, 1920–1925* (December 1925): 53–60.

A more recent biographer, who claims to be in possession of first-hand evidence relating to Lincoln's boyhood, declares that Abraham as an infant had a melancholy disposition, and another writer affirms that there was not a day in his childhood life when he enjoyed a degree of happiness. These statements would imply that there were hereditary tendencies largely responsible for this morbid condition. The evidence supporting these claims is not good; there is no reliable source which would allow one to learn very much about the childhood disposition of this boy.

It shall be the purpose of this paper to make a study of certain established events taking place in the experiences of Abraham Lincoln, which would develop, in a perfectly normal way, the spirit of melancholy which seemed to exert over him such a tremendous influence. My method of approach will be inductive rather than deductive, and I hope to arrive at a conclusion free from traditional contributions, and one which may be of some historical value.

In seeking color for this task we could have chosen no time of year more favorable than the Autumn, and no location offering a more satisfactory environment than Lincoln City. The season is in tune with the melancholy note which the writer has chosen to sound, registered in the poetic mind by that prophecy of passing time: "The melancholy days have come, the saddest of the year."

This place is the site of a memorial which helps us to travel back one hundred and six years, to a day when a little boy holding tightly to his father's hand, trudged his way from a mound on the hill to a motherless home. Memories that now crowd in upon us, should place us in a proper mood to approach a study of this most dominant characteristic in the life of the Martyred President.

Writers have had a tendency to emphasize the story-telling ability of Lincoln, until he has become the Mark Twain of the White House. It must be granted that anecdote became a powerful weapon in the hand of Lincoln, and also a vehicle of laughter in some tense moments when relief was necessary to save the situation. It is true also that in periods of relaxation he tried to revive his dejected spirit by seeking such associations as would make for good cheer. Lincoln, however, was no clown, and frivolity was not in his vocabulary. He was the mirthful, melancholy man, but mirth was superficial while melancholy was profound.

One need but study the many portraits of Lincoln, to discover the real Lincoln. His serious, sober and solemn disposition allowed him to evaluate the needs of men and cultivate a broad sympathy for all humanity.

Abraham Lincoln loved five women. For each one of these women he had an affection peculiar to itself, and no two of them excited in him the same appreciation. Yet we cannot feel that his love for any one of them was more pronounced than for the others. Three of these five women at one time lived in this very community, and two of these three lie buried here.

The first woman that Lincoln loved was his mother, Nancy Hanks Lincoln. The pioneer mothers were not given to mirth. Transient and inadequate homes, continued loneliness, and the constant fear of the approach of the savages[1] gave them subdued spirits. It was the pioneer mother that suffered most in the birth of western civilization, and a monument erected to Daniel Boone without Mrs. Boone by his side is a false picture of the "winning of the west."

The first great sorrow that came into the Lincoln home was the death of the third child, an infant named Thomas. Abraham was about two years old at the time of this child's birth, and while its death may not have influenced him directly it must have cast a gloom over the home and especially over the mother. Abraham must have come to know his mother in these first years of observation as a sad-eyed guardian whose love was revealed through tears rather than laughter.

The Lincoln family moved from Kentucky to Indiana in the fall of 1816. There is a tradition current, that on the way they stopped at Little Mount Cemetery in Larue County, Kentucky, where the infant child was buried. Here Nancy, as she kneeled on the small mound marking the site of her buried hopes, poured out her heart as she left the scene forever. Abraham, then a boy of seven years, must have been deeply touched by this demonstration, and undoubtedly remembered the sorrow of leave taking and his own childish grief.

Less than two years after the arrival of the Lincoln family in Indiana the mother became one of the many victims of an epidemic known as "milk sickness," then prevalent in the community. The death of the mother and the crude preparations for burial must have left a very deep

---

1 Here the term "savages" is a racist term that was applied to Native Americans, portraying them as wild or less than fully human. The word comes by way of French from the Latin word *silvaticus*, said of someone who lives in the woods.

scar on the heart of this nine-year-old boy. His appeal to David Elkins, a minister back in Kentucky, to hold a funeral service for the mother is a well known tradition. The writer has personal acquaintance with the grandson of this same David Elkins, and the tradition current in the family coincides with the Indiana version of the story.

In the death of Nancy Hanks Lincoln we feel that we have discovered the first tragedy which directly contributed to the melancholy of Abraham Lincoln. His own testimony in later years suggests how deeply he was influenced by both her life and her death when he said, "All that I am or hope to be I owe to my angel mother."

The love which Abraham Lincoln had for his sister Sarah must have been greatly accentuated by the double role she was now to play in his life, that of both sister and mother. Upon the death of Nancy this little eleven-year-old girl became the mother of the household consisting of her father and her brother and a waif by the name of Dennis Hanks whose foster parents had also been claimed by the dreaded disease. That Abraham came to love this little mother, who was also his playmate, with a most tender devotion we cannot doubt, and here the setting was laid for the second tragedy.

Before Sally Lincoln reached the age of twenty years she was married to Aaron Grigsby. This wedding may have been a season of rejoicing for all the guests, but for Abraham it meant separation from the one who had been his constant companion from birth. In less than two years after this wedding, and before Sarah had reached her twenty-first year, she joined her mother in the great beyond. The influence of this second tragedy upon Abraham can best be judged from an excerpt of the *Indianapolis News* of April 12, 1902, contributed by Captain John W. Lemar:

> A great grief which affected Abe through life, was caused by the death of his only sister, Sally. They were close companions and were a great deal alike in temperament. About a year after her marriage to one of the Grigsbys she died. This was a hard blow to Abe who always thought her death was due to neglect. Abe was in a little smokehouse when the news came to him that she had died. He came to the door and sat down, burying his face in his hands. The tears trickled through his large fingers and sobs shook his frame. From then on he was alone in the world, you might say.

Although Abraham Lincoln was not yet out of his teens he had seen both his mother and his only sister borne away to their final resting places.

The third woman Lincoln loved was his stepmother, Sarah Johnston Lincoln. Some biographers have taken occasion to sneer at Thomas Lincoln for bringing into his home, one year and three months after the death of his first wife, a new mother for his children. From the viewpoint of the writer this was a worthy and commendable act, especially so when we remember that Mrs. Johnston was a widow with three children.

It might be in harmony with our discussion to here present a picture of the Indiana home, in which Abraham Lincoln grew to maturity, or at least mention the personnel of the home. It consisted of the father, Thomas Lincoln, and his second wife, Sarah Johnston Lincoln; the two children of Thomas, Sarah and Abraham; the three children of Mrs. Lincoln, John D., Matilda and Elizabeth Johnston; and also Dennis Hanks. There is a possibility that some Hall children were also taken into the home, although this fact cannot be substantiated. With three sets of orphan children, and possibly four, under one roof, we might have what we could call the first orphanage in the State of Indiana. The many mouths which had to be fed may account for the fact that Thomas Lincoln was not able to set aside an accumulation for his old age.

We should not forget that while many children gave Lincoln plenty of playmates, yet there was something akin to pity surrounding the home which really was the remnant of three pioneer families. There was no tragedy associated with this foster mother, however, that had direct bearing on Lincoln, unless it was the tragedy of her oldest son, who became a parasite on Thomas and Sarah Lincoln and brought into the world at least one child who was no credit to the family. Abraham Lincoln loved his stepmother with an affection that apparently surpassed that of her own children.

The Lincolns left Indiana for Illinois on March 1, 1830, Abraham then having arrived at his 21st year. He was now a man, but he did not leave all the memories of this Indiana residence behind. He carried in his heart two deep scars which apparently were never healed.

After a visit to this community in 1844 he was inspired to compose these lines:

> My childhood's home I see again,
>   And sadden with the view;
> And still, as memory crowds my brain,
>   There's pleasure in it, too.

O memory! thou midway world
    'Twixt earth and paradise,
Where things decayed, and loved ones lost,
    In dreamy shadows rise;

Near twenty years have passed away
    Since here I bid farewell
To woods and fields, and scenes of play,
    And playmates loved so well;

Where many were, but few remain,
    Of old, familiar things;
But seeing them to mind again
    The lost and absent brings.

The friends I left that parting day,
    How changed! as time has sped,
Young childhood grown, strong manhood gray,
    And half of all are dead.

I hear the loud survivors tell
    How naught from death could save,
Till every sound appears a knell,
    And every spot a grave.

I range the fields with pensive tread,
    And pace the hollow rooms,
And feel (companion of the dead),
    I'm living in the tombs.

The fourth woman Lincoln loved was his sweetheart, Ann Rutledge. There are so many conflicting traditions about this courtship of Lincoln's that the writer will not attempt to unravel the contradictions nor present a new interpretation of this attraction which Ann had for Abraham. We are not interested in learning if Ann had other admirers before Lincoln came upon the scene nor whether Lincoln was a first or second choice of Ann's. Her own sister, Sarah Rutledge Sanders, in a recent interview with Dr. W. E. Barton, among other interesting details of this early courtship, made this one statement which will be sufficient for our purpose. She said, "Lincoln loved Ann sincerely and she gave him undivided affection."

This affection paved the way for the third great tragedy in the life of this great soul. It may be that it brought a greater sadness than any of his other experiences. Maturity gave him a keen appreciation of the impassable barrier of death, and one woman has said that Lincoln told her in speaking of the grave of Ann Rutledge "My heart lies buried there." Upon the tombstone over this grave one may read the following inscription:

> Out of me, unworthy and unknown,
>   The vibrations of deathless music;
> "With malice toward none, with charity for all,"
>   Out of me forgiveness of millions toward millions,
>
> And the beneficent face of a nation
>   Shining with justice and truth.
> I am Ann Rutledge who sleeps beneath these weeds,
>   Beloved of Abraham Lincoln,
>
> Wedded to him, not through union,
>   But through separation.
> Bloom forever, O Republic,
>   From the dust of my bosom.

January 7th, 1813   August 25th, 1835

The last one of the five women loved by Abraham Lincoln was Mary Todd, who became his wife and the mother of his children. This courtship was not a period of exuberant joy; by this time he had already become the victim of an increasing depression which made him approach this new affinity in a spirit of reluctance. We cannot accept the conclusion of some writers that he was a cowardly suitor, who slunk away unannounced from the first attempt to conduct the wedding ceremony. But undoubtedly this melancholy man was not a gallant lover, and there was something pathetic about his new affection.

The later experiences of Lincoln, while not responsible for his pronounced dejection, did accentuate it. The death of a son and the hurling of the nation into civil strife filled the cup of sadness to overflowing, and a tragedy as the climax of his own life was inevitable.

Of the five women Abraham Lincoln loved, his mother, his sister, and his sweetheart were all taken from him at times when it would be difficult for him to become reconciled to their departure. Events associated with the other two, his stepmother and the mother of his children, were such as would arouse in him the deepest sympathies. In the great struggle between the states it was the constant appeals of the war mothers from both sides that moved him with the deepest and most genuine sorrow.

If we are students of William James instead of William Herndon we shall not prowl around in the dusty attics of traditions nor shake the genealogical tree of either the Lincoln or Hanks families in hopes that some spoiled fruit will fall to explain the mystery of Lincoln's melancholy, but we shall conclude from the evidence in hand that the grooves of sorrow made in the plastic mind of the boy Abraham, were made deeper and deeper by each successive tragedy, until each thought wave passed through a valley of sadness. So it was that the life of Abraham Lincoln was touched and moved by the spirit of melancholy.

LOUIS A. WARREN (1885–1963) was a Lincoln scholar who directed the Louis A. Warren Lincoln Library Museum in Fort Wayne, Indiana, from 1928 to 1956. His acclaimed work, *Lincoln's Youth* (1959), remains the classic study of Lincoln's Indiana years.

12

★ ★ ★

Lincoln and the Wool-Carder's Beautiful Niece

JESSE N. WEIK*

Beginning about 1880, Jesse Weik made several trips to southern Indiana to collect stories from those who knew Abraham Lincoln.[1] The account here came from John M. Lockwood of Princeton, Indiana.[2] In August 1827, according to Lockwood, a young girl named Julia Evans caught Lincoln's eye, her "bewitching" beauty so powerful that she captivated Lincoln for several years.

Either Lockwood had an excellent memory, or he could tell a good story (or perhaps both). He told Weik that when he talked with Lincoln thirty-one years later in Mount Carmel, Illinois, Lincoln remembered the 1827 incident. This paper provides the most complete account available of the alleged encounter and, if true, provides insight into a rarely seen facet of Lincoln's personality.

THE DAY OF THE OLD-FASHIONED WOOL-CARDER IS GONE, IN fact, but few people now living have ever seen that primitive and cumbersome but very useful machine which prevailed so extensively in the early part of the last century, when our forefathers, with patient and

---

* Weik first published this paper in *Success Magazine* in December 1902. Mrs. Lotta Edson Strain, granddaughter of John M. Lockwood, read it at a Southwestern Indiana Historical Society meeting in Newburgh, Indiana, on 27 May 1925. A copy is part of the *Southwestern Indiana Historical Society Annuals*, Vol. 1: 56–62, at the Evansville-Vanderburgh Public Library. The story, summarized, appeared in the *Indianapolis Star* on 7 February 1909, p. 39. Weik included a letter from Lockwood about the incident in his book *The Real Lincoln* published in 1922 by University of Nebraska Press (appendix I, p. 365)

1 Jesse W. Weik to Albert J. Beveridge, 23 May 1923, Albert Beveridge Papers, Library of Congress, Washington, DC. A copy is in the Beveridge File, Lincoln Boyhood National Memorial, Lincoln City, Indiana.

2 Princeton, Indiana, is located about forty miles northwest from Lincoln's boyhood home.

laborious care, carded the wool into rolls, and our grandmothers after-wards, with swift and nimble fingers, spun it into yarn. In each town or village, in those days, some man was usually selected to operate such a machine, generally propelled by horse power, to which the people, com-ing from every direction far and near, would bring the season's supply of wool to be disentangled and carded into shape for the spinning-wheel and the loom. Being the leading, and frequently the only manufacturing concern in a locality, it was not only the principal source of commercial and industrial activity, but also the public market place or forum, where all the great and perplexing questions that stirred the village community were analyzed, discussed, and disposed of, when it had finally attained these lofty and important proportions, it was known as the carding-mill.

An institution of this kind was in existence in the year 1827, in the vil-lage of Princeton, Indiana. The owner, James Evans,[3] had entrusted its operation to a bright and industrious young man of eighteen, who, with his parents, had emigrated nine years before from Westchester County, New York, and whose conduct and management of the industry com-mitted to his charge had, in the highest degree, won the confidence and approval of his employer. Evans himself spent but little time about the mill, so that the young man at once exercised the functions of the pro-prietor, superintendent, operator, and cashier. His name was John M. Lockwood and the same zeal and devotion to duty has characterized his life ever since; for, although almost seventy-five years have elapsed since the days of the Evans carding-machine, he is still enjoying, in an unusual degree, at the advanced age of ninety-three years, full possession of all his faculties. While engaged in the service of Mr. Evans, an accident oc-curred, the nature and result of which are best understood if we adhere to this wool-carder's version.

HE RODE THIRTY MILES WITH A LOAD OF HAY
"In the afternoon of a particularly warm, dry day, in August, 1827," is the testimony of Mr. Lockwood, "a tall, beardless, long-legged boy about

3 James Evans (d. 1834) cultivated a large farm in addition to his wool-carding business. His brother was Robert M. Evans (1782–1842), namesake of Evansville, Indiana. *A Biographical History of Eminent and Self-Made Men of the State of Indiana*, vol. 1 (Cincinnati, OH: Western Biographical Publishing, 1880), 20.

my own age, dressed in a suit of well-worn brown jeans, the trousers
of which he had long before outgrown, and wearing a woolen hat and
coarse, heavy, plain-cut leather shoes of the style then in vogue among
the backwoods people, came riding up to the mill. Behind him, tied over
the horse's back, was a bunch of wool, which, after dismounting, he carried across the road and dropped at my feet, asking if it could be carded.
I answered in the affirmative, but added that people who patronize the
wool-carder, like those who carried their grain to the grist mill, had to
await their turn; but, when he told me that he had ridden from a point
in the interior of Spencer County, at least thirty miles away, I relented
somewhat and decided that, in his case, I would be justified in waiving
the ordinary rule. On account, therefore, of the long return journey that
lay before him, I promised that his work should be done in advance of its
turn, and that it would be ready for him before the close of the afternoon,
an announcement that evidently yielded him great relief.

In response to my request, he gave me his name, but, being a new one
to me, and one I had never heard before, he looked over my shoulder and
carefully spelled it as I wrote it down in the little book which contained
the history of the day's transactions. There were two ways, I explained to
him, of settling for the work; either by paying cash or taking the requisite
toll, "But I have no money," he interrupted in a melancholy tone of voice,
"so that you will have to keep out wool enough for your pay."

"For some time he lingered about the place, watching the machine
do its work, occasionally clucking to old Davey, the veteran sorrel
horse whose dignified but uncertain movement save when under the
strict surveillance of an overseer, furnished the motive power for the
mill; finally he left, strolling down the road toward the other end of
the village. Later in the afternoon he returned, finding his wool properly
carded into rolls and ready for delivery. It was wrapped in the same sheet
and fastened at the top and ends with the same thorns which had held
it in place on the long journey from Spencer County. I remember that
he had eighteen pounds, and I 'tolled' one-sixth of it, or three pounds."

"After I had handed him the little ticket or slip containing his name
and the bill, or figures, of the transaction usual in such a case, he started
to go; but, before he reached the door, he halted, turned about, dropped
his bundle to the floor, and, by motion of his head, beckoned me aside,

indicating by look and gesture that he had something significant as well as private to say to me. I stepped back a few paces so as to avoid as much as possible, the noise of the machine. "I don't want to keep you away from your work," he said; "but, before I left town, I thought I would like to ask you if you know Julia Evans," mentioning the name of my employer's niece.[4] "Yes, I know her well," I responded, "and she is not only among the handsomest, but also one of the best girls in town."

"It was then that he confided to me, with some secrecy, the fact that he had passed Miss Evans in the street a short time before; that she had bowed to and saluted him, as was then customary even between strangers, and that from a passer-by he had learned her name. It was very evident that he was thoroughly captivated by her beautiful face and figure, for she was, indeed, a charming girl, and admittedly the village belle. Although it was late in the afternoon, and a long ride lay before him, he seemed somewhat reluctant to go. The glimpse of Julia Evans's face had clearly upset him. His bundle lay where he had dropped it on the floor, and, under pretense of stopping, now and then, to get a drink of water before he started, or of repairing a broken strap in his horse's bridle, he continued to linger about the mill, occasionally renewing his questions to me about Miss Evans and every way manifesting the deepest interest in her.

"My endorsement of the girl and my testimony as to her sweetness of character as well as her beauty had, evidently, found a ready and deep seated lodgment in the young swain's heart, for he finally expressed a purpose to return, and, wonderingly, asked me if I thought she would consent to an introduction. I cannot specifically recall the fact now, but I have no doubt that I felt warranted in promising to arrange and secure the coveted presentation to the girl in case he should return. I shall never forget the earnest, anxious look on his face, and I confess that I laughed, after he was gone, when I thought of the impression on his tall, awkward figure, his coarse, home-spun attire, and his rude, backwoods manners would set on the heart of pretty Julia Evans, who, considering the time, and place, had enjoyed somewhat superior advantages, and, although

---

4 Julia's father was Robert M. Evans (1782–1842), the namesake of Evansville, Indiana. Joseph P. Elliott, *A History of Evansville and Vanderburgh County, Indiana* (Evansville, IN: Keller Printing, 1897). Robert's brother James owned the wool-carding business.

living in a new and undeveloped country, was, nevertheless, in view of
her surroundings, far above average in beauty, education, and womanly
accomplishments.

"At length, having left the mill, he crossed the road, mounted his horse,
fastened the bundle of wool behind him, waved me adieu, and rode away.
At a turn in the road he disappeared from view and I returned to my
work. I could not help thinking all the afternoon of that solitary traveler
and the long journey through the thirty or more miles of thick and lonely
forest that lay between Princeton and his backwoods home in the wilds
of Spencer County."

IN THOSE DAYS, SUCH A JOURNEY WAS NOT REMARKABLE

Time passed on,[5] thirty-one years had elapsed, and the west rocked in
the throes of that memorable agitation against the further extension of
human slavery. A great political meeting was held at Mt. Carmel, a town
in Illinois on the bluffs over the Wabash River, in September, 1856.[6] To
this meeting repaired many of the people from Princeton, Indiana, distance only ten miles, among them John M. Lockwood, no longer James
Evans's young wool-carder, but a man of wealth and influence in the
community, and deeply interested in the great and momentous political
questions that then agitated the nation. To the tall, earnest man who,
by his eloquent and impassioned protest against the further encroach-
ment of the arrogant slave power, sought, that day to arouse the people
to the needs of the hour, he listened with deep and reverent attention.
The reader need hardly be told that the speaker was none other than
Abraham Lincoln. In that sad, earnest face, that giant figure swaying
and vehement with righteous indignation, Lockwood recognized a man
he had seen before.

5 Julia Ann Evans eventually married Silas Stephens, sole proprietor of the only saddlery in
Evansville, Indiana. After selling his business to Joseph Peter Elliott and Dr. William M. Elliott,
Silas Stephens engaged in the sawmill business on the riverfront. He owned the first steam sawmill
built in Vanderburgh County and later farmed. Silas and Julia had one daughter, Jane E. Scantlin.
See Joseph Peter Elliott, *A History of Evansville and Vanderburgh County, Indiana* (Evansville, IN:
Keller Printing, 1897), 349.

6 Lincoln visited Lawrenceville and Olney, Illinois, on 19 and 20 September 1856. These towns
are less than thirty miles north of Mount Carmel. See Earl Schenck Miers, ed., *Lincoln Day by Day:
A Chronology 1809–1865*, vol. 2 (Washington, DC: Sesquicentennial Commission, 1960), 179.

After the close of the meeting, he made his way to the platform and was introduced to him. "So you're from Princeton?" inquired Lincoln. "Well, I was in Princeton myself once," he continued, "but it was a good many years ago, when I was a boy, I rode there, over thirty miles across the country, on a flea-bitten mare, with a bunch of wool which my mother had sent along to have carded. There was nothing remarkable about such a journey in those days, and I might, in the course of time, have forgotten it, but for one incident. While waiting for the wool-carder, I strolled about the village and happened to pass, on the street, a very beautiful girl—the most bewitching creature, it seemed to me, I had ever seen. My heart was in a flutter. The truth is that I was so thoroughly captivated by the vision of maidenly beauty that I wanted to stop in Princeton forever, and it was only with the greatest difficulty that I succeeded in persuading myself to leave the place at all. When I finally overcame my passionate yearning and set out on the long journey homeward, it was with the fixed purpose to return. I knew my garb and manners proclaimed my backwoods origins and training; but, in spite of all my imperfections and delinquencies, I was determined to see more of the Princeton girl."

On hearing this, Lockwood ventures to observe that he was the man who had carded Lincoln's wool, whereupon the latter's face assumed an expression of the deepest interest, and he warmly grasped the informant's hand a second time, "Did you return and meet the girl?" inquired Lockwood. "No, unfortunately, I did not," laughingly answered Lincoln. "I suppose I justified the wisdom of Shakespeare, who contended that it is folly to trust in the 'madness of a wolf, or a boy's love.' During that long tiresome ride away from Princeton, some of the sentiment, doubtless, eased out of me, and, after reaching home, other and conflicting things soon arose to claim my attention. What prevented my return I do not now recall, but, so deep an impression had the Princeton girl made on me, I remember that it was several years before her image was effaced from my mind and heart."

JESSE N. WEIK (1857–1930) was a native of Greencastle, Indiana, who collaborated with Lincoln's law partner William Herndon in writing Herndon's *Lincoln*, published in 1889. Weik wrote the text using letters and reminiscences collected by Herndon.

13

★ ★ ★

Word Pictures of Pioneer Families and Lincoln Contemporaries

BESS V. EHRMANN*

Ehrmann contends that Abraham Lincoln was not the only successful man to grow up in frontier southwest Indiana. Here, she discusses other men who experienced the same pioneer conditions as Lincoln and achieved success as businessmen, lawyers, judges, and members of the Indiana General Assembly.

THE NOTED PEOPLE THAT I HAVE CHOSEN TO SPEAK ABOUT were all residents of Spencer County during the fourteen years that the Lincolns lived there, and it was my privilege to see them, to talk to them, and to note what type of people they were.

The first one that I shall tell you about was a Luce Township man, Mr. William Richardson.[1] The Richardson family was one of the best known, one of the wealthiest, and one of the most outstanding families in their township. I went with my mother to their home. I remember so well what a very hospitable and energetic man Mr. Richardson was. As I recall him, he was not very tall, rather heavy in build, with a very kind

---

* Ehrmann delivered this paper on 30 October 1928 and published it in *Indiana History Bulletin 6*, extra no. 3, *Proceedings of the Southwestern Indiana Historical Society during Its Ninth Year* (August 1929): 119–121. The original piece also featured two additional contributions by Mrs. Albion Fellows Bacon and Mrs. Charles T. Johnson not included here.

1 Born in Hardin County, Kentucky, on 6 February 1809—just six days before Lincoln was born in the same county—Richardson came with his family to Perry County in 1815 and moved to southwestern Spencer County in 1829. He was elected to the Indiana House in 1849 and 1853 before being elected to the Senate in 1854. Richardson died in 1896.

and pleasant face. His home was one of the finest in the entire county in the early days. It was well furnished and they had the comforts of that time. Certainly the home of this man doesn't answer the description given by a recent historian when he said: "The cabins of these wood folks were often ill-kept, dirty in the extreme, infested with vermin."[a]

Then I will paint for you a word picture of his wife, Mrs. Richardson.[2] Well do I recall her sweet face, her hair parted in the middle, combed smoothly back, neatly dressed. She was a large woman. She, too, was so hospitable, welcoming everyone to her home, and such hospitality was never found greater in any other place than it was in the Richardson home. The descendants of that family are living in our county today. They have always been representative people. They have owned large farms, and have been people of force. So those are the first that I take pleasure in testifying for, who were not the type described above.

The next was a judge who lived here in Rockport. Judge Harman Barkwell[3] was a very small man, as I remember him; very wrinkled and withered looking. He always wore a tall silk hat, and a king-tailed coat, and carried a cane. How well I remember seeing him stepping along the street in his brisk manner. I know I used to think as a child, that the wind would blow him away because he was so shriveled, and yet I felt instinctively that Judge Barkwell was a very intelligent man, and I have heard since that he was educated in law at New Harmony. He lived his earliest days very close to where Lincoln worked at the ferry at Anderson Creek, and I feel that undoubtedly Lincoln and Judge Barkwell knew each other in their younger days.

The next man I shall speak about is the Honorable James Gentry.[4] Mr. Gentry has been recorded in history many times as having been a friend of the Lincoln family. I do not know how much schooling Mr. Gentry may have had, perhaps no more than Abraham Lincoln

2 Mary Ann Luce (1816–1884) married Richardson in 1833. The Luces were prominent in early Spencer County.

3 Barkwell (1807–1889) was born in Kentucky and came to Indiana (Troy, Mt. Vernon, and Rockport) "after reaching his majority"; thus, he arrived sometime after 1828. He settled in Rockport in 1839 and was a member of the state legislature and the 1850 Indiana constitutional convention.

4 James Gentry, father of this James Gentry, brought his family to Spencer County in 1818 and founded Gentryville. The younger James Gentry (1819–1905) grew up a short distance from the Lincoln farm. Like Lincoln, he served in his state legislature (1870–1873) but as a Democrat.

had. Many of our pioneers didn't have any more education in the way
of schooling than Lincoln had, but I am going to quote what Judge Cur-
ran DeBruler said of Mr. Gentry before the latter's death: "I have never
talked with any man who understood better than Mr. Gentry the political issues of the day. He could talk more understandingly on all of the
important questions of the day than any man I know." That was the statement of a college man, a graduate of Harvard. I remember Mr. Gentry as
a very kind-faced man, a polite gentleman, walking along the streets of
Rockport, neatly dressed, speaking to his friends, showing by his bearing
that he was a man worthwhile. And the Gentry name in Spencer County
has always stood for the very best type of citizen.

The next picture, that of my grandmother, is not in accord with the
statement that when Lincoln lived in Spencer County "everybody,
women and preachers included,"[b] drank and smoked. When I read that
I could see my dignified old grandmother, and the very thought that she
would drink or smoke was something that I could not bear to think of.
She is only one of the many who lived here then, who were of the same
type.[5] My grandmother was a little above medium height, rather a large
woman. I never saw her when she was not neatly dressed, even if it was
but a calico dress, with either a frill of lace, or a collar about her neck, held
together with an old-fashioned pin. She always wore a little black lace cap
with ribbons hanging down over the shoulders. She was very particular
about what her grandchildren should say and do, and I remember very
well some of the punishments that were received by the children in that
day, because their deportment was not just as grandmother thought it
should be. I feel that she was typical of the womanhood of that time,
brave, indeed, to stand the hardships of the pioneer life. Their home,
too, was a home of comfort. The next person is Mr. Joseph Richardson,[6]
"Uncle Joe," as the Rockport people liked to call him. Mr. Joe Richardson was a schoolmate of Lincoln and lived out near the Lincoln home
in his boyhood. He afterwards came to Rockport to live. He was very
fond of his personal appearance and he always looked very neat. I was

5 Probably Evaline Bayliss Britton (1808–1892).
6 Joseph Richardson (1816–1892) was born in Kentucky. His family moved to Indiana in 1817
and lived near the Lincolns in the Little Pigeon community. He became a local businessman and
was twice elected clerk of Spencer County Circuit Court.

too small to know that he always wore a wig, as I have been told by others was his custom. He was not, as Mr. Beveridge described the pioneer, without thought of personal appearance, and rough and rude in manner. Mr. Richardson had very beautiful manners. All he did showed that he had been a man of affairs. Of course, he was a very old man when I knew him.

In closing my pictures, I want to tell you one thing that my mother-in-law, who was the daughter of Judge Lemuel Quincy DeBruler, told me. She remembers well so many of these well-known people of that early time. But this recollection is to my way of thinking rather an outstanding thing because it shows that the influential and cultured people in southern Indiana traveled about from county to county, and therefore could have been known by everyone. My mother-in-law told me of the impression made upon her by Mrs. Robert Dale Owen, of New Harmony. When my mother-in-law was a very small child her father gave a dinner party in Rockport in honor of Mr. and Mrs. Robert Dale Owen.[7] Her whole attention was caught and held by the beautiful Mrs. Owen. She had on a black velvet dress with a tight basque and a full flowing skirt that rippled around her. She had a very beautiful white lace collar with a large cameo pin at her throat. Her hair was parted in the middle and combed down over the ears. Robert Dale Owen and his wife came to Spencer County in an early day and mingled with the people. Therefore, they no doubt went to other counties, and I trust and feel sure that the Lincolns knew of the great good being done in an educational way at the little settlement of New Harmony.

EHRMANN'S NOTES

a. Beveridge, Albert J., *Abraham Lincoln*, I, 50 (Boston and New York, 1928).
b. Beveridge, *Abraham Lincoln*, I, 51–52.

BESS V. EHRMANN (1879–1963) was a Rockport, Indiana, native who dreamed that Spencer County would receive deserved recognition

---

7 Eugenie DeBruler Ehrmann (1859–1943) was Bess Ehrmann's mother-in-law. This event doubtless occurred in the 1860s or early 1870s since Mary Jane Robinson Owen (born 1813) died on 12 August 1871. Mrs. Owen was a citizen of New York when Owen met her in 1831.

in the Lincoln story. She wrote a number of books including *Missing Chapter in the Life of Abraham Lincoln*. Ehrmann was instrumental in creating Lincoln Pioneer Village in Rockport, served as president of the Southwestern Indiana Historical Society, and was curator of the Spencer County Historical Society.

14

★ ★ ★

Interviews with Spencer County Pioneers about 1895

T. H. MASTERSON*

T. H. Masterson interviewed Spencer County residents about 1895. Thirty years later, though he was unable to find his notes, he shared what he remembered. He recorded his memoirs and sent them to the Southwestern Indiana Historical Society where Edna Brown Sanders read them in February 1928.

WHEN I WAS A YOUNG MAN I WAS GREATLY INTERESTED IN everything relating to Lincoln, and particularly that part of his life spent in southern Indiana. That was thirty-odd years ago, about 1895. There were still living at that time near Gentryville a few persons who had been his companions and I felt that their recollections of the great president should be preserved. I visited them, talked with them and recorded as fully and accurately as possible their memories. My purpose was to let them tell in their own way the things they remembered of Lincoln, and to report their recollections faithfully.[a] Unfortunately, I have lost my original notes and the copies of these stories and thirty years have erased much of the matter from my mind. I hesitate to give my dimmed and incomplete recollection of what those old people told me, but as you think they may have some worth, I will do the best I can.

---

* First read by Sanders on 23 February 1928. Masterson published these recollections in *Indiana History Bulletin* 6, extra no. 3, *Proceedings of the Southwestern Indiana Historical Society during Its Ninth Year* (August 1929): 56–59.

I called on Aunt Elizabeth Hesson[1] first (I think I have her name correctly). John O. Chewning[2] was with me, if I am not mistaken. My recollection is that she lived some distance south and west of Lincoln City. I had heard that she was Lincoln's first sweetheart, at least his first regular "company." She was about eighty-five years old when I saw her; she was in good health, with an active mind, and not at all impressed with the fact that Lincoln had been her "beau." She talked freely of him as she would have done about any country boy she had known in her youth. My recollection is that she first met Lincoln at Pigeon or Little Pigeon Baptist Church. At least, that was the beginning of their "keeping company." She was sitting on a split log or puncheon bench toward the back of the church and Lincoln came in and sat down by her. She shared her songbook with him and, in a way young people had a hundred years ago and still have, they got acquainted. After the long sermon was over, "Abe" asked to see her home and she agreed. They walked out of the little clearing along the woods path a hundred yards or so, then sat on a log and took off their shoes, for shoe leather had to last a long time in those days. "Abe" carried both pairs of shoes.

They trudged along barefooted the three or four miles to her home. The old lady smiled at the recollection, for "Abe" lived two or three miles on the other side of the church and he hadn't known just where she lived when he asked to see her home. He stayed to dinner and no doubt did ample justice to it. He must have felt the long walk was worthwhile for he asked her to let him call again and he "kept company" with her for several months.

I wanted to know what broke off the affair and Aunt Elizabeth said her father objected. She was reluctant to tell me why he objected, but finally said that "Abe" had gotten too much cider or applejack one time and fell in a branch on his face and almost drowned. She went on to say that "Abe" was not a regular drinking fellow, and she never heard of his doing it again. Her father was very strict about drinking, however, and would never forgive that one lapse.[b] Soon afterward the Lincolns moved to Illinois.

1 He probably refers to Elizabeth Tuley Hesson (1811–1896) who came to Indiana in 1824. See Louis A. Warren, *Lincoln's Youth, Indiana Years, Seven to Twenty-One, 1816–1830* (New York: Apple-Century-Crofts, 1959), 156.

2 John O. Chewning (1852–1939) owned the *Rockport Journal*.

John Tuley[3] was over eighty-five years old when I saw him; he lived south of Gentryville some distance. He said "Abe" Lincoln was a little older than he, but that they were playmates. Lincoln was at the Tuley home once in the early winter. It was very cold and the ground was covered with a deep snow. He and "Abe" had set some traps in the woods two or three hundred yards from the house; they wanted to go out to the traps, but they were barefooted and were afraid they would freeze their feet. They finally figured out a plan. Each one got two thick clapboards and stood them up before the roaring fire in the fireplace and let them get hot clear through. They then wrapped them in a cloth and raced through the snow to the traps and stood on the boards while they robbed and baited the traps. They had to stop once or twice going back to warm their feet, but they didn't get frostbitten.

I asked Uncle John why they didn't wear shoes or boots in such cold weather, and he said they did not have any. In those days, he continued, traveling shoemakers made all the shoes for the whole community, which was sometimes miles in length. The cobbler would start at one end of the community and work his way down. He booted and shoed the whole family in each place, so that his progress was pretty slow. The first families got their footwear early in the fall and wore them out before spring. The last customers might not get theirs until almost Christmas or New Year and their shoes carried them through the spring thaw. It was an equitable arrangement. They might get their chilblains early or they might get them late, but they all got them. I asked Uncle John if "Abe" was different from the other boys and he said, "No, except he was mighty strong and was always reading when he could get any books."

Aunt Rachel Grigsby[4] was also another of the old ladies who knew Lincoln. I am not certain that her name was then Grigsby; my recollection is that her maiden name was Ray. She was one of the brides that figured in the infare when the double wedding occurred in the home of Reuben Grigsby. The story of this celebration is known to all students

3 John Tuley (1816–1899) came to Indiana in 1824.
4 Elizabeth Ray (1813–1901) married Reuben Grigsby Jr. on 16 April 1829. They were one of the couples involved in the *Chronicles of Reuben* story. See William E. Bartelt, *There I Grew Up: Remembering Abraham Lincoln's Indiana Youth* (Indianapolis: Indiana Historical Society, 2008), 166.

of Lincolniana, and the "Chronicles of Reuben" that told of that famous event. She said that the story of the "mix-up" in a part of the proceedings was substantially true. I do not know which one of the Grigsby boys was her affianced, but he came for her at her father's house between New-tonville and Grandview, and she rode behind him to the Grigsby home near Gentryville. His brother had also ridden to Perry County to get his bride.[5] The two couples were married in the Reuben Grigsby home and a celebration of unusual merriment and distinction occurred. The party was held downstairs, or rather on the first floor, for there was no stairs. Aunt Rachel said she climbed the row of pegs in the wall to the loft or upper story when she went to her bridal chamber. She remarked that she always liked "Abe," notwithstanding the embarrassment caused by the prank which he was reported to have engineered.

I am afraid that these few facts will add nothing to the materials relat-ing to Lincoln's life in Indiana. They are merely glimpses of a simple, crude era in the development of America. But out of these primitive sur-roundings, springing from those plain, homely conditions, there came one of the sublime men of history. Lincoln spent his formative years in that environment, and the qualities of mind and heart that raised him to such precious preeminence were fixed there in the wooded hills of Spencer County, Indiana. He grew up among a plain people who knew no pretense; candid, straightforward folks, whose hard, dangerous life had made it necessary to face realities, to look straight into the heart of things, to grasp the controlling facts of any situation and to act ef-fectively at the decisive moment. But that is only a part of the picture. Hard-headed and hard-fisted they were, but permeating all of their prac-tical nature was an idealism, a spiritual penetration, that looked through facts on to the eternal truth. Profoundly religious, almost mystic in their belief that right would prevail, their moral natures had the toughness and tenacity that sustained them to the end.

Growing up among such people, living their life, drinking in their spirit, is it not understandable that Abraham Lincoln became the most practical idealist, and the most ideal practicalist the modern world has known? Phillips Brooks said of Lincoln that, "In him was vindicated

5 The brother, Charles, married Matilda Hawkins of Dubois County, not Perry County.

the greatness of real goodness and the goodness of real greatness," and the foundation of that goodness and greatness was acquired among the plain, simple neighbors in southern Indiana.

MASTERSON'S NOTES

a. These interviews with Lincoln's boyhood friends appeared in the *Chicago Times Herald* or the *Indianapolis Journal* about 1895.

b. I do not relate this incident with any desire to tarnish the fame of a great man. Bedaubing the great dead seems to me to be a contemptible sport, but I feel that I must tell you just the things this old lady told me.

T. H. MASTERSON (1875–1952) was a native of Spencer County, Indiana, and studied law before moving to Kennett, Missouri, in 1922. He never practiced law seriously but became an insurance and farm-loan agent.

15

★ ★ ★

Early Days in Spencer County

ELBERT DANIEL HAYFORD*

Elbert Hayford (1872–1947) originally wrote this as a letter to his sister, Amy Hayford Osborne, in order for it to be read at a meeting of the Southwestern Indiana Historical Society. Although the letter primarily presents a recitation of facts, it recounts some of Hayford's firsthand conversations with Indiana neighbors and friends of Abraham Lincoln.

WHEN THOMAS LINCOLN MADE HIS HOME IN INDIANA IN THE autumn of 1816 the site of his settlement was within the limits of what was then Perry County. This county was formed in 1814 and included the eastern half of present Spencer County, the west line of Clay and Hammond townships being the west line of Perry County. The population of the county in 1816 was 1,720, or about three percent of the population of the new State. Southern Indiana was rapidly filling with people and in 1818 Spencer and Vanderburgh Counties were organized by the legislature, one on each side of the present Warrick.

In 1814 many settlers had come into the county, members of whom made their homes along the road that was that year surveyed from Darlington, at or near the present site of Newburgh, to Troy, then county seat of Perry.[1] In the spring of the following year, 1815, the trees on the line of

---

* The envelope containing this letter was postmarked 13 November 1925 from Bangor, Maine, and mailed to Amy Hayford Osborne's address in Evansville, Indiana. Bob Varable eventually came to own the original letter and donated it to the Spencer County Historical Society, which then published it in its newsletter in September 2009 (issue 80).

1 Darlington, Indiana, at one point the county seat of Warrick County, no longer exists as a municipality. It was located on property now owned by Alcoa Aluminum just south of Indiana Highway 66.

this road were blazed and cut and some of the streams bridged. Among those who settled upon or near this road in that year were Uriah Lamar, a native of North Carolina, a justice of the peace, county tax collector of Perry County and later a merchant of Rockport. There was also Aquila Huff, of Maryland antecedents, who came from the neighborhood of the Lincolns, in Kentucky; and there was also the father of John Romine. All these settled east of the present site of Rockport. At or near Rockport were Daniel Grass, legislator, whose descendants, mostly under other names, are numerous in Spencer County today; Azel W. Dorsey, at one time a teacher of Abraham Lincoln; W. R. Hynes, a generous donor of land and money at the time of the establishment of this county seat; William H. Ellis, Willis Snyder, a soldier of the War of 1812; William Bennett, a native of Preble County, Ohio; Enoch Berry; Martin Stuteville; and James and Henry Small. The six latter, in 1818, contributed $ 250.00 to build a bridge over Lake Drain so that "the upper settlements can pass with certainty and facility."[2]

In the western part of the county among others was David Luce, formerly of Muhlenberg County, Kentucky, later to give his name to the township; Ebenezer Richardson and Alfred Myler, the latter a native to Tennessee. James G. Hammond, a native of Maryland, had already settled on the site of Grandview in 1809, and George Huffman, born in Pennsylvania, and a soldier of the second war with England, had established himself a few miles north of Troy in 1812.

Another principal road in the county was the one extending northwest from Troy. The northern part of the county was probably not settled so rapidly as the part parallel to the river. For two or more generations the Lincolns had been accustomed to a rolling country. The region where Thomas Lincoln settled was a hilly, well-drained area. The name Gentryville was not applied to the little town nearby until after 1818, in which year James Gentry Senior purchased and moved upon a large tract of land there, containing more than one thousand acres.

The writer, between 1895 and 1897 visited and talked with a number of people of Spencer County who remembered the Lincoln family. Mrs. Charles Grigsby, who lived with her daughter, Mrs. Inco, I saw at

2 This quote appears to be from an article in the *Rockport Weekly Umpire* on 6 June 1867.

their home north of Grandview. Her maiden name was Ray and she and her sister married brothers, Reuben and Charles Grigsby.[3] The Rays lived at or near the present site of Maxville. An imposing infare dinner was served at the Grigsby home, near Gentryville, the day after the marriage, the two couples proceeded on horseback to that point.[4] Abraham Lincoln did not receive an invitation to attend this wedding dinner. When I asked Mrs. Grigsby if, as has been charged, Lincoln was not invited for the reason that he was not considered in the social strata of the Grigsbys', she vehemently asserted that this was not the case.[5]

Wesley Hall has related to me the incident that he has given in greater detail to Mr. Murr, relative to the time he stopped at the Lincoln home overnight on his way home from [the] mill, at which time Abraham showed him the new book he owned, the *Life of Benjamin Franklin*. He also recalled seeing Lincoln work at the carpenter's bench, as an assistant to Thomas Lincoln, his father.

Capt. John W. Lamar told me he particularly recalled an incident of Lincoln's visit to Indiana, in 1844. They were riding along the road together when Mr. Lincoln asked him to stop the horse. Mr. Lincoln went off the road and searched a few moments and pointed out an old saw pit and asked Mr. Lamar if he recalled the time when an ox fell into this pit and he and the Captain, with others, lifted it out. It was on this trip in 1844 that Mr. Lincoln spoke in Rockport, and I think in Boonville, as well.[6] The great issue that year was the annexation of Texas. Thomas H. Benton, Senator from Missouri, had been sent by the Democrat party

3 In 1828, about eighteen months after Aaron Grigsby married Abraham Lincoln's older sister Sarah, she died of childbirth. Some assert that Lincoln resented Aaron for not calling sooner for medical help. In spring 1829, two of Aaron's male relatives married in a double wedding.

4 "Infare dinners" were second-day dinners that typically followed a wedding. It likely originated from an Old World custom of feasting for several days after a special event.

5 According to tradition, none from the Lincoln clan were invited to the double wedding. Whether in retaliation or just for good-natured fun, Abraham Lincoln allegedly arranged for each of the bridegrooms to be escorted to the wrong wedding bed. Although the deception was immediately discovered, Lincoln kept tongues wagging through a satirical poem titled, "The Chronicles of Reuben." The poem, written like a Bible verse, proved to be a humorous topic of conversation in the community for many years afterward.

6 According to local tradition, Abraham Lincoln made several other speeches around Spencer County in 1844 (and allegedly spoke in Knox, Daviess, and Warrick Counties). However, the Rockport address is the only southern Indiana speech corroborated with a contemporary source. Lincoln also visited his boyhood home and the graves of his mother and sister. This would be Lincoln's first and only return to his childhood home since leaving Indiana in 1830.

to speak at Boonville, where a great meeting was held. I have always thought that Mr. Lincoln was sent into Indiana to answer Mr. Benton. Mr. Lincoln did all he could to aid in the election of Henry Clay, but Indiana cast a large majority for James K. Polk electors.

General James C. Veatch has told me that he was present when Mr. Lincoln spoke for Mr. Clay in Rockport, in 1844, and was at that time so much impressed with his ability that he went to Chicago in 1860 as a delegate to the Republican National Convention with firm determination to do all in his power to bring about the nomination of Mr. Lincoln for President.[7] General Veatch traveled by boat to Cairo and hence to St. Louis. Here he met Edward Bates, of Missouri, and other delegates from the state and together they traveled by rail to Chicago, the General continually urging upon Mr. Bates and others Mr. Lincoln's eminent claims as a candidate for president.

Southern Indiana was settled by a hardy, progressive and intelligent people. In a new and sparsely settled community, and there were of course, limited educational advantages, but there must have been many more books in the surrounding country than has generally been thought possible.

My great-grandfather, Samuel Brown, brought a few books from Augusta County, Virginia to Dubois County in the spring of 1818. One of these, a pocket atlas, lies before me as I write. Abraham Lincoln said he read every book he had heard of in a radius of fifty miles of his home in Indiana. This book was within that radius, but there is no evidence that Lincoln ever read it. The descriptive matter in this book is good and the maps are usually accurate for a publication of that period. Samuel Brown, who owned this book, entered land at Portersville, but did not long survive, contracting milk sickness in October, 1818, he died, and the same dreaded disease carried off his eldest son, William. Precisely at this time a few miles away milk sickness [deprived] the boy Lincoln of his mother. Margaret, the widow of Samuel Brown, and the second son, Samuel Gibson Brown, my grandfather, remained on the land they occupied and succeeded in establishing themselves in gaining a competence.

7 General James C. Veatch (1819–1895) was a prominent Rockport citizen, serving as adjutant-general of Indiana and collector of internal revenue for the first district of Indiana. See *The Rockport Journal*, 27 December 1895.

I may well close this paper with a quotation from a pocket atlas of my great grandfather, as it so well applies to the intrepid pioneers of southern Indiana. Relating the trials of the Pilgrims in 1620, it says: "They bore their hardships with unexampled patience and persevered in their pilgrimage of almost unparalleled trials, with such resignation and calmness, as gave proof of great piety and unconquerable virtue."

ELBERT DANIEL HAYFORD (1872–1947) was a native of Rockport, Indiana. He practiced law in Evansville before moving to Maine. Hayford served several terms as auditor of Maine and was a writer and historian.

PART 3

LINCOLN'S NEIGHBORHOOD
AND ENVIRONMENT

16

★ ★ ★

The Lincolns and Their Home in Spencer County, Indiana

C. C. SCHREEDER[*]

In the 1920s, as the Indiana Lincoln Inquiry educated the public about the importance of Indiana in Abraham Lincoln's life, the State of Indiana was working to create a proper memorial or shrine where he lived for fourteen years. With the help of a private group called the Indiana Lincoln Union, citizens raised money to buy much of the Lincoln farm, create a cabin-site memorial, and build a stone memorial building in what became known as the Nancy Hanks State Memorial. A recreational area known as Lincoln State Park was established just south of the memorial. In 1962, the Nancy Hanks Lincoln Memorial became part of the National Park Service, and we know it today as Lincoln Boyhood National Memorial. Of course, Schreeder had no idea of the development to come when he wrote this paper in 1929.

IN LINCOLN CITY, SPENCER COUNTY, INDIANA, THERE STANDS a small monument on which appears the inscription: "Spencer County Memorial to Abraham Lincoln who lived on this spot from 1816 to 1830."[1]

Abraham Lincoln was seven years of age, when in the fall of 1816 his parents removed from Hardin County, Kentucky, and settled in Spencer County, then a part of Perry County, Indiana. Thomas Lincoln, his father, had visited Indiana in September, that same fall, and located a quarter-section, 160 acres, of government land near Little Pigeon Creek

---

[*] Schreeder delivered this paper on 5 June 1929. A copy is part of the *Southwestern Indiana Historical Society Annuals* 4: 157–169 at Evansville-Vanderburgh Public Library.

[1] This stone was moved to a spot between the cabin site and memorial building when a cabin-site memorial was erected.

and about sixteen miles north of the Ohio River. From the opening statement of this article, one is correctly to infer that what became known
as the Lincoln Farm is now the site, in part, of Lincoln City, a railroad
junction town in southwestern Indiana. It was on this farm that the
Lincoln[s] lived for fourteen years, and then sold out and migrated to Illinois. This contribution is written mainly to describe the scenes, homes
and experiences of the Lincoln family during the fourteen years of their
sojourn in Indiana. The plural term, homes, is here used advisedly, for
the Lincolns really had three habitations in Indiana, as we shall later see.

It was in Washington County, Kentucky, that Thomas Lincoln and
Nancy Hanks were married on the 12th day of June, 1806. The marriage
ceremony was performed by Rev. Jesse Head. At the time of their marriage, Thomas Lincoln and Nancy Hanks were 28 and 23 years of age, he
being her senior by five years. They were destined to become the parents
of a son, who would rise to great heights of achievement and be elected
the sixteenth president of the United States. A description of these parents cannot be without interest to the inquiring mind. "Tom" Lincoln
is said to have been about five feet and ten inches in height, strongly
built, weighing about 180 pounds, and having coarse black hair and hazel
eyes which looked from a round face. Nancy Hanks Lincoln was taller
than the average woman. Her body was slender and her weight about 130
pounds. She had dark skin, dark brown hair, gray eyes, and outstanding forehead, and accented chin and cheek-bones. Abraham Lincoln
bore very little resemblance to his mother and still less to his father.
Tom Lincoln was somewhat sluggish in both mind and body, while his
wife was quick and active. He was quiet in manners, and unemotional;
she was more talkative and responsive, gentle and trustful. Her judgment
was acute; his was really poor, and for this reason he was a poor manager.
At no time in life did he possess much worldly wealth, but his family was
never in the lap of poverty. In Kentucky Tom Lincoln did carpentry and
farmed in a small way, but he made no noteworthy progress. So when
word came back to him from friends who had gone from Kentucky to
Indiana that they were doing well in the latter state, and that rich land
could be obtained there from the Government at two dollars per acre,
he decided to seek his fortune across the Ohio River. Accordingly he
directed his course toward the frontier in which is now Spencer County,

Indiana. There he selected, as already stated, a quarter-section of land, at the four corners of which he piled brush-heaps as markers, under the requirement of the law, to indicate to all others that the land had been claimed for entry. Mr. Lincoln did not file his claim in the land office at Vincennes until about a year later, the exact date being October 15th, 1817, and ten years afterward he received from the Government a patent, not for the full quarter-section, but for the west half of the Southwest Quarter of Section 32, Town 4 South, Range 5 West. The supposition is that he found that he could not pay for the whole 160 acres and relinquished to the Government one-half of it. This farm he deeded to Charles Grigsby, February 20th, 1830, in consideration of $125.00, a less sum than he paid for it at the hands of the Government. Subsequently, the land passed through other hands, and in 1872 when the town of Lincoln City was laid out, it became a part of the town plat.

When the Lincolns came to Indiana, the family consisted of the parents and two children, a daughter, named Sarah, and a son, whose name was destined to shine with luster upon the pages of American history. Sarah was the older of the children. She was born February 10th, 1807, in Elizabethtown, Kentucky, where her parents lived for about two years after their marriage. Thence they removed to a farm about two and a half miles from Hodgenville, Hardin County, Kentucky, and there Abraham Lincoln was born February 12th, 1809. A third child, little Thomas, was born unto Thomas and Nancy Hanks Lincoln, but it died in infancy and was buried in Kentucky. Sarah and Abe Lincoln spent their first but only few school days in Kentucky.

The exact date of the arrival of the Lincoln family in Spencer County, Indiana, cannot be established, but it was some time between Thanksgiving and Christmas, 1816, when with scant worldly possessions they reached the spot on which they were to live for nearly fourteen years. It was in the midst of the dense virgin forest that they settled, on one of the many low-rolling hills of southwestern Indiana.

In order to provide for his family a shelter against the chilly blasts of approaching winter, Tom Lincoln built a three-sided shed, constructed of poles, not having time for erecting a more substantial structure. According to tradition, two trees, standing apart about fourteen feet east and west, were selected as strong supports for the pole shed. Against these trees a stout pole was lodged, each end resting in a forked post that extended slantingly to the ground. Parallel to this horizontal pole another pole rested in the forks of shorter posts, thus to give slant to still other poles that were placed on top of the supporting poles, thus forming a roof. Poles were then placed, ends to the ground, so as to lean against the framework. Only three sides of the structure were thus closed, the fourth, which was to the south, was left open. The shelter has been described as a "half-faced camp." The roof and the three closed sides were made more or less rain and wind proof by brush, dry grass and autumn leaves bound in place by additional poles. Leaves on the ground floor gave warmth and softness for beds of skins and comforters. In front of the open side, a wood-fire was kept burning night and day, reflecting into the camp heat and light, and at the same time serving to keep away wild animals at night, Among the wild animals were the bear, wolf, fox and raccoon. Wild game, including the deer, squirrel and turkey, was abundant, hence the family need not want for fresh meat.

In this pole shelter-camp, the Lincolns lived their first winter in Indiana. But in 1817, a cabin of round logs was erected. It was about 12 by 14 feet, inside measurement, covered with riven oak boards, the earth forming its floor. A single door, on the south side, was the only opening. A stick and clay chimney stood at the east end.[2]

A pole or open-faced camp was left standing, some 30 yards from the log cabin. It served to shelter an aunt and uncle of Mrs. Lincoln, Betsy and Thomas Sparrow, and their nephew, Dennis Hanks, who came from Kentucky and joined the Lincolns in 1817. The aunt and uncle died the following year, and were buried on the same hill where Mrs. Lincoln was buried but a few weeks later, the three of them dying of milk-sickness, a fatal disease contracted by drinking milk from a cow that had eaten the foliage of the white snake root, a plant that grew in damp and shady places. The plant transmits its poison to the milk of the cow.

Mrs. Lincoln was sick only a few days. She realized death was near and called her children to her bedside. She asked them to love their father and each other, and to put their trust in God. She died in the log cabin

---

2 As discussed in other essays in this collection, researchers disagree about how many structures the Lincolns occupied in Indiana and when the buildings were constructed.

on October 5th, 1818, and was buried in a coffin made by her bereft husband. She was buried by the side of her aunt and uncle who had practically reared her. There was no ceremony at the cabin or the grave, for no minister was near enough at hand, whose services could be obtained. In the following spring a minister came from Kentucky and preached a funeral sermon at her grave.

The grave of Nancy Hanks Lincoln was neglected for many years. In 1879, P. E. Studebaker, a friend of her son, erected a monument at her grave and placed an iron fence around it.[3]

Little Sarah Lincoln was but eleven years old when her mother died, and bravely she tried to take her mother's place. At last, her father sought a second wife, and at Elizabethtown, Kentucky, married on December 2nd, 1819, Mrs. Sarah Bush Johnston, a widow having three children, John, Sarah, and Matilda.[4]

Thomas Lincoln returned home with his new wife and her children, the second Mrs. Lincoln, bringing with her considerable household goods of convenience and comfort, which the Lincolns had never known to enjoy. The Lincoln family was now eight in number, including Dennis Hanks. More house room was a necessity, and Lincoln built in 1820 a hewn log house, 12 by 24 feet, having two rooms, a front and back door, two front windows, and a puncheon floor. Its stick and clay chimney was at the east end of the house. This house stood a few feet in front of the log cabin, and the two were used at the same time by the Lincolns.

The home of the Lincolns stood for over a half-century, or until 1874, when it was sold to Capt. William Revis of Evansville, Indiana, who tore it down and shipped it by rail to Rockport, Indiana, and thence on barges by way of the Ohio River to Cincinnati where it was worked up into relics of the Lincoln home and sold to the general public.[5]

In the latter part of that same summer the writer hereof paid his first visit to Lincoln City. The Lincoln home was not then standing. I found one log, which had been left on the site of the house because it was thought to be too much decayed for removal. From this I secured a piece

3 Fifty Spencer County citizens paid for this fence.
4 The Johnston children were John, Elizabeth, and Matilda.
5 This is the cabin the Lincolns probably were building when they left Indiana; most likely the family never inhabited it. It is referred to as the 1829 cabin.

of sound timber, which was about six feet long and four inches thick. This I kept in my possession for over a half century, declining several generous offers for it. About two years ago, I had the piece of timber squared, and polished on three sides. It proved to be white-oak of finest quality. I had it cut into six inch blocks, and all of them I have given away to historical societies and museums, save one, which I purpose [propose] to give for placement in the proposed Lincoln Memorial building of which mention is made further on. One of the blocks was presented to the State Historical Museum in the Capitol at Indiana, and the hammer of a gavel, presented to the Southwestern Indiana Historical Society was made out of one of the blocks. One block I gave to Captain Ellrod of Washington, D. C., whose large collection of Lincoln relics, including the bed on which President Lincoln died and other furniture in the room, was recently sold to the Government.[6]

In describing the pole shed or "half-faced camp," which Tom Lincoln hastily built on coming to Indiana with his family, one must rely largely upon tradition. But the cabin in which his wife died, and the larger one, built after his second marriage, stood many years, and there has come down to us from several persons who saw these cabins, such information as enables us to describe them with fair accuracy. For a description of the first log cabin, which the father of Abraham Lincoln built, we are largely indebted to Redmon T. Grigsby,[7] who directed Mrs. Bessie Harrel, during her school days at Chrisney, to make a drawing of the cabin. This drawing has been reproduced and copies are extant.

Mr. Grigsby was a descendant of Reuben Grigsby, Sr., who was living a few miles south of where Tom Lincoln settled, when the latter came to Indiana. It was to Charles Grigsby of the same family that Tom Lincoln sold his home just before the Lincolns removed to Illinois. James Gentry afterward owned the Lincoln farm. The photographs of the second Lincoln cabin, which are extant, show it to have a porch clear across the front, but this was probably built onto the house by some subsequent owner after Tom Lincoln sold it. These illustrations do not show the first cabin and probably for the reason that it was torn down long before any photograph of the Lincoln home was made. The earliest one, now in

6 One of these blocks is in the collection of the Evansville Museum of Arts, History, and Science.
7 Redmond T. Grigsby (1848–1927) was grandson of Reuben and Nancy Grigsby.

existence, was taken in 1860, the year in which Abraham Lincoln was a successful candidate for the presidency.

There was standing in Spencer County an historic building with which the Lincolns were identified, namely, the old Pigeon Baptist Church, which stood less than two miles southwest of where the Lincoln home stood. This Tom Lincoln helped to build in 1819,[8] and it is said that his son, Abe, then ten years of age, did his part. His father built the doors, windows and pulpit. Under its white weather-boards were the original hewn logs, of which it was constructed. The records of the church organization show that by letter Thomas Lincoln was admitted to membership on June 7, 1823, and that he was afterward a trustee of the church. At the old Pigeon Church the Lincolns worshipped. There is no record showing that Abraham Lincoln was ever a member of this or any other church.

It was in the graveyard at Pigeon Church, that Sarah, the sister of Abraham Lincoln, was buried. She had married Aaron Grigsby at the age of nineteen, and was twenty-one when she died January 20, 1828. Her grave, like that of her mother, was neglected many years. At a comparatively recent date, the people of Spencer County erected at her grave a monument.[9] Many tourists each year visit the last resting places of the mother and sister of the Great Lincoln.

Lincoln Park, state owned and maintained, surrounds the grave of Nancy Hanks Lincoln. It embraces no part of the land which constituted the Lincoln farm. This park lies near the present town of Lincoln City, which is located on the Evansville and Huntingburg branch of the Southern railroad, and on the Indiana State Road, No. 62, about 35 miles east of Evansville. Recently an Indiana state-wide organization was formed, with Mrs. Studebaker Carlisle of South Bend, as its president, the purpose being to make a drive for funds wherewith to erect a suitable Lincoln Memorial building at or near the Lincoln Park, and this is, indeed, a commendable movement.[10]

8 Although the decision on the building site was made in 1819, the plans for the building were completed only in 1821.

9 A simple fieldstone marker at Sarah's grave was replaced with a granite one in 1916. The Indiana Lincoln Route Commission initiated the effort.

10 Governor Jackson appointed 125 Indiana citizens to the Indiana Lincoln Union on 22 December 1926. The Great Depression reduced the success of the drive begun in 1929. For a complete review of the Indiana Lincoln Union, see *The Indiana Lincoln Memorial in Spencer County, Indiana, a Report by the Indiana Lincoln Union*, 1938.

The cabins, built and occupied by the Lincolns in Indiana, were types of those erected by Pioneer settlers of forest covered lands of the Middle-West. Few of them are now found, especially in southern Indiana, into which hardy pioneers began to arrive more than a century ago.

It is true that Thomas Lincoln was a carpenter, as well as farmer, and his afterward illustrious son, worked with him. No doubt, they assisted in erecting numerous buildings in the Indiana community in which they settled. But one must not expect to find such buildings still standing as landmarks. The fence-rails, such as Lincoln split with proverbial skill in his early life, have given place to wire-fencing. The splendid timber for lumber, which abounded in southern Indiana when the Lincolns crossed the Ohio and took up residence in the Hoosier State, has almost entirely disappeared. The low rolling hills, and their valleys have been cleared of their timber and dense undergrowth, and developed into productive farms, save here and there. The Lincolns developed only a part of their 80 acres, and like other farmers of their day in Indiana, their principal crop was corn, and corn-bread was their main "staff-of-life." The land must be cleared of the trees, and plowed with the "shovel plow," which did scarcely more than scratch up the soil. Young Abe Lincoln followed the plow as it cut through roots that often would fly back and crack his shins. It was no easy task, and required not only the strength of a study [sturdy] plow-man, but the proverbial "patience of Job." Lincoln biographers have neglected to tell us whether Abe Lincoln ever uttered a "cuss word" when he plowed "new ground." But they draw upon their imagination, telling us that he was wont to have with him a book when he went to the field to plow. They tell us that at nights he read by the light of burning pine knots, yet they do not name the pine among other trees that grew in southern Indiana, which were the oak, elm, maple, beech, gum, hickory, sycamore, poplar, dogwood, sassafras, and now and then the cedar and pine.

In clearing land trees were cut down, and their trunks and main branches cut up into logs, which were dragged, by oxen or horses, into clusters, and then men with strong pieces of saplings called "hand-spikes," rolled the logs into heaps. Hence is derived the term "log rolling." The work required strong men, and often men on these occasions vied with each other in lifting heavy timbers, one at one end of a hand-spike, and the other at the other end. No doubt Abe Lincoln engaged in such tests of physical strength. It is said of him that he was a "powerful man." The logs thus piled into heaps were burned to get rid of them, and the result was that millions of feet of fine timber were thus destroyed.

Of logs not only dwelling houses but barns, mills and storehouses, were built of logs in that early day. These logs must be laid, one upon another, and the work was called "house-raising" or "barn-raising." At these raisings, as well as at "log-rollings," neighbors helped each other without pay. But bountiful meals were served, and the whiskey jug presented. Abe Lincoln aided in these community co-operations, but historians do not tell us whether or not he "tipped" the whiskey jug. Perhaps he did, but if so, he did it in moderation, as was usual with men of that early day.

Attention has been called to these things, simply to suggest the necessities which led to Abraham Lincoln's skill in swinging the axe, the maul, and the plow. When he became a candidate for the presidency, he was called "the rail-splitter," and if so in derision, the result was opposite that intended, for the appellation served to popularize him with the farmers, who polled the majority vote in that day.

As to the few school days which were those of Lincoln, and as to his love for books, and in regard to the men with whom he came in contact in early life, others have written at length, and the present writer shall not attempt to recount Lincoln'[s] opportunities for an education or the influence of his early environments. Sufficient has been here recorded to suggest that he was reared amid pioneer scenes, and learned the useful lessons of toil and perseverance, that in youth and early manhood he lived the simple life, that he lived close to nature and gained from her noble ideals. It was in Indiana that he laid the foundation of a great character, and by responding thereto, in after life, he became a great lawyer and statesman, the president and preserver of his country. But let him tell us the source of his greatness, as implied in the great tribute he paid to the memory of his mother. While in the White

House Lincoln said: "All that I am, or hope to be, I owe to my angel mother."[11]

Kentucky, the native state of Lincoln, gave him to Indiana when he was but seven years of age. The next fourteen years of his life were spent within the borders of Indiana. When he reached his majority, Indiana gave him to Illinois, and Illinois gave him to the Nation.

When in the spring of 1830 the Lincolns left Indiana for Illinois, bidding farewell to true and tried friends, they left the mother of a future president sleeping beneath the sod of a little knoll not far from the home whose walls had echoed her sweet voice, and the dust of his beloved sister in a churchyard not far away. The family, as it journeyed forth to Illinois, consisted of seven souls, namely, Thomas Lincoln and his son Abraham, the second Mrs. Thomas Lincoln and her children by a former marriage, namely, John, Sarah, and Matilda Johnston, and Dennis Hanks.[12]

One cannot study the history of the Thomas Lincoln family without being impressed that the step-mother, who came into the life of Abraham Lincoln when he was but ten years old, was a noble character. Bush was her maiden name. She was born and reared in Kentucky, of sturdy German stock. Her disposition was, in many respects, opposite that of Nancy Hanks Lincoln, in that she was a more determined character, and inclined to direct her family affairs with sterner hand. But with all this she was kind and gentle. We are told that little Sarah and Abe Lincoln soon learned to love her after she came into their lives, and that she returned love for love. Some writers have implied that she was even more indulgent to Abe than to her own son. She is quoted as saying of him: "He was the best boy I have ever known." She lived to see him elected President, while his father died nine years before the highest honor within the gift of the American people was bestowed upon his son.

The data herein incorporated has been gained from various sources and persons, but for the lack of space the writer must forego the pleasure of mentioning those who have aided him in getting together facts

11 Lincoln's law partner, William Herndon, recalled this comment being made to him in the early 1850s. See William H. Herndon and Jesse Weik, *Herndon's Lincoln*, ed. Douglas L. Wilson and Rodney O. Davis (Champaign: University of Illinois Press, 2006), 16.

12 The party comprised thirteen members. Here again, Elizabeth, who married Dennis Hanks, is called Sarah. Not included are the five children of Dennis and Elizabeth Hanks, Mathilda's husband, Squire Hall, and their one child.

herein stated. To all these he is truly grateful, and this contribution is, with modesty, submitted in the hope that it may prove, at least, of some measure of interest and value. I hereby acknowledge the assistance given me by various parties of whom special mention is due:

MR. GEORGE HONIG,
MR. GEORGE R. WILSON,
MR. JAMES ATLAS JONES
and MR. NOAH SPURLOCK.

C. C. SCHREEDER (1847–1930) was born in Germany and immigrated to the United States in 1852 with his mother. Following his service in the Civil War, he became a prominent Republican politician; he was elected to the Indiana House of Representatives for five terms and was instrumental in securing battlefield monuments to Indiana troops. Schreeder was commissioned colonel on the staff of a number of Indiana governors.

17

★ ★ ★

An Interview with James Atlas Jones on the Lincoln Cabin in Spencer County

GEORGE H. HONIG*

With the exception of a stovepipe hat, no icon is more closely associated with Abraham Lincoln than the log cabin. George Honig elaborates on the Indiana Lincoln cabin in this article. Most researchers agree that the Lincolns lived in several structures during their fourteen years in Indiana and were building another cabin when they left. The first structure was the "half-faced camp" hastily constructed on their arrival in late 1816. Whereas some historians contend the Lincolns lived in this cabin for a year, evidence suggests that by early February they dwelled in a round (not hewn) log cabin also quickly built but providing more shelter. Then, probably in 1818 or 1820, they constructed a more substantial, somewhat-hewn log cabin with loft; it served as home for the Lincolns during most of their time in Indiana.

John Hanks told Herndon the first cabin was a rough, unhewn one; the second, "sorter" hewn (no longer standing by 1860); the third, hewn but not occupied by Lincolns.[1] In September 1865, William Herndon visited the site and wrote that the house he saw the Lincolns built but never lived in. He said the first and second Lincoln homes no longer existed.[2] Thus, the cabin Jones describes here is one the family never lived in.

THIS INTERVIEW WITH JAMES ATLAS JONES WILL BE BASED entirely on Mr. Jones's experience while living in the Thomas Lincoln cabin in Spencer County during part of the year 1862.

---

* Honig delivered this paper on 23 February 1928; it was first published in *Indiana History Bulletin* 6, extra no. 3,*Proceedings of the Southwestern Indiana Historical Society during Its Ninth Year* (August 1929): 37–39.

1 WHH interview with John Hanks, 1865–1866, *Herndon's Informants*, 455.

2 WHH interview with Nathaniel Grigsby et al., 14 September 1865, *Herndon's Informants*, 116.

On February 4, 1928, I visited Mr. Jones's home at Rockport, Indiana. The conversation became so interesting that I missed several cars. Mr. Jones was born in 1844, below Rockport, Spencer County, and in 1861, at the age of seventeen, the patriotic impulse moved him to volunteer for service in the army. Being very small for his age as well as young, he was made drummer boy and, with his company, shipped off to Indianapolis. "Here," said Mr. Jones, "they weeded out the runts and I was shipped back home."

In the spring of 1862, James Atlas Jones, Thomas Wilmot, and Lewis Morgan, all of Rockport or the vicinity, were engaged by Atwell Morgan (called Boone Morgan) to work on his farm, which was the Thomas Lincoln farm where Lincoln City now stands. These three young men, owing to the shortage of beds, were compelled to sleep in one bed. They got along very well and felt justly proud of the fact that at night they were sleeping in perhaps the same corner of a cabin where Abraham Lincoln, then president of the United States, had many nights rested his tired body.

Mr. Jones recalled that many visitors came at that time to take a look at the cabin and carry away some of the walnut rails on the fences. He said: "Old Sam Graham, of Rockport, came, and as he placed a walnut rail on his wagon, said that he was going to make a cane out of it." Judge Lemuel Q. DeBruler and his brother, Dr. James P. DeBruler, and many others came to get rails.

Atwell Morgan had bought the land from the Gentrys, and not being able to pay for it, the land later reverted to Mr. Gentry. Mr. Jones's description of the "Lincoln Cabin" agrees with the photographs I have in my collection, and which most people have seen printed at different times.

It was a hewn-log cabin and might be called a "Mansion" (was so called in that day), but it was not a two-story cabin. At that time it had two windows on the south side. There was a door on the south side and another opposite on the north side, so that when both doors were open you could see through the house into the back yard. There was a porch on the south side facing the hill about a quarter of a mile away, where now rests Nancy Hanks Lincoln. As Abraham Lincoln freed many souls, his mother might be called the "Mother of Liberty."[a] Mr. Jones describes the interior as having two rooms; in the east room on the north end was a kitchen, and on the east side was the fireplace. When the outside doors were open it was possible to see from the front of the log cabin into the back yard, and glimpse part of another smaller cabin of unhewn logs. It was about 10 by 12 or 12 by 14 feet, about half the size of the larger cabin, standing with about five feet of ground between the two buildings. This smaller cabin was on a line with the east side of the cabin and stood directly north of it.

At this point I asked Mr. Jones if this smaller cabin was not the first cabin built by Thomas Lincoln and the one in which Nancy Hanks lived and died. Mr. Jones did not know for certain, but was inclined to think as I did, that Nancy Hanks died in the smaller cabin, and when Thomas Lincoln married Sarah Bush it was necessary to build the larger cabin, called at that time a "mansion." As Abraham Lincoln's new stepmother brought her children along, the family of Thomas Lincoln now numbered eight persons, including Dennis Hanks.

John Hevron, a relative of Mr. Jones, lived in this Lincoln cabin during 1866, 1867, and 1868. In 1867, Mr. Jones married Miss Lydia Snyder, and at this time he and his wife visited the Hevrons. As to the disappearance of the Lincoln cabin, Mr. C. C. Schreeder will give us a splendid story for our program when we meet at Gentryville for the spring meeting.

In 1862, James A. Jones re-enlisted in the army and served until 1865. At the present time, February 4, 1928, he is enjoying the best of health, and has a keen mind. Mr. and Mrs. Jones, with their daughter, Miss Bonnie, live in a fine old home, the only house in that block, and located on the top of a small hill facing the college building, which was built about 1857.

Mr. Jones's statement helps to throw a new light on the spot or location of the cabin which was the second of the three homes that Thomas Lincoln had in Spencer County. The first home was an open-faced camp of leaning poles, covered with straw and dried leaves, with three sides to it. Have we located the spot where the cabin stood in which Nancy Hanks Lincoln lived and died? In the photograph which I have, taken about 1860, the west end of a cabin can plainly be seen through the two open doors.[3] This leads me to believe that we have found the spot where Nancy Hanks Lincoln died.

HONIG'S NOTE

a.   Said by W. W. Webb, May 30, 1874, as he stood at the grave of Nancy Hanks; published in the *Evansville Journal*, June 2, 1874.

GEORGE H. HONIG (1874–1962), a Spencer County native, was a student of Lincoln's Indiana history all his life. He was a well-known Evansville artist and sculptor whose work is still evident around the city. Honig was very active in the Lincoln Inquiry project and the creation of Lincoln Pioneer Village in Rockport.

---

3 For a complete discussion of Lincoln's Indiana cabins, see John E. Santosuosso, "A Survey of Lincoln Boyhood National Memorial and Lincoln City," n. p., 1970: 3–28. This unpublished report, including a detailed account of the cabin and gravesites, may be found in the library at Lincoln Boyhood National Memorial. Santosuosso concludes that all the photographs, including the one mentioned here that Honig used for an engraving, are of the cabin the Lincolns built but never lived in. Scholars generally refer to it as the 1829 cabin.

18

★ ★ ★

The Lincolns' Eastward Environment

THOMAS JAMES DE LA HUNT*

In this presentation Perry County historian Thomas de la Hunt views the panorama around the Lincoln farm. To the west lay New Harmony on the Wabash River, site of the Harmonist religious communal society (1814–1825) followed by the short-lived Owen utopian experiment. To the east lay Corydon, state capital from 1816 to 1825. Naturally, Lincoln knew about both communities; indeed, the most direct road between the two ran along the southern boundary of Thomas Lincoln's farm. But we have no solid evidence the young Lincoln visited either town.

When Thomas Lincoln's brother Josiah came to the Corydon area (Harrison County) in 1812, Thomas may have visited there before or while living in Spencer County. Certainly, Abraham kept up with political events in the state capital and possibly made the trip. As a boy, Lincoln heard about the educational experiment some fifty miles to his west. Dennis Hanks recalled in 1889 that "ox teams and pack-horses went through Gentryville" traveling to New Harmony. Hanks also recalled Lincoln saying, "'Denny, thar's a school an' thousands o' books thar, and fellers that know everything in creation,' he'd say, his eyes as big 'n' hungry as a hoot-owl's." Yet, Abraham did not visit this educational utopia, and "put it out o' his mind, after awhile."[1] Thomas Lincoln briefly owned land in Posey County east of New Harmony; in fact, this land was part of the property he relinquished to gain clear title to his Spencer County land.[2] No firm evidence supports a Lincoln visit to Posey County.

---

* De la Hunt delivered this paper on 30 October 1928 and published it in *Indiana History Bulletin* 6, extra no. 3,*Proceedings of the Southwestern Indiana Historical Society during Its Ninth Year* (August 1929): 114–118.

1 Eleanor Atkinson, *The Boyhood of Lincoln* (New York: McClure, 1908), 30–32.

2 For a complete treatment of Thomas Lincoln's Indiana land activities, see William E. Bartelt, "The Land Dealings of Spencer County, Indiana, Pioneer Thomas Lincoln," *Indiana Magazine of History* 87 (September 1991): 211–223.

The essay focuses on the area immediately east of the Lincoln neighborhood. In 1816, when the Lincolns arrived in the new state of Indiana, their
home was in the western part of Perry County. The Ohio River town Troy was
not only the county seat but also the site of the area's post office. Effective
1 February 1818, with the creation of Spencer County, the western boundary of Perry County was moved twelve miles eastward to the Anderson
River. Thus, for about fourteen months, Lincoln resided in Perry County.

ABRAHAM LINCOLN'S OWN STATEMENT THAT DURING HIS
boyhood years of residence in southwestern Indiana he had read every
book available within a radius of fifty miles around, is quoted by so many
of his biographers as to stand for itself without further reference toward
its verification here.

In analyzing the cultural influences probably felt by the youth's plastic
mentality, more than one writer and speaker has stressed the fact that
New Harmony was within this imaginary circle, near enough to make
its impression upon him. They point out in support of this theory the
friendship of mature life that existed between Lincoln and that other
great soul, Robert Dale Owen.[3]

Thomas Lincoln's Spencer County farm was at a point approximately bisecting the distance between the state's two towns—villages,
rather—that were of major importance during Abraham Lincoln's formative years, Corydon and New Harmony. Naming them in such order
of precedence is intentional here. Is there not reason to assume that
the lad whose inherited Americanism already went back six generations
would feel the influence of the territory's capital in Harrison County,
settled by native-born Anglo-Saxon stock, more powerfully than that of
the exotic Posey County community founded by George Rapp and carried on by the extraordinary "Boatload of Knowledge" whose intellectual
cargo represented diverse lands and tongues?

Conceding without argument the hypothesis that Lincoln's "environment" extended to the westward through Warrick County as far as
Gibson, Posey, and Knox counties, is there no analogy for supposing

3 Robert Dale Owen (1801–1877) was the son of the founder of the Owen utopian experiment.
During the Civil War, Owen was well known in the White House.

that the boy and man may have felt some cultural influence from east of
Anderson Creek, a region which most historians have, perhaps inadver-
tently, omitted to consider?

In Perry County in 1816 lived Hananiah Lincoln, and in Harrison
County, Joshua Lincoln, the former a cousin and the latter a brother of
Thomas Lincoln. Some writers have chosen to draw an inference that it
was the earlier migration of these kinsmen from Kentucky to Indiana
which brought Thomas Lincoln to Indiana in the first place. Be that as
it may, no one should ignore the fact that when Thomas Lincoln took up
his land claim on Indiana soil he became first a citizen of Perry County,
with Troy as the county seat. It would seem improbable that the contacts
then formed with that little village should be wholly broken off by the
organization of Spencer County two years later.

Among outstanding citizens of Troy prior to 1830, many of whom
are still represented by direct descendants a hundred years afterward,
might be named Reuben Bates (lineal ancestor of Mrs. Sallie Logan
Bergenroth of Troy), a man of education and considerable wealth, whose
stately old brick Georgian mansion, built in 1822, was only demolished
in 1927; Francis Posey, of the Virginia Posey family, who had surveyed
the town site in 1815, and with whom "'Tom' Lincoln spent his first night
in Indiana";[a] Jacob Protzman, tavern-keeper at the time of the Lincolns'
near-by residence, an educated Pennsylvanian, whose wife belonged to
the Lewis family that gave General Andrew Lewis to Lord Dunmore's
War;[b] Dr. Robert G. Cotton, the local physician, whose practice was
countrywide, a cultured gentleman of Virginian descent through Kentucky; his wife, a Dorsey of Maryland, springing from the celebrated
Nicholas Greenberry.[c] Joseph Wright, recorded as a major on William
Henry Harrison's staff; John Bowie, James McDaniel, and John Daniels
were other men of prominence in early Troy.

James Taylor, Abraham Lincoln's employer in the ferry trade, belonged
to a fine old southern family; as late as 1895, his son, Green B. Taylor,
gave personal information to Miss Tarbell when she was beginning her
investigations.[d] It was Green Taylor with whom Lincoln roomed in the
original Taylor homestead, long since destroyed, on the Ohio just east of
the mouth of Anderson Creek. This is substantiated by Judge Edward A.
Lorch, of Evansville, and is not a mere tradition, such as the legend that

calls one of two ancient houses on the river bank at Maxville the abode where Lincoln stayed when operating the ferry. In the democracy of pioneer life a "hired hand" shared accommodations with his employer's family, so it was the natural thing for the two youths, "Abe" and "Green," to room together.

The Shoemaker family of Perry County were men of strong character. Adam Shoemaker, who lived at Troy, has been called "a boon companion of 'Tom' Lincoln.[4] He was one of the few known teachers of young Abe."[e] Lincoln himself related this fact to a nephew, John Chapman Shoemaker, whom he met in Indianapolis when on his way from Springfield to Washington for his inauguration in 1861. Shoemaker was then representing Perry County in the state senate.[f]

Solomon Lamb, first sheriff, recorder, and clerk of Perry County, by appointment in 1814, held the first office only two years, but served twenty-two years in the other capacity. He was a native of Albany County, New York, and a son of the revolutionary veteran, John Lamb, buried in the Tobinsport "Upper Cemetery." His superior penmanship in official record-books at the Cannelton courthouse shows him a man of education; this is further evident through volumes in Latin and French that had been in his library and descended to his great-granddaughter, the late Helen Morgan Baumgaertner, of Rockport.

Farther upstream than Troy lived the Weatherholts, Tobins, Winchels, and the Polks. The most conspicuous of the last-named family was the Reverend Charles Polk, whose biography was presented before the Southwestern Indiana Historical Society at Rockport, October 11, 1921.[g] He was Perry County's delegate to the first constitutional convention at Corydon in 1816. He served on two committees, the one relative to elective franchise and elections, the other, relative to the distribution of the powers of government.[h] He was one of southern Indiana's pioneer Baptist ministers, and the founder of old "Gilead" Church at Tobinsport in 1817. It is far from unlikely that he was personally associated with members of "Old Pigeon" congregation to which Thomas Lincoln belonged, only some thirty-odd miles away.

---

4 Adam Shoemaker (1779–1849) is described as "an ardent abolitionist." Lincoln probably knew him as a preacher and perhaps met him when Lincoln lived briefly in Troy. Neither Lincoln in his autobiographical statements nor Herndon informants list him as one of Lincoln's teachers.

At Rome, ten miles above Tobinsport, after the county seat was re-
moved there in 1819, lived families of good blood and fair education.
Some of these were: Huckeby, Groves, Connor, Ewing, Reynolds,
Wheeler, Thompson, Cummings, and other substantial citizens; farmers, merchants, or followers of law and medicine; average men of their
day and generation. In northern Perry County were the Esareys, Ewings,
Deens, Fosters, Reilys, Cunninghams, Minors, Wheelers, Lashers, and
Van Winkles, typical Anglo-Saxon stock who made their influence felt.
This latter group lived nearer the road leading west from Corydon toward Gentryville and Boonville, so there is perhaps stronger logical reason for their inclusion in the Lincolns' eastward environment than those
families of Perry County who dwelt along the Ohio River above Troy.

Whether or not Abraham Lincoln ever actually borrowed books at
Corydon may always remain a matter of pure surmise, but a quaint advertisement culled from the *Indiana Gazette* (Corydon) for October 28,
1819, shows that the loan of volumes was not unknown at the time. It
also affords contemporary proof that the pioneer sheriff, who had been
a dauntless Indian fighter and was afterward a United States senator, was
not lacking in literary and military taste during his years of residence in
Corydon. The advertisement read as follows:

RETURN MY BOOKS AND I WILL LEND AGAIN

The persons who have borrowed of me, Scott's *Military Discipline*, with
the plates; *The Naval History of the U. S.*; Duane's *Handbooks for Infantry
and Rifle Corps, History of the Late War*, Webb's *Monitor*, Steuben's *Military
Guide*, and *The Trial of Gen. Hull*, will confer a favor by returning them
immediately.

John Tipton

Classic Corydon, indeed, in its period of preeminence as territorial and
state capital, is an intellectual factor to be reckoned with in any serious
consideration of southwestern Indiana's early status, and the immigrants
who came to that place to lay the foundations of our commonwealth
were pioneers of distinction. They were not illiterates to whom learning
had been denied; they were not outlaws escaping the restraints of higher
civilization.

The Corydon which Thomas Lincoln may have known, and to which he might have taken his young son, Abraham, has been effectively sketched for us by the brilliant Charles Washington Moores:[i]

> Where William Henry Harrison and John Tipton and Isaac Blackford and many a comrade and friend of Washington used to gather and James Monroe and Andrew Jackson received a royal hospitality, and while men were still talking of Napoleon, Indiana's tiny capital rested in village simplicity among sheltering elms and nestling hills. . . . It was an easy-going, old-fashioned Virginia village, with an ambition to be decent and to cultivate the social spirit. Its older houses were log cabins, but it had some generous brick colonial residences, which still stand. Democracy had become a social ideal everywhere. The man in the big colonial house and the man in the log cabin neither patronized or toadied. . . .
>
> One way to judge the character of a town is by its representative men. Old Corydon as a social study calls for a broader view, for the student must consider the things done there and the men who did them; those whose labor drew them there from time to time as well as those to whom Corydon was home. Of the men who lived in Corydon while it was Indiana's capital, Dennis Pennington, John Tipton, Spier Spencer, and Isaac Blackford were probably the leaders, and of those whose duties brought them there often and kept them there, mention may be made of Governors William Henry Harrison, Jonathan Jennings, and William Hendricks, Treasurer Samuel Merrill, Secretary of State Robert A. New, and Judges Benjamin Parke, James Scott, and John Johnson. . . .
>
> It was but a village. Its biggest men would be counted young to cope with such responsibilities in our modern day. They were young, but they possessed scholarship and character. Harrison, Jennings, Blackford, New, Merrill, and Benjamin Parke were classical students—several of them teachers by profession and by choice, readers and gatherers of the best books. And Pennington and Spencer and Tipton were men of valor and character. These pioneer patriots gave of their own character to the State whose foundation they laid. They were young for such genuine achievement. In 1816 Jennings was 32, Hendricks 33, Tipton 30, Blackford 30, Ratliff Boon 35, Samuel Merrill 24.

> "They all are gone—gone, gone adown the years;
> And Corydon itself has passed since then
> Into new paths of broad prosperity
> Through virile agriculture, business sense,
> And noble service in the rural life."[j]
> "And so, from out the forest, swamp and glen,
> From out a thousand obstacles, these men
> And women, our grandparents, shaped
> The State. And now, with folds of Glory draped,
> The Century's monuments greet the dawn;
> The curtain drops, the passing years roll on."[k]

DE LA HUNT'S NOTES

a. Letter of Dr. Logan Esarey to Hon. John E. Iglehart, February 3, 1928.

b. Ibid.

c. Ibid.

d. Tarbell, Ida M., "Abraham Lincoln," in *McClure's Magazine*, VI. No. 1, 8 (December, 1895).

e. Esarey to Iglehart, February 3, 1928.

f. Ibid.

g. See *Proceedings of the Southwestern Indiana Historical Society*, Bulletin No. 16, October, 1922.

h. Dillon, John B., *History of Indiana*, 557–58 (Indianapolis, 1843).

i. Moores, Charles, "Old Corydon," in *Indiana Magazine of History*, XIII, 20–22, 41.

j. Langdon, William Chauncy, *The Pageant of Corydon*, 41 (New. Albany, Ind., 1916).

k. Leible, Arthur B., in "The Pageant of Indiana University," 1916.

THOMAS JAMES DE LA HUNT (1866–1933) was a lifelong resident of Cannelton, Indiana, and spent his later years researching and writing the history of Perry and surrounding counties. His newspaper column, "The Pocket Periscope," appeared in the *Evansville Courier and Journal*. He served as president and secretary of the Southwestern Indiana Historical Society.

19

★ ★ ★

Some Early Troy History

SALLIE BERGENROTH*

In 1815, Troy, Indiana, was surveyed into ninety-six lots. It grew because of its location on the Ohio River and because it served as county seat of Perry County, the county wherein stood the Lincoln home until the creation of Spencer County in 1818. By 1818, Troy had some twenty log cabins and was an important commercial river port in the 1820s.[1] The 1826 *Indiana Gazetteer* notes Troy "contained (in Aug. 1826) 19 families, 120 souls, 1 tavern, 1 store, 2 blacksmiths, 1 cabinet maker, two shoemakers, 1 physician, a tan-yard, a warehouse, and a post office."[2] This was the time Abraham Lincoln worked for James Taylor on the Taylor farm and operated the ferry over the Anderson River at Troy. Indeed, this river village served not only as a source of income for Lincoln but also as an opportunity for education, as he met river travelers from around the country and saw newspapers from cities up and down the Ohio and Mississippi Rivers. The character and appearance of Troy resembles those of New Salem, Illinois, where Lincoln lived five years later.

ON FEBRUARY 12, 1809 A BABE WAS BORN IN THE WOODS OF Kentucky amid hardships and poverty—educated in the University of Nature and associated his name with the enfranchisement of labor— with the emancipation of millions—with the salvation of the Republic. He is known to us as Abraham Lincoln. Nothing is greater than to strike

* Bergenroth presented this paper on 1 June 1928; a copy is part of the *Southwestern Indiana Historical Society Annuals* 3: 29–33 at the Evansville-Vanderburgh Public Library.

1 *History of Warrick, Spencer and Perry Counties, Indiana* (Chicago: Goodspeed Bros., 1885), 668.

2 John Scott, *The Indiana Gazetteer or Topographical Dictionary*, 1826 (reprinted Indianapolis: Indiana Historical Society Publications, 1954).

the shackles from the limbs of men—A nation is not great because it covers vast territory or its ships that cover the sea or its flag that floats in all lands. A nation to be great must produce men and women of genius.

Then as pioneers of Kentucky, his father left that home and in the fall of 1816 Thomas Lincoln immigrated to Indiana territory landing at Troy near the mouth of Anderson River. Then Troy was the county seat of Perry, being also the oldest as well as the largest town in the Pocket except Vincennes.[3] Thomas Lincoln remained at the mouth of Anderson River until the fall of 1817 and during his stay here attended a ferry established by James McDaniel but at that time owned by James Taylor.[4] Here Abraham Lincoln assisted in the ferry transfer. The wood yard was the goal of all river men. My grandfather Reuben Bates coming from Virginia with the first white settlers landed at Troy just above the lowlands of Anderson River called the Pond Field and that piece of land remained in the family—transferred to his youngest son Reuben Bates. With him came the Willians brothers and sisters of my grandmother all of whom crossed the river just opposite my home now. They bought land in Kentucky—two brothers one Thomas Willian born in 1799 and died in 1871. One James Willian remained in Troy—was a tanner on a large scale. He is buried in Rockport and many of the citizens remember him.

A sister of the Willians married and moved to Marion Co. Kentucky near Lebanon. She lived to be ninety-nine years of age. She sat in the door of her own home all night and listened to the Battle of Perryville having in that engagement with Braggs Army her husband and one son who came out without a scratch. Many were the trips she made back to Troy on horse back—the trail being through Hardinsburg and stopped over for the night.

The Dills Farm joined the Willians and it was here that John T. Dill had the exclusive right to operate a ferry from the Kentucky shore of the Ohio River, to set passengers across the river in either direction.

At this time Abraham Lincoln was living in the home of James Taylor on the Indiana shore (1826) as hired help and the work did not keep him busy at all times he was employed to run the ferry and slept with a son

3 The "pocket" was a name for southwest Indiana popular in the 1920s.
4 Although scholars accept that the Lincolns crossed the river near the area, both Herndon and Lincoln himself contradict local lore about the Lincolns staying in Troy for almost a year.

of James Taylor named Green B. Taylor. Now the proof positive of this is that in after years of successful steam boating Capt. Taylor's second wife was my mother's oldest sister who lived to be ninety-four years old—mind bright and clear and was buried from my home in the Bates lot. She said the Lincolns came to Indiana as a cousin lived here. I have in my possession an old Ledger of Reuben Bates, my grandfather, who opened the first store of any consequence here and the name Hananiah Lincoln a charge of two plugs of tobacco 75 cents, 8 pounds of sugar $1.00, one-pound copper as 12 cents. Most every entry of charge would be to cash 75 cents up to $10.00 as money was very scarce in those days.

Now another episode of Lincoln came up with the Dills as they contested the rights of Abraham who had at different times interfered with his business, notably in one case when he took a passenger from the Indiana side and delivered him aboard a steamer that stopped mid-stream to the financial loss of Dill.[5] A case was called in the home of squire Pate. Dill was sworn and his testimony corroborated that of his brother. Squire Pate heard this evidence with strong predisposition to find for the plaintiff. He knew the essential facts as the Dill Bros operated the ferry from land owned by him and paid rental. The Dill boys were neighbors and the squire would prefer to please them. But he would not pronounce judgement until he had heard what the defendant had to offer. Just then Squire Pate became conscious that others were present. A number of neighbors or strollers had heard of the trouble on the river bank and had come over to see how things were going. Pate looked at Lincoln but softened a little the judicial tone in which he addressed the defendant, "Are there any witnesses for the defendant; does he desire to testify?" Abraham Lincoln rose to his full height almost knocking the floor beams above the courtroom—so tall was he and answered that he had no witnesses, that the facts were as had been stated, but he would like to ask a question. "Do the rights of John T. Dill under this license forbid other

5 This story of Lincoln as a defending litigant in Kentucky appears nearly eighty-six years after the incident in a 1913 *Louisville Courier-Journal* article reporting everyone in the "immediate vicinity" was "thoroughly familiar with the above story, and most of the neighbors know the exact room in which the trial took place." Cleburne E. Gregory, "Lincoln Defendant in First Case at Bar," *Courier-Journal*, 16 February 1913, section 4, page 1. See also William H. Townsend, *Lincoln the Litigant* (Boston: Houghton Mifflin, 1925), 34–38. The Pate home is the only extant structure associated with Lincoln's Indiana years. Ironically, it stands in Kentucky.

persons to operate a ferry from the Indiana bank to the middle of the river"? The squire replied that the entire width of the river belonged to Kentucky but the defendant pressed his point. "I did what these men say I did", said Lincoln. "A man came to the bank of the river to catch a passing boat. The boat could not land because of low water, but stopped in the middle of the river. John Dill was not in sight and his boat on the other side of the river. Somebody had to take that man from the Indiana shore to the boat, or the man had to miss the boat. I was there and the man offered to pay me to take him out to the boat and I did it, but did not set the man across the river as Dill claimed. I only set him half way." It was this offending act that had got him in trouble with the Dills. In years afterward, he told this was the first whole dollar he ever earned in a day. The money he often sent to his father who lived sixteen miles away.

Now a little more history of Troy as a few weeks ago I received a card notifying me that I would be eligible to become a member of the Pioneers if any of my people had lived in the state before the year 1830. At that time my Grandfather Reuben Bates was building the second brick home here. The first my mother was born in and the second she was married in. The old brick on the hill was a ten-room house with hall running through the house 15 feet wide. In this hall the main stairway run up. On the left of the house the family room was located. A stair led to the girls' room with no opening door in upstairs hall. Only last year was this house raised [sic] and the workmen found a receipt from the land office at Vincennes dated May 14, 1838 for the S. E. quarter of section 18 containing 160 acres sold to Reuben Bates for $200.00 or $1.25 an acre.

Now in 1848 Grandfather had two sons and a nephew in Bloomington College and only last year Miss Mary Burke, Superintendent of our school in Troy, wrote me to send her something old or relating to the early history of Indiana and I have here the letter I sent and her reply.

SALLIE BERGENROTH (1863–1934) was born in Kentucky but came to Troy, Indiana, as a small girl. Interested in Troy's history, she was active in the Southwestern Indiana Historical Society.

20

★ ★ ★

Early Agriculture in Spencer County, Indiana

DAVID H. MORGAN*

As pioneers pushed westward into Indiana, they subsisted on whatever they could find. Nearly all of a family's needs in terms of food and clothing were supplied by farm, forest, and stream. Living in rough lean-to or one-room log cabins, most early pioneers hunted game. If they succeeded at farming, often they produced enough for only their immediate family. This portrait by David Morgan, a teacher and surveyor from Spencer County, summarizes the challenging environment Lincoln's family faced after they first moved to Indiana.

PEOPLE WHO LIVE IN THE FINE AGRICULTURAL SECTION OF Indiana, known as Spencer County, cannot realize, and few can believe, what this fine country was a hundred years ago. This beautiful place covered with modern homes, its people surrounded by all the appliances, conveniences and luxuries of modern civilization seem to think little, and care less, for all the trials, privations, sorrows and troubles that it took to convert a vast solitary wilderness into this veritable "Garden of Eden".

That you may realize the difference now and then is the object of this article. Let me first name a few of the things that were not then even dreamed of. There were no automobiles, tractors, gang plows, mowing

* Morgan first presented this paper to the Southwestern Indiana Historical Society on 24 June 1926. A copy is part of the *Southwestern Indiana Historical Society Annuals* 4: 57–69, at the Evansville-Vanderburgh Public Library.

machines, hay rakes, binders, steam threshers or mills of any kind, surfaced roads, railroads, traction cars, telephones, telegraph, wagons, carts, buggies, horses, cattle, hogs, sheep or poultry, carpets, rugs, stoves, etc. I could name hundreds of things that you now enjoy that they knew nothing of but I guess I have stated enough to cause you to think and realize how grateful we ought to be to our ancestors for their trials and privations and to the great God of the Universe for his loving care and kindness in looking over us and caring for us, allowing us to live and enjoy so many great blessings, forgiving us our sins against ourselves and our trespasses against our neighbors, our partaking of so much happiness and giving so little in return.

As late as 1830 most of the homes in Spencer County had no floors save the bare ground. Some had puncheon floors of slabs hewed on one side, edged up and laid side by side on sleepers. A few had plank floors. These plank had to be hand sawed. The log was first rolled up on a scaffold and one man worked on top and the other on the bottom side dragging the saw up and down through the log, cutting one board at a time. This was a very slow way of getting lumber. The houses were made mostly of round logs with notches cut in each end in such a manner as to hold them together. The open spaces between the logs were stopped by pieces of wood wedged in between the logs, called chinking. To farther stop the openings, clay was mixed into a stiff mud and daubed over the chinking on both the inside and outside of the house. A door was generally cut in the middle of one side of the house and the fire was at first made in the center of the room and the smoke escaped out of a hole left uncovered in the roof. Later an opening was cut, generally in one end of the room, and a fireplace built of small logs and topped with small pieces of poles built up above the level of the roof of the house for a chimney for the escape of the smoke. This entire fireplace was then covered with a stiff mud made of clay and a fire started and kept burning until the clay was hard like brick. This was the old stick and clay chimney. Fire was carefully preserved and not allowed to go out by carefully burying good live coals in dry ashes. Fire would keep in this manner for days but when fire had to be started from the beginning, the following things were necessary: punk, which was the inside part of a knot which was in a state of decay, was obtained from the knots of ash timber; a piece of flint, which was not a product of this part of Indiana.[1] Most of the flint used to make fires was Indian arrowheads picked up in the woods; powder which was a very scarce article as well as an important one and was more important than any other one article. To make a fire, a piece of punk was placed in a good position, a little powder poured on the punk, from a piece of dry wood a few shavings were made and placed ready at hand, then with the flint in one hand and a piece of steel in the other, a person would strike the flint with the steel in such a manner as to cause the sparks to ignite the powder and the flash set the punk on fire, then by blowing and carefully coaxing, a blaze was made in the shavings, so you can see the making of a fire was a slow process and no easy job.

Another important thing at first was a roof over the house. Imagine a man now trying to make a roof without lumber, shingles or nails, yet our fathers did it. Here is how it was done. The house was made in such a manner that the roof logs reached from end to end of the building, each log being a little higher as you approached the cone of the house. The first houses were covered with clapboards which were rived out of oak timber. These boards were from three to four feet long and were laid on in rows across the roof and weighted down with poles, nails being scarce and expensive. I might write much more about the farmhouse and its contents but will leave that to someone else. But just one word about the farmer's wife and what she had to do with. Her tableware consisted of a few iron knives, forks and spoons and a few pewter or tin plates. Her kitchen utensils of a dutch oven, a cast iron skillet, a frying pan and a Johnnycake board. Few people now living ever saw a Johnnycake or know of what and how it was made.[2]

I will now describe some of the implements that were necessary to successful farming in the time of our fathers from 1800 to 1820. The most important article was his rifle and its equipment which consisted of a powder horn and charge, a bullet pouch, a string of small square greased

1 The term *punk* typically refers to the dry insides of rotten tree trunks used for kindling. It serves as an easily combustible material that can help ignite fires by rudimentary methods.

2 Pioneer women in Indiana performed far more labor-intensive chores than did their counterparts in the east, leaving them in perpetual fatigue. With few commercial stores in rural areas of southern Indiana, women often made the family's soap, candles, clothes, and shoes—long, tiring tasks. Also, women assisted with livestock, gardens, and home maintenance. These tiring cycles they combined with frequent childbearing and childrearing.

cotton pieces called patching, a ladle to melt lead and a pair of bullet molds to manufacture bullets and a skimming knife. This rifle was the old fashioned muzzle loading, flintlock type.[3] To load it you had to pour the powder from the horn into the charge from there into the muzzle of the gun, then place your cotton patch over the muzzle of the gun; take a bullet; put it on the patch and force it into the gun and with ram rod, which was a long hickory stick carried on the underside of the gun, drive the bullet down the inside of the barrel. If you will go to some of the museums of the great cities you can yet see this remarkable old type of gun that played such an important part in the history of the early settlement of our country.

The farmers' most important implement was an ax and a hoe, neither of which was the fine tool you now see carelessly thrown around on the farm. With his ax he cleared a small place for his house and garden (I will not call it a farm), cut the poles to build his cabin and deadened the timber on a small tract of land. It took from two to four years to get the deadening into such shape that nay kind of a crop could be raised and then from ten to fifteen years to rid the land of stumps. Let me just drop a remark here and you can easily verify it. If the timber that originally stood on Spencer County was sawed into lumber and sold at the present price, it would bring at least ten times as much money as the real and personal property would if all turned into money. The [hoe] was an important farm implement and all the first crops in this county were planted and cultivated with it as they could be planted with nothing else. The first crops were corn, beans and pumpkins, all planted on the same land. They planted corn from March until July so that they could have roasting ears as early and as late as possible, green corn being an important article of food; beans were used both green and dried, corn and pumpkin was also dried for winter use. Cotton and flax were among the first crops raised, neither of which was extensively raised. It was quite

3 Long rifles became popular among settlers in North America. The rifled muzzle loader weighed from seven to ten pounds and was used extensively in the American Revolution and the War of 1812. Their users often referred to them as Pennsylvania rifles or Kentucky rifles. See John G. W. Dillin, *The Kentucky Rifle: A Study of the Origin and Development of a Purely American Type of Firearm* (Washington, DC: National Rifle Association of America, 1924).

a job to seed cotton and break flax by hand and after [obtaining] the fibre to hand card and spin, dye and weave it into cloth, all of which was done by hand, and nearly all of the work was done by the women and children.

Now laugh if you choose for I am going to tell you gourds were very extensively raised and used and our fathers could ill afford to do without them. They were found in every household used as dippers to drink from or as ladles for various purposes. One was always found hanging at the well or spring. They were used as containers for almost everything from sugar to soft soap. One of the great sources of contentment was the thought that there was "Whiskey in the demijohn and sugar in the gourd". There was also a kind of gourd that would hold from a peck to a bushel. These were also used as containers of various kinds and many peck and half bushel measures were made of them. For some reason the rats, mice and other varmints would not try to gnaw through the hard shell of a dry gourd, consequently they made safe receptacles for seed corn, beans and other seed that had to be carried over from fall to spring.

The first plows used were "bull tongues". The bull tongue was a kind of shovel plow about fourteen inches long and four inches broad at the upper end. This was fastened to a rude kind of a stalk and drawn by one horse (horses were used in Spencer County before oxen). Later came the jumping shovel which had a cutter to break the roots or jump the shovel over them. According to the best evidence, Richard Brown made the first turning plow in the county. It was a rude affair with a share much like a present plow but the mold board was made of wood. Vincent Brown, a son of "Uncle Dickey", lived for many years about two miles west of Rockport and although many years older than myself was one of my most intimate friends. Times without number have I slept under his roof and many a good meal have I eaten from his table (Peace be to his memory). Vincent Brown kept one of these old plows until his death and it was in his barn that I saw it. I had William Pullen take a picture of it for me but the picture, like the plow, has passed to the Great Beyond.

Probably the first wagons and cattle were brought to this county from Tennessee in the year 1814 by Isaiah Horton who settled near Darlington, the first county seat of Warrick County. Some of his descendants still live near Yankeetown. I got my information about the Hortons coming from Tennessee to Indiana from Sarah Woodruff who was a daughter of Isaiah Horton and was fourteen years old when they landed in Spencer County and after her marriage, lived for many years on the present site of Hatfield. They left Tennessee sometime in the year 1813 with two wagons drawn by oxen. The men folks managed the teams and wagons while the three daughters rode horses and drove the rest of the cattle. They arrived at Yellow Banks, now Owensboro, in the year 1814, ferried the river there and cut their way through the bottoms to the Indiana highland. They could not move straight north on account of the black slash and other sloughs but moved up the river to the Berry settlement above the head of the little island. Berry and Grass with others were at that time starting, or about to start, the town of Darlington which was the first county seat of Warrick County and probably induced the Hortons to move to that settlement.[4] Let me digress here and state that salt was manufactured at Darlington in 1815 and all the southwest corner of Spencer and the southeast corner of Warrick counties are underlaid with salt water and salt could probably be manufactured here as cheaply as anywhere in the U. S.

Now a little about those wagons; they were nothing like the present farm wagon. There was no such thing as a thimble skein, but the axle extended from the outer end of one hub to the outer end of the hub on the opposite side of the wagon. A narrow strip of iron was bent over the end of the axle and passed back so as to extend entirely through the hub to a bolt on the axle. This was the old fashioned skein. On the outer end of each axle there was a hole for the linchpin. This pin was to prevent the wheel from rolling off when the wagon was in use. The hubs were much larger and the wheels higher than the present wagon. The bed was fourteen feet long, four and one-half feet wide and thirty inches deep. Every wagon was equipped with a bucket of pine tar which hung on the coupling pole immediately behind the rear axle and was used for the same purpose that axle grease is used for now and a wagon hammer, the principle use of which was to remove and replace the linchpin when the wheels had to be taken off. The wagon was a heavy, clumsy affair and when in use, when tar was scarce and the axles dry, made almost as much noise as a calliope and about as much music.

---

4 For a brief period in 1814, Evansville actually served as the first county seat of Warrick County.

It is not known who brought the first chickens and hogs to Spencer County but it is known that William Spencer, the first settler in Luce Township, raised both hogs and chickens. I talked to both Wilson and William Huff, early settlers in Huff Township, and both remembered that as early as 1825 there were horses, cattle, sheep, hogs and poultry in Huff Township but neither knew who first brought them there. Chickens were tolerably plentiful in Spencer and Warrick Counties in the year 1816 for there is an authentic account of a trading boat on the Ohio River in that year trading flour for chickens at the rate of one barrel of flour for three dozen chickens. Three dozen chickens would buy much more flour at the present price. Flour was a scarce article and little wheat was raised and mills were far away. The wheat raised was harvested with reap hooks and threshed with flails. The first mill of any importance that ground wheat near here was built at Henderson, Ky., in the year 1817 and farmers of southern and western Spencer County took their wheat there to be ground into flour, making the trip in skiffs and dinky boats.

Few, if any, farmers raised wheat to sell on the market as it is sold now. Most of them raised just wheat enough that they might have wheat bread on Sundays or when they had company or when they wanted to make pies which were generally made of pumpkin or berries. The wheat, when harvested, was placed in stacks and let remain in the straw until needed for flour. It was then pounded out of the straw with a flail, the chaff and dirt winded out of it when it was ready to be carried to the mill. In any early day large quantities of sugar was made in Spencer County. It was manufactured by the farmers from the sap of the black or sugar maple trees which grew all over the county except in the river bottoms. The trees were tapped, generally in February, when the sap began to raise, with an ax or an auger and a spigot placed in the wound in such a manner as to conduct the sap to troughs, gourds or other receptacles. This sap was then gathered in buckets, carried to the camp and boiled down to sugar or syrup. Sugar is necessary to the growth of all vegetable life. What a wonderful provision in nature (if not an intelligence in the vegetable kingdom) that trees and other plants are able to extract from the soil such large quantities of this article that is so necessary to animal life and place it within our reach. Great God our Heavenly Father, How wonderful are the works of thy hand. How far beyond human comprehension

are all thy ways. Now, "Lest we forget, lest we forget" make us to realize
how much we are dependent on Thee and on one another.

Who planted the first fruit trees in Spencer County will probably
never be known. In 1870 I made an endeavor to discover this fact and
interviewed all the old settlers of my acquaintance but was unable to
locate the proper party. There was an old orchard on a farm just west of
Rockport now owned by Allen Gentry. Jacob Young lived there from
1834 to 1877. He told me that the trees were there and bearing apples and
pears when he bought the place in 1834. There was another orchard on
the old Morgan place just west of Youngs. Mrs. M. E. Proctor, who was a
daughter of John Morgan, thought her mother planted this orchard but
she did not remember when. There was another orchard just north of
this on the old Wm. Wilkinson farm but I could not learn who planted
it. There was an old orchard near Santa Claus and Allen Kincheloe told
me he bought apples there to treat one of his first schools. He thought
it was planted by Jonathan Greathouse but did not know. Uncle Hugh
Hamilton, who came to Spencer County in 1809, told me that he planted
fruit trees many times after he was married but could not remember
the dates. Probably the first fruit trees planted in Ohio Township were
planted by Uncle Hugh and Aunt Maria Hamilton. They also raised bees
and among other things raised a family of fifteen children, most of whom
grew to manhood and womanhood and became useful citizens. There
were several old orchards in Luce Township, one on the Ford Wilkinson
farm, but I could not learn their origin.

There was a bunch of old pear trees in Huff Township and I saw them
in full bloom and while I stood there admiring their beauty and enjoying the odor of their blossoms, wondering and dreaming whose hand
had planted them, an old settler by the name of Masterson came along.
I meekly inquired if he knew who planted the trees. He informed me
that they had stood there just as they were as long as he could remember
and for all he cared or knew might have been there a thousand years. I
am willing to risk my reputation as a historian that they were the first
pear trees planted in southern Indiana if they had been there a thousand
years. In thinking of the early apples do not imagine that they were Jona-
thans, Grimes Golden, King Daviss, Starks Delicious, Missouri Pippins,

etc., for the[re] were not such apples but the early settler probably enjoyed them as much as we do the fruit of our day.

Excuse me, but I just have to tell you this story before I stop. In returning after inspecting the old orchards and trying to locate the first one, I came to Spring Station (now Chrisney) just a little before noon, met my old friend John Kramer and we both headed for the home of our mutual friend John B. Christney [sic] because we knew that at twelve o'clock the dining table would be covered with everything good to eat that could be found in Grass Township and John B. never liked to eat by himself. After dinner we headed for the main attraction which was the manufacturing plant that stood by the spring and proceeded to sample some of the very first output of the old establishment and while thus enjoying ourselves one of the old settlers of Grass drove up and I, being chock full of "Old Orchard", proceeded to interview him. I have forgotten who the old man was and would not tell his name if I knew, but he told me that many years before that time when he was a young man and people scarce and game plentiful, he had killed a wild goose on his farm and in its crop he found a plum seed which he planted. It grew to be a tree and bor [sic] fruit and at that very minute it was in full bloom and gave promise of an abundant yield although a very old tree. This, he said, was the origin of the famous wild goose plum. This story I believed and about thirty years afterward, at a banquet of a Horticultural Society in Topeka, Kansas, I told the Toastmaster that I knew the man that killed the goose from whose crop came the seed that produced the wild goose plum. Now the Toastmaster happened to be versed in natural history and seeing how well the crowd were taking my wild goose story, informed us that fruit was no part of a wild goose's diet, that it would eat grass, green wheat and many other things even to fish or gravel but that it had never been known to pick plums, and more than that no goose had any such thing as a crop in its makeup. Now I don't know much about the anatomy of a wild goose and less about its dietary or social habits, but I found out that my Grass Township friend—baseball parlance—put a goose egg over on me and I cheerfully admit that as I believed his story he likewise cooked my goose.

This is probably a good place for me to stop. I realize that I have not handled the subject properly and that I have not written what I started out to write about, but before you criticize me too severely, try to write an article of this kind yourself.

DAVID H. MORGAN (1852–1939) was a teacher and surveyor in Spencer County, Indiana, before moving to Kansas. In 1922, he was elected to the Kansas House of Representatives. Morgan frequently wrote about his memories of Spencer County.

21

★ ★ ★

Materia Medica of Pioneer Indiana

BELLE V. KNAPP*

When pioneers like the Lincoln family moved to southern Indiana, they brought with them a pressing need for medical expertise that often went unmet. Those willing and able to provide medical services did so with rudimentary methods and tools. This paper offers insight into medical practices common during Indiana's pioneer days.

THE STORY OF INDIANA AND HER PIONEER DAYS, AND THE OLD herb doctor has its beginning hundreds of years ago. Men of science have, after long years of study learned to read the pages of nature's book, and have told us the story of what Indiana was long before man appeared to write down his own history.

In pioneer days Indiana was lavish in her supply of medical value. An industry that we hear little about today is the gathering of wild herbs and roots for medical purposes. They say ointments that were made fifty years ago and took fifteen days to make then, will take only fifteen minutes to make now. It is an important industry, and in Indiana today is to be found one of the largest medicinal herb jobbing houses in the world. They say that to visit this house one is reminded of the pioneer days, when almost every piece of root, bark or herb was of some value.

The old doctor is no more to be found, and few home remedies are needed. Still there are more than two hundred and fifty species of roots,

* Knapp first presented this paper to the Southwestern Indiana Historical Society on 10 June 1924 and published it in *Indiana History Bulletin* 3, extra no. 1, *Proceedings of the Southwestern Indiana Historical Society during Its Sixth Year* (December 1925): 12–17.

herbs, and barks that are found valuable in manufacturing drugs. In pioneer days a prescription did not call for a trip to the drug store, but for a trip to the woods, where roots and herbs were gathered and prepared in the manner prescribed. Every old lady had some special prescription to offer, such as a catnip tea for the baby; cherry bark, rock candy and whiskey for colds; jimson leave salve for infection; polk root for rheumatism; Golden Seal for the stomach; blood root for coughs and colds; Mayapple as a laxative; Indian turnip for carbuncles; bog onion for white swelling and carbuncles; sarsaparilla as a spring tonic and blood purifier; camomile tea for hives; slippery elm for nausea and dysentery.

Some of the most important herbs, roots and barks used by the pioneer doctor still play an important part in the composition of some of our specific medicines today; some, of course, are obsolete. Golden Seal is a very valuable medicine and one very much used. It could be found in pioneer days growing wild in every well drained woodland of Indiana, and today the commercial demand for the plant is large. It is one of the best liver stimulants, and is used by our modern physicians extensively; the dry leaves sell for about five dollars a pound.[1] Crude drugs are hard to secure in these days, for two reasons. One reason is that Indiana woodlands are fast disappearing, another is that in this day of automobiles it is beneath the average person to go about digging roots.

The life which was most adapted to the root gatherer was the life lived by the shanty boatman, along the river. The professional root and herb gatherers enjoy nature in her most primitive abode. They seem to always have an inherent love for nature, and great compensation comes to the gatherer in the beautiful sunsets that he sees, and the great out of doors that he enjoys, while hunting for the patches to be found here and there.

One of the remarkable phases of the demoralization of the Indians was the prostitution of Indian medical knowledge, and the increasing practice of "Black Art" [a technique or practice considered mysterious and sinister]. I suppose the patients in those days had cures with auto suggestion to aid the

1 Goldenseal (*Hydrastis canadensis*) is a low plant with palm-shaped leaves. A single white flower appears in the center of each set of leaves, turning into one red berry with about ten seeds. It remains one of the most popular herbs in the United States, often combined with echinacea to treat or prevent colds. But we have no scientific evidence it works or treats any condition. See "Goldenseal," University of Maryland Medical Center, at https://www.umm.edu/health/medical/altmed/herb/goldenseal (accessed March 2018).

physician, just as we have today. The Indians were proverbially poor nurses, but the medicine man knew numberless useful practices and remedies.

The pioneer physician did most of his traveling horseback. After the roads were somewhat improved he used a sort of an open buggy. In riding horseback he carried his medicines in a pair of saddle bags. His trips often kept him from home a week at a time, and each patient was visited according to his order on the "call book". A doctor was always welcome in any home and when on the road stopped at any house that he happened across at meal or bed time. "These were good days to live in."

"A part of the life of every community in pioneer days was the pioneer doctor," whose life was shortened by hardships and exposure to weather but whose "humanity triumphed even over the severity of the winter storm. His journey by night may have been by the stars or by a flash of lightning. Still he traveled on through the forest, tireless, sympathetic, and ever ready to relieve the distressed and suffering."[a]

The first doctor of Dubois County was Dr. Crillus, whose long active life seems to have been spent at Jasper, and whose remains are in the old pioneer cemetery at Jasper today.[b] In 1850 there were but seven physicians in Dubois County.

It is said that Dr. J. H. Hughes had an extensive practice, much of it along the Patoka River and its tributaries. In the summer and fall months Dr. Hughes would have flat boats built at various water-mills, and load them with hoop-poles, staves, corn and such other products as the new country afforded, taken in payment of doctor bills. When the floods came the boats were taken down south as Dr. Hughes usually spent his winters at New Orleans, on account of his health. The pioneer period was rife with privation and hardships. The period of construction that followed was no less full of hard and difficult problems of institution making and revision. We should enter with appreciative insight into the experiences of the builders who wrought so well in their day and generation. We should also feel a strong sense of obligation to the pioneer physicians of the commonwealth; their contribution to the moral and material greatness of our Indiana was neither small or insignificant.

In the early history of the state but little consideration was given to the water supply except from a standpoint of convenience. "There is an account of a construction in Madison in 1816 which is believed to have been the first public water works in the State of Indiana." There was a contract let to a certain man at Madison to lay a water main, and this main consisted of long sycamore logs, which were made hollow. These were telescoped and laid in trenches through the town, with uprights at certain intervals. These uprights were also hollow, with wooden faucets placed in them at a certain distance from the ground. These faucets were plugged; people desiring water could pull out the plug and place their container beneath the faucet and catch all the pure water they desired.[c] This water supply was furnished from a spring on a hill above the town, and the owner of the spring was given five hundred dollars a year for the town water supply.

The early settlers of Indiana, in their task of subduing nature and hewing out a civilization were handicapped by ignorance of germs and germ causes of diseases. The pioneer doctors were compelled to fight against the ravages of smallpox, chills, typhoid, consumption and many other mysterious diseases, without the demonstration and acceptance of the knowledge of preventive medicine and public health as we know it today.

"Preventive medicine had its real beginning with the discoveries of Pasteur, whose active life period was from 1860 to 1890. Pasteur proved that so-called contagious diseases were due to germs, mostly minute vegetable organisms, and he said, 'It is within the power of man to drive all contagious and infectious diseases from the earth.'[d] We must admit that even before Pasteur's discoveries, some progress had been made in the prevention of diseases caused by germs, even though the germ cause was not recognized."[e]

Discovery of vaccination as a preventative of smallpox was published in England as early as 1798 and knowledge of this discovery reached the United States at the beginning of the nineteenth century. It is believed beyond doubt that the first native to be vaccinated was "Little Turtle", the famous Indian Chief. It is related that while he was on a visit to Washington he learned of vaccination and at once had himself and the members of his party inoculated, and carried the prevention to his people. This was prior to the organization of Indiana as a state, since Little Turtle died in the year of 1812.[2]

2 Little Turtle, or Mihšihkinaahkwa (c. 1747–1812), was a Miami chief and one of the most famous Native American military leaders of his time as a result of several victories against US forces in the 1790s. See Harvey Lewis Carter, *The Life and Times of Little Turtle: First Sagamore of the Wabash* (Urbana: University of Illinois Press, 1987).

Public health rests upon three activities, legislation, organization and education. The belief of the fathers of medicine of pioneer days in the efficiency of elaborate resolutions seems to have been exceeded only by their childlike faith in the integrity of the legislature. At a meeting of the doctors in 1851 there was a committee appointed, whose duty it was to prepare and present to the legislature a memorial setting forth the evil and dangerous results of the use of patent medicines.[3] But the patent medicine fraud continued to flourish and still flourishes today. New patent cure-alls appear every week, and the supply seems to equal the demand, while the unholy partnership between commercialized medical fraud and the advertising departments of the public press, on which the whole miserable fabric rests, continues to extort a constantly increasing toll of "blood money" from the frailty and weakness of every community.[f]

In an issue of the *Western Sun*, published at Vincennes in 1808 is to be found the first summons to a community effort on behalf of public health, and the first health ordinance was passed by the Trustees in 1819, only a few years after the admission of Indiana as a state.[g]

The town constable became the first Health Officer. The first state health officer was thought to have been appointed in 1863. "The first medical society in the state was formed at Vincennes June 2, 1817, being organized in conformity to an act of the Legislature passed December 24, 1816, entitled 'An Act to regulate the practice of physic and surgery'. This Society was known as a 'district Society' because it included only a judicial district."[h]

Up to 1830 and later the district medical Society for southwestern Indiana embraced the counties of the judicial districts, which included Spencer County, and most if not all of the counties embraced within the Southwestern Indiana Historical Society at this time. Delegates were sent from the annual district meeting to the state organization.[i] It thus appears that during Lincoln's life in Indiana there was the same free communication between the counties in the medical fraternity as

3 Popular throughout the nineteenth century, "patent medicine" refers *not* to medicine that has been patented but to proprietary (i.e., "secret formula") and unproved remedies advertised and sold directly to the public. Marketing pieces frequently asserted these patent medicines could cure various ailments, though specific ingredients were rarely disclosed. See Stewart A. Holbrook, *The Golden Age of Quackery* (Boston: Macmillan, 1959).

existed in the legal fraternity, including judges, prosecutors, and practicing lawyers.

After years of comparative scientific isolation the doctors organized a county medical Society in Marion County in 1845 or 1846. History records no scientific discussion emanating from this Society.[j] The present state Society was organized in 1849, and thirty years later the Legislature enacted the first vital statistics law. The first public admonition from the organized medical profession is found in the constitution of the first medical Society, which declared that physicians should never neglect an opportunity of fortifying and supporting the good resolutions of patients suffering under the bad effect of intemperance and vicious lives. I think the medical profession finds it necessary to cry out against the same evils today.

There have been transactions published by the Indiana State Medical Society since 1849. So far as known there has been but one complete set of these transactions on file and they are in the Indianapolis city library. Dr. Luther D. Waterman set himself the task of collecting and preserving this most valuable and interesting record of the state. Public Health is synonymous with preventive medicine. There was a Board of Health in Bloomington as early as August, 1833. A report signed by Dr. C. P. Hester as Secretary gives an account of an epidemic of smallpox in Bloomington in that same year. It is said there was a Board of Health organized in Ft. Wayne in 1842.[k]

It is said that after the first Board of Health was organized (1850) there was so much ill feeling among the members of the organization that they did no good until Dr. Jameson became a member a few years later and put the organization into working order.[l]

The first Public Health Board of Indiana was held in Gov. Albert G. Porter's office November 3, 1881, with Dr. John W. Compton of Evansville present. Dr. Thaddeus Stevens, was selected as the first Secretary. Dr. Stevens served two years, and was succeeded by Dr. E. R. Hawn, who died in the same year, and was succeeded by Dr. E. S. Elder 1883–1885. He was followed by Dr. Metcalf who served for eleven years, and was succeeded by Dr. John N. Hurty, who gave about twenty-three years of faithful service to the people of Indiana.[m]

KNAPP'S NOTES

a.   George R. Wilson, *History of Dubois County*, Jasper, 1910, p. 110.

b.   Wilson, *Dubois County*, p. 110.

c.   Dr. W. F. King, "One Hundred Years in Public Health in Indiana", *Indiana Historical Society Publications*, vol. 7, no. 6, pp. 279–280.

d.   King, p. 272.

e.   King, p. 277.

f.   King, pp. 287, 285.

g.   King, pp. 273–274.

h.   King, p. 283. See also Dr. G. W. H. Kemper, *Medical History of Indiana*, Chicago, 1911, pp. 10, 18, 49.

i.   *Evansville Gazette*, 1822. See *History of Vanderburgh County*, edited by John E. Iglehart, vol. 3 of Esarey's *History of Indiana*, pp. 120 and 122. See also Kemper, pp. 19–20, 42–44, 48.

j.   King, p. 283.

k.   King, p. 279.

l.   King, p. 279.

m.   King, p. 287.

BELLE V. KNAPP (also known as Mrs. H. C. Knapp) (1874–1950) was a native of Spencer County, Indiana. She lived in Huntingburg, Indiana, when she wrote an article for the Southwestern Indiana Historical Society.

PART 4

LINCOLN AND THE LAW

22

★ ★ ★

Environment and Opportunities of Lincoln in Indiana

ELBERT DANIEL HAYFORD*

Abraham Lincoln rooted much of his persona in the law. It served as the center of his professional life and the platform for his political career. But who or what inspired his love for law and the legal profession? In several papers, the Indiana Lincoln Inquiry examined this issue. Here, Hayford provides an overview of the legal environment during Lincoln's youth and his opportunities to study and learn the law.

THE ENTIRE EIGHT COUNTIES OF SOUTHWESTERN INDIANA, including Lincoln's county of Spencer, were all in the same judicial circuit for judges and prosecuting attorneys, and the lawyers, the leading men of the time, as lawyers and commonwealth builders as well, followed the judge on the circuit on horseback, and during Lincoln's time practically all of the leading lawyers in these counties, including also frequently lawyers from Vincennes and occasionally from Henderson and Louisville, practiced at Rockport and Boonville, where Lincoln attended court. Judge James Hall,[1] one of the most competent

---

* Based on handwritten notations on the original, we presume this paper to be by Hayford who presented the paper to the Southwestern Indiana Historical Society on 17 November 1925. It is now part of the Southwestern Indiana Historical Society Collection at Willard Library in Evansville, Indiana.

1 James Hall (1793–1868) was one of the earliest US authors to write about the American frontier. Hall served in the War of 1812 and later worked as lawyer, circuit judge, newspaper and magazine editor, state treasurer of Illinois (1827–1831), banker in Cincinnati, and writer of history and fiction. He was well known for sketching life in the French settlements of Illinois and describing the region's backwoodsmen and voyageurs. "James Hall (1793–1868)," *The Biographical Encyclopaedia of Ohio of the Nineteenth Century* (Cincinnati: Galaxy Publishing, 1876), 660–661.

and impartial writers of that time, who was for many years circuit judge in southern Illinois among people whom both he and Eggleston describe as much the same in southern Ohio, Indiana, and Illinois, where they settled near the river, in describing court scenes in this section of the country during Lincoln's time, says:

> The seats of justice were small villages, mostly mere hamlets, composed of a few log-houses, into which the judge and bar were crowded, with the grand and petit jurors, litigants, and witnesses, and, in short, the whole body of the country—for in new counties everybody goes to court.[a]

O. H. Smith,[2] describing the interest of the people of Indiana of the early time when the population was settled chiefly in the southern third or half of the state, says the people came hundreds of miles to see the judges and to hear the lawyers plead, as they called it.[b]

The court records in these counties usually showed the admission to the bar of lawyers upon their first appearance in the court, and always when lawyers from other counties came before the court to transact law business. Unfortunately the records of Spencer were destroyed by fire, the entire record of the admission of lawyers during Lincoln's time in Spencer County was destroyed,[3] but Perry County, lying east of Spencer, farther removed from Vanderburgh and Gibson Counties, where most of the lawyers in the counties mentioned lived during Lincoln's time, has preserved its record of admission to the bar; so has Warrick County; and the list taken from the latter counties may be fairly assumed to describe men who practiced during the same period at Rockport in Spencer County. From these sources and from the record of various particular trials in local history it is established that the leading lawyers were frequent, and many of them regular, practitioners at Rockport in Spencer County during Lincoln's time.

2 Oliver Hampton Smith (1794–1859) was born in New Jersey and lived in Pennsylvania and New York before settling in Indiana in 1817. He was admitted to the bar in 1820 and served as a US Representative from 1827 to 1829 and 1837 to 1843. Following his service in Washington, Smith moved to Indianapolis to resume his law practice. Oliver H. Smith, *Early Indiana Trials and Sketches: Reminiscences by Hon. O. H. Smith* (Cincinnati: Moore, Wilstach, Keys, 1858).

3 Fire destroyed many of Spencer County's earliest records in 1818; nine years later, the first county courthouse also burned. Information about the early history of the county is therefore scant. Bess V. Ehrmann, comp., *History of Spencer County, 1939* (n.p.: Spencer County Historical Society, 1939), 5–6.

John A. Breckenridge [*sic*][4] was one of the distinguished lawyers of the southern Indiana bar during Lincoln's time.[c] It is well settled, and it has never been doubted as a matter of family history and local history among the old settlers of Spencer and Warrick Counties, that Lincoln was a frequent visitor at the residence of John A. Breckenridge in Warrick County, that he heard him plead at the bar at Boonville, borrowed law books from him, and Rev. J. Edward Murr, author of *Lincoln in Indiana*,[d] quotes Wesley Hall as stating that young Lincoln frequently made pilgrimages to Breckenridge's home, borrowed his law books, sometimes remaining throughout the day and night and reveling in the mysteries of the law, and also that Lincoln obtained his first opportunity of reading Shakespeare on these visits, and that he, Hall, had heard Lincoln recite Shakespeare.[5] Mrs. Raleigh in her sketch of Brackenridge says that the latter loaned Lincoln law books, and a friendship was established between them which was never broken.[e] On Rev. Murr's having his attention called to the fact that his authority for the statement above mentioned in his *Lincoln in Indiana* was not stated with definiteness, he wrote me a letter stating that his authority for the statement was Wesley Hall, who made the statement to him, and that Hall was a man of the highest character for integrity and truth, and his word was reliable.[6]

4 Throughout this essay Hayford incorrectly spells John A. Brackenridge's surname as *Breckenridge*.

5 Contrary to Hayford's claim, many of these stories draw considerable skepticism. Warrick County judge Roscoe Kiper wrote in 1924 that he doubted the extent of Brackenridge's importance (Roscoe Kiper to Albert J. Beveridge, 25 September 1924). Former US senator Albert Beveridge, a Lincoln historian, also threw cold water on the extent of Brackenridge's influence—see Albert J. Beveridge, *Abraham Lincoln, 1809–1858*, vol. 1 (Boston: Houghton Mifflin, 1928), 91n2. Most notably, Lincoln historian Louis Warren doubted Lincoln witnessed one of Brackenridge's murder trials and disputed the Boonville connection, believing Lincoln's contact with Brackenridge more likely occurred in Rockport than Boonville. See Louis A. Warren, *Lincoln's Youth: Indiana Years 1816–1830* (Indianapolis: Indiana Historical Society, 1959), 198–199. But as annotations to the companion piece on Mr. Brackenridge indicate, new evidence supports the possibility of greater Brackenridge influence on Lincoln.

6 John Edward Murr (1868–1960) was a Methodist minister who grew up with Lincoln's cousins in Harrison County, Indiana, and who preached a circuit from 1897 to 1902 that included Spencer County, Indiana, where frequently he interviewed persons associated with Lincoln. Murr probably had the closest relationship with the old residents of any of the region's early interviewers and provided a good view of day-to-day life in the Little Pigeon Community. For these stories, Murr relied heavily on Wesley Hall, a boyhood friend of Lincoln (Lincoln being two years older). Hall's father, a Kentuckian, moved to Indiana and settled about four miles from the Lincoln cabin. See Murr's article "Lincoln in Indiana" in *Indiana Magazine of History* 13, no. 4 (December 1917): 307–348; 14, no. 1 (March 1918): 13–75; and 14, no. 2 (June 1918): 148–182.

Mrs. Raleigh on being interrogated for definite evidence of her statement says that the fact that has always been recognized as family history in the Breckenridge family, has never been doubted, and is indignant that at this late date after all of the witnesses of the time are dead there should be any question made about it.[7]

From 1824 to 1830 the fourth judicial circuit in Indiana was composed of the counties of Dubois, Pike, Gibson, Posey, Vanderburgh, Warrick, Spencer, Perry and Crawford, and one judge and one prosecuting attorney filled the office in all of those counties, and with two terms of court a year, as Judge Hall says, the judge and prosecuting attorneys and lawyers following them around the circuit were much of the time on horseback. David Hart, a descendant of one of the Hart brothers of Richard Henderson & Company fame, was presiding judge in those counties from 1818 to 1819, when he resigned, having disqualified himself to hold the office under the constitution of Indiana by issuing a challenge to fight a duel.[8] He was succeeded as president judge by Richard Daniel of the Princeton bar, who held the office from January 2, 1819, to February 21, 1822. He was succeeded in February 1822 by James R. E. Goodlett, who held the office till December 31, 1831. When these judges were not upon the bench they were practicing as lawyers at the bar.

The prosecuting attorneys of Spencer County were from August 9, 1[8]24, to August 14, 1826, Amos Clark, who was succeeded on the latter date by Charles I. Battell, who held the office of prosecuting attorney till December 30, 1832.

Judge Hart died about 1820, and his widow and children returned to Kentucky.

Richard Daniel was a leading practitioner of the bar in all of the counties named during all of Lincoln's time in Spencer County. Amos Clark

7 When challenged to support her assertions that Lincoln knew Brackenridge, Raleigh admitted she could not prove it, but argued she could not prove her own birth either. Later, she signed a deposition saying that "Abraham Lincoln knew my Uncle John A. Brackenridge, walked miles to hear him plead law and borrowed books from him." Deposition handwritten by Raleigh to Iglehart, 10 April 1935, box 5, folder 4, John E. Iglehart Papers, 1853–1953, Indiana Historical Society, Indianapolis, Indiana.

8 David Hart, an attorney from Gibson County, was elected president judge of the new circuit on 27 January 1818. See Leander J. Monks, Logan Esarey, and Ernest V. Shockley, eds., *Courts and Lawyers of Indiana*, 3 vols. (Indianapolis: n.p., 1916), 1:63.

was the leader of the Evansville bar during all of Lincoln's time in Indiana, and for more than ten years later, when he removed to Texas.[f]

During Lincoln's life in Indiana, after he was old enough to take an interest in politics, Ratliff Boone [sic] was congressman for the district including Spencer County, a fact of much importance in the life of Lincoln, and a life of Ratliff Boone is now in preparation, and will be published before long.[9]

In the legislature of Indiana Spencer County was represented by Daniel Grass in 1818 as representative, who was succeeded by John Daniels, representing Spencer, Perry, Dubois and Warrick in 1822; by David Edwards representing Spencer, Perry, Dubois Counties, and Lewis Township, part of Warrick County, in 1823; William McMahan, same counties 1824; John Daniels, the same, Spencer, Perry and Dubois Counties, 1825 and 1826; Isaac Veatch, representing Spencer and Perry Counties in 1827. Isaac Veatch was the father of General James C. Veatch, a very able and distinguished citizen of Rockport.[g] Samuel Frisby represented the same counties, 1828; Richard Polk, same counties, 1829; John Pitcher, same counties, 1830.

The senators were Ratliff Boone, representing Posey, Vanderburgh, Spencer and Perry Counties, 1818 to 1822; Daniel Grass, representing Perry, Spencer, Dubois, and part of Warrick, 1822 to 1825; Daniel Grass, representing Perry, Spencer and Crawford Counties in 1826; John Daniels, representing the same counties from 1827 to 1830.

Of the comparative influence of John Pitcher[10] and John A. Brackenridge[11] on Abraham Lincoln during his life in Spencer County, there is

9 Ratliff Boon (1781–1844)—state legislator, second governor, and Congressman—was one of the most prominent members of Lincoln's community. (Hayford incorrectly spells Boon as *Boone* in this essay.) The Warrick County seat in Boonville was named for Ratliff's father, Jesse. See Linda C. Gugin and James E. St. Clair, eds., *The Governors of Indiana* (Indianapolis: Indiana Historical Society Press, 2006).

10 John Pitcher (1795–1892) served as lawyer, Spencer County sheriff (1826–1830), state representative (1830–1831), and candidate for US representative from Indiana in 1837. He was a member of Indiana state senate from 1841 to 1844, candidate for presidential elector for Indiana in 1848, and candidate for delegate to the Indiana state constitutional convention in 1850. Pitcher was perhaps best known for lending law books to the young Abraham Lincoln. See his profile in two subsequent chapters.

11 John A. Brackenridge (1800–1862) is profiled in a companion piece titled, "John A. Brackenridge," by Eldora Minor Raleigh. Brackenridge was a well-known attorney who practiced law in Warrick County, Indiana, and allegedly lent books to Lincoln, books of law and Shakespeare. Years later, some locals contended Lincoln walked miles to hear Brackenridge plead in court, most notably in an alleged murder trial about 1828.

at this late period no means of accurately knowing. Pitcher, like Brackenridge, was a man of excellent ancestry, had the best education for his time, and came from Connecticut, where he studied law with Judge Reeves, the well-known law book writer, before coming to Indiana to practice. Pitcher was a man of anti-slavery, Brackenridge of pro-slavery sentiments, and in view of the importance of the slavery question during the time mentioned, it is more than likely that Pitcher exercised a good deal of influence over Lincoln in that direction, and in pointing out clearly correct ideals and in discussing questions of interest at the time in conversation with Lincoln.[12] Pitcher was a fine conversationalist, and easy of access, although he never acquired the social habit of the westerner, more readily acquired by Breckenridge, but throughout his life maintained always a stern and dignified reserve. He was one of the great trial lawyers of Indiana, altogether the ablest man in public life who lived in Spencer County during Lincoln's time. My judgment is that both Pitcher and Breckenridge exercised important influence upon the ideals and life of Lincoln during this important formative period.[h]

Daniel Grass was probably more of a commonwealth builder with political influence in Spencer County than any other man in it from the earliest history of Rockport until Lincoln left Indiana.[13] There can be no serious doubt about Lincoln's knowledge of him, and acquaintance with him, although there is no direct testimony of which I have knowledge to that particular point, but the circumstances of Grass' life and his relation to matters of public interest justify this conclusion.[i]

The life of Daniel Grass has been written and will be published in the proceedings of this Society.

Joseph Lane was one of the distinguished men of southern Indiana, was a rival of Ratliff Boone and Robert M. Evans in public life. When Vanderburgh County was created, Boone legislated him out of his

12 Some evidence suggests Brackenridge was in fact anti-slavery or at least sought to help slaves. In October 1835, Brackenridge was indicted (along with John A. Graham and William McKinney) in Spencer County for "harboring negroes." Although Indiana remained a free state, it was still illegal to assist blacks fleeing slavery.

13 Daniel Grass (1774–1836) was the second man to take a land grant in Spencer County and the first to own land in Rockport. He was lawyer, judge, member of the Constitutional Convention of Indiana in 1816, state senator in the first Indiana state legislature (1817–1818), state representative, state senator again (1822–1826), and sheriff of Spencer County (1833–1836). In 1828, Lincoln stayed with Grass while waiting for Allen Gentry to build a flatboat they floated to New Orleans.

legislative district, putting his farm into Vanderburgh County, which accounts for the irregular eastern boundary of Vanderburgh County.[14] Lane was intimate with Grass, Boone, Evans and Hugh McGary, who in a conference settled their rivalries sufficiently to permit the creation of Vanderburgh County as it now exists so as not to interfere with the ambitions of Grass in Spencer County and Boone in Warrick County. Lane's account of the organization of Vanderburgh County is the only reliable one in existence.[j]

Lane worked in the clerk's office in Warrick County soon after the organization of Warrick County, was very active in politics in the third decade, was Justice of the Peace in Vanderburgh County, member of the legislature defeating Robert M. Evans for the place, was in the Mexican War, appointed Governor of Oregon, and became United States Senator upon the admission of Oregon to the Union, and was candidate against Lincoln and Hamlin in 1860 with Breckenridge, the ticket being Breckenridge and Lane. It is probable that Lincoln knew Lane, as he probably had the opportunities, and Lane was one of the foremost popular men in this section in the third decade, during Lincoln's time in Indiana.

John M. Lockwood was a member of the family of the wool carder Evans, wool carder at Princeton, and knew Lincoln very well. The circumstance of their meeting with a romance incidental to Lincoln's visit to the wool carder Evans at Princeton has been fully described.[15 k]

I remember John M. Lockwood very well. My father knew him well. He lived in Evansville from 1830 until a later period, when having accumulated a fortune he went to Mount Vernon, where he died, having acquired prominence in that community. He was a giant size, as I remember something like six feet four inches high, and was probably as tall as Lincoln when the two as young men met together at the wool carder's house and place of business in Princeton.

14 Because Joseph Lane's (1801–1881) popularity threatened Ratliff Boon, when Vanderburgh County was carved out of Warrick County, Boon helped ensured that Lane's farm ended in Vanderburgh, not Boon's home county. William Fortune, *Warrick and Its Prominent People* (Evansville, IN: Courier Company, 1881).

15 In August 1827, allegedly Lincoln was "thoroughly captivated" by the "beautiful face and figure" of Julia Evans in Princeton, Indiana. See the companion piece in this book by Jesse W. Weik, "When Lincoln Met the Wool-Carder's Beautiful Niece."

The leaders of the English Settlement in north Vanderburgh County are recognized as men of prominence in this section by the early historians, including George Flower, who wrote a history of the English Settlement in Edwards County, Illinois. Among others were the Hornbrooks, Maidlows, Ingles, Wheelers, Hilliards, Potts, James Cawson, and Dr. Hornby. Very recently a substantial portion of the library of James Cawson, a civil engineer and school teacher from London, who came into the English Settlement in 1818, with a library brought from England, to which he added continuously while in America, was donated by one of the living representatives of his family, related to his wife, Mrs. Bertha Cox Armstrong, great granddaughter of George Potts, who married a sister of Mrs. Cawson, and who was a partner with Cawson in business, into whose custody the library of the Cawson family came. This library is now in the possession of the Vanderburgh County Museum and Historical Society, and will be the subject of proper description by one of the ablest members of that Society.[1]

General W. Johnson was well known throughout all of the counties in southwestern Indiana, including Spencer County, practiced in all of the counties, was one of the most prominent men in the organization of Indiana Territory and the State of Indiana, was a land speculator in many of the counties, and was one of the most influential and active men in Indiana Territory.[16] His services in putting the anti-slavery clause in the first constitution of Indiana were of the greatest value.[17] It is probable that Lincoln knew him and his work.[m]

Elisha Harrison, who was a second or third cousin of William Henry Harrison, was one of the most influential men in southwestern Indiana from 1816 to 1825, about the period of his death. He was in the lower house

16 General Washington Johnson (1776–1833) was the first postmaster in Vincennes (1800), first lawyer in Vincennes, organizer of Knox County Bar Association, member of the first territorial legislature (elected in 1810), member of the first board of trustees for Vincennes University, adjutant-general of Indiana Territory, three times chairman of the borough of Vincennes, twice president judge of the court, member of the state legislature for several terms, and during the seventh session Speaker of the House of Representatives. He was auditor of the Indiana Territory and treasurer when it became a state.

17 According to Wilson, "General W. Johnston represented a pro-slavery constituency, and often voted its wishes, but he afterwards declared he was always morally opposed to the introduction of slavery in Indiana." See George R. Wilson, "General Washington Johnston," *Indiana Magazine of History* 20, no. 2 (1924).

of the legislature when Vanderburgh County was created, at the time Boone was in the state senate. He was very ambitious in politics, whereby he incurred the enmity of Ratliff Boone, who succeeded in preventing him realizing his political ambitions.[18]

Robert M. Evans was a man of great prominence in southwestern Indiana.[n]

Dealing with the facts known to exist during Lincoln's life in Indiana which are relevant to this inquiry, and summarizing them generally, my conclusion is that the movement of people and trade north, south, east and west in southwestern Indiana, influencing the people of Spencer County in the third decade and connecting them directly with Boonville, Evansville, Princeton, New Harmony and Vincennes, furnished full opportunities necessary for a man of Abraham Lincoln's type, as the world now knows him, to obtain the experience, information and knowledge which he is found to have acquired when he reached the state of Illinois, and for the existence of which no other explanation has been or can be given. By this I mean that for the space of fifty miles or greater, in all directions from the Lincoln farm, contact with people and sources of information were accessible to Lincoln. Vincennes was still the mother city of a large territory. Nearly all of the public men of Indiana, commonwealth builders, were then living in southern Indiana, a substantial number of them in Vincennes and Corydon, some of them in New Harmony, Princeton, Evansville, Boonville and Rockport. There was a stage line from Evansville to Vincennes from 1824, continuously making two trips each way a week till railroads were built. Evansville was the receiving and discharging point for New Orleans, and the Ohio River traffic for Vincennes and southwestern Indiana and intermediate territory, as well as a wider territory, as newspaper advertisements of the time show.

New Harmony was during that time at its zenith, a point of worldwide importance, where resided men of national reputation, where high intellectual standards were maintained both in magazine and

---

18 Elisha Harrison (died c. 1826) established and maintained the Evansville *Weekly Gazette*, built the first courthouse in Vanderburgh County, and engaged in various business enterprises. He was also brigadier general in the militia. *Indiana Magazine of History* 15 (1919): 120.

newspaper literature then published.[19] In 1822 a road was built from New Harmony to Boonville, across Vanderburgh County, in two sections, one section extending from the Warrick County line to the Posey County line, centering in Saundersville, the heart of the first British Settlement in Indiana.

Corydon was the state capitol till 1825, and after the capitol was moved to Indianapolis it was the residence of many prominent people, and travel was continuous between that point and Vincennes and Evansville by roads which went past the Lincoln farm.

As appears from the foregoing statement, the entire eight counties in this Society, including Spencer County, were all in the judicial circuit for judges and prosecuting attorneys, and the leading lawyers practiced in all of the counties. Lincoln was a Jacksonian Democrat when he left Indiana in 1830, and his representative in Congress was Ratliff Boone, who is described as an excellent campaigner, very suave and polite in his address among the people, though very combative with his political opponents, a political boss, who ruled practically without interference in southwestern Indiana during Abraham Lincoln's residence in Spencer County. He was in Congress during all of Jackson's time, and from 1824 to 1838 except one term of two years when he was beaten one vote.

There were published from 1820 to 1830 weekly newspapers in Evansville, New Harmony, Vincennes and Corydon, the files of which are now accessible, perhaps for other periods, though complete files are not preserved.[o]

What I regard as a very important, if not the most important, unfinished work in this direction is a series of biographies beginning with families in Spencer County, to whom definite reference is made by Mrs. Ehrmann.[P]

In addition, it is in contemplation by some of our ablest workers to have sketches more or less complete as facts justify on a large number of the prominent families living between Corydon and New Harmony, and north as far as "Jasper, then called Enlow's Hill. There was free communication between the Lincolns and the Enlows. This would aid in building up the intellectual side of Lincoln's environments. It would furnish side lights that led Lincoln in his search for knowledge."

Corroborative of the interpretation and conclusions arrived at in our vision of this work, and relating to the opportunities which were presented to Lincoln in his environments in Indiana, is a recent article by Meredith Nicholson,q in which one of the ablest of our Indiana writers deals with the factor of what he calls "a healthy curiosity which winged the genius of Lincoln for immortality", and he correctly states that what a youth really seeks and finds and assimilates for himself, whether he has known the stimulus of college training or has done his own exploring, leads into a field where standardization and method are helpless. Mr. Nicholson is plowing in the same field with us.

HAYFORD'S NOTES

a. *Legends of the West*, Preface to Second Edition, by James Hall.

b. *Early Indiana Trials and Sketches*, by Hon. O. H. Smith, p. 7.

c. History of Warrick, Spencer and Perry Counties, 1885. Also Sketch of John A. Breckenridge, by Mrs. Eldora Minor Raleigh, one of the leading historical writers of the Southwestern Indiana Historical Society, whose mother was a sister of John A. Breckenridge, Bulletin 16, Indiana Historical Commission, 1922, p. 60. See also Indiana Magazine of History, Vol. XVII, p. 147. ld. Vol. XV, p. 141.

d. Indiana Magazine of History, vol. XIV, p. 159.

e. Bulletin 16, Indiana Historical Commission, p. 63.

f. For a sketch of Amos Clark see Esarey's *History of Indiana*, Vol. III, Vanderburgh County, edited by John E. Iglehart, p. 57.

g. *History of Spencer County* (1885), p. 489.

h. Indiana Magazine of History, vol. XVIII, p. 145, 146 and 147.

i. It is upon the doctrine of probabilities that Butler founds his argument in favor of natural religion.

j. *History of Vanderburgh County*, 1889, p. 101. One of Woollen's finest sketches is of Jo. Lane, p. 412.

k. The daughter of John M. Lockwood, deceased, has furnished an account to the Vanderburgh County Museum and Historical Society of Lincoln's visit to the wool carder Evans at Princeton, with whom Lockwood worked in 1827 and earlier. Mr. Jesse W. Weik published in December, 1912, Success, Magazine, "When Lincoln Met the Wool Carder's Niece". A copy of the article was read at the meeting of the Southwestern Indiana Historical Society at Newburgh, May 1925, by Lockwood's granddaughter, Mrs. Lottie Edson Erwin.

l.   See Ida Tarbell's reference to the influence of this settlement upon Abraham Lincoln in her book, "In the Footsteps of the Lincolns" (1924), p. 150. See also Indiana Magazine of History, vol. XV, p. 89.

m.   See the paper by George R. Wilson on General W. Johnson read before this Society on February 1924, Indiana Magazine of History, Vol. XX, p. 123, a valuable contribution to the history of the State.

n.   Sketch of Robert M. Evans is found in Esarey's *History of Indiana*, Vol. III, Vanderburgh County, edited by John E. Iglehart, p. 47. For a sketch of Elisha Harrison see Id. p. 53.

o.   Indiana Magazine of History, vol. XV, p. 138–143, and notes. Bulletin 18, Southwestern Indiana Historical Society, p. 73 et seq.

p.   *The Lincoln Inquiry*, Indiana Magazine of History, March No. 1925, p. 5. See list, *History of Warrick, Spencer and Perry Counties* (1885), p. 258, et seq.

q.   Is our Great National Motive Power being Educated Out of Us? An article in the Evansville Sunday Press, July 19, 1925, one of the Pre-Eminent Author Series of articles by foremost American writers.

ELBERT DANIEL HAYFORD (1872–1947) was a native of Rockport, Indiana. He practiced law in Evansville before moving to Maine. Hayford served several terms as auditor of Maine and was a writer and historian.

23

★ ★ ★

John A. Brackenridge

ELDORA MINOR RALEIGH*

John Adams Brackenridge (1800–1862) was "one of the foremost pioneer lawyers of southern Indiana" who, some sources say, provided early legal influence on young Lincoln.[1] In this essay, Brackenridge's niece Eldora Raleigh presents an overview of his ancestry, life, and family. An oft-repeated legend suggests Lincoln traveled about fifteen miles to Boonville, Indiana, to hear Mr. Brackenridge speak in court, noting in particular Brackenridge's defense at a murder trial in 1828, which allegedly inspired Lincoln to practice law.

Nearly all variations of the Brackenridge story derive from the statement of S. T. Johnson to William Herndon, Lincoln's law partner,[2] or Herndon's later biography of Lincoln.[3] Ms. Raleigh and the rest of the Lincoln Inquiry sought to promulgate the Brackenridge story because it increased the importance of this area to Lincoln's career and success. In *Lincoln's Youth,*

* Ms. Raleigh first presented this paper to the Southwestern Indiana Historical Society on 31 January 1922 and later published it in the *Indiana Historical Commission Bulletin* 16, *Proceedings of the Southwestern Indiana Historical Society* (October 1922): 60–66.

1 *History of Warrick, Spencer, and Perry Counties, Indiana: From the Earliest Time to the Present; Together with Interesting Biographical Sketches, Reminiscences, Notes, Etc.* (Chicago: Goodspeed Bros., 1885), 26.

2 Mr. Johnson told Herndon that Lincoln attended court in Boonville, became acquainted with Brackenridge there, and gave Brackenridge "calm intelligent attention" during one of Brackenridge's murder trials in 1828. According to Johnson, Lincoln did not see Brackenridge from 1828 to 1862; however, when Brackenridge allegedly traveled to Washington, DC, in 1862, Lincoln "instantly recognized" him and told him that trial "formed a fixed determination to study the law and make that his profession." According to Johnson, Lincoln said, "It was the best speech that I, up to that time, ever heard. If I could, as I then thought make as good as speech as that, that my Soul would be satisfied." See S. T. Johnson (WHH interview) in *Herndon's Informants: Letters, Interviews, and Statements about Abraham Lincoln,* ed. Douglas L. Wilson and Rodney O. Davis (Urbana: University of Illinois Press, 1998), 115.

3 See William H. Herndon and Jesse Weik, *Herndon's Lincoln,* ed. Douglas L. Wilson and Rodney O. Davis (Champaign: University of Illinois Press, 2006).

Louis A. Warren cast doubts on Brackenridge's influence,[4] but perhaps
Warren ignored or overlooked at least one murder case S. T. Johnson had
in mind.[5] Either way, Lincoln undoubtedly interacted with Brackenridge.

THE NAME OF BRACKENRIDGE CARRIES US BACK TO THE "BON-
nie braes" of Scotland, where the "bracken," or large fern flourishes, and
covers the hillsides. The coat of arms of one branch of this family was a
bunch of the fern on a bar or pole, with the device, "Virtutas et Industria"
(Virtue and Industry).

Their date of migration to this country I do not know, but several
brothers of that name settled in Pennsylvania, where their name is held
in some repute—authors, writers and a supreme judge being among
them, historically.

One of these pioneer brothers, John Brackenridge, and his daughter, Nancy, were massacred by Indians on his plantation in Woodstock
Valley in 1781. John and James, two small boys, escaped by hiding in
the brush. John became a Presbyterian minister and was sent to the
Federal City. The First Presbyterian Church of Washington, D. C., other
churches, schools and a seminary were the result of his labors.[6]

He married Eleanor White, daughter of Zachariah White of Maryland. Three sons and two daughters were born to them. The graves of
the Rev. John Brackenridge, his wife, Eleanor, and their little daughter,

4 Warren states that no murder trials are recorded in Warrick County in 1828 or 1829. Also,
he disputes the Boonville connection and argues that Lincoln's contact with Brackenridge was
more likely in Rockport than Boonville. Moreover, Brackenridge probably never made the trip
to Washington in 1862; instead, his son George met with Lincoln in 1863 before George's appointment to a post in the US Treasury. Louis A. Warren, *Lincoln's Youth: Indiana Years 1816–1830*
(Indianapolis: Indiana Historical Society, 1960), 198–199.

5 By the 1830s Brackenridge served as Warrick County prosecutor. One of his earliest cases
involved defending an attempted murder charge against Pinkney Anderson between 1826 and 1829.
It stands out because the trial may have been one Lincoln witnessed. Many local residents surely
discussed the case.

6 Brackenridge was elected chaplain of the United States Senate and held that position from
1811 to 1814. Later, he served as chaplain of the House of Representatives from 1822 to 1823.
Marilyn Mcadams Sibley, *George W. Brackenridge: Maverick Philanthropist* (Austin: University of
Texas Press, 2013). A sermon he preached in the House chambers in midsummer 1814 accurately
predicted that the British would reach and burn federal buildings in the new capital city. Robert C.
Byrd, *The Senate, 1789–1989* (Washington, DC: Government Printing Office, 1982), 301.

Mary—enclosed in cement walls—are located in the Soldier's Home near Washington.

John A. Brackenridge, a son, and his sister, Attilia Ann, who had married Edward G. Handy in Washington, came to Indiana. The brother had been educated at Princeton University and now came to Indiana to practice law.[7] One of the sons of Attilia Ann was John Brackenridge Handy, whom many of you will remember as a successful Warrick County lawyer and a just judge.[8]

At the age of twenty-seven, John A. Brackenridge married Isabella Helena McCullough of Boonville.

Any account of this Brackenridge family would be incomplete without referring to the pedigree of the mother, and to do this you must go with me to Virginia, where the Rev. John Craig, a native of Donagor, County Antrim, Ireland, and a graduate of the College of Edinburgh, came in 1734, and in 1737 became the pastor of Augusta Church, near Staunton, Va., which was then called Beverly Mills.

Augusta County, organized in 1738, included all the territory embraced in the present states of Kentucky, Ohio, Indiana, Illinois and the greater part of West Virginia.

Dr. Craig and his congregation with their own hands built "The Old Stone Church," which still stands and is the oldest house of worship in the Valley of Virginia. The limestone was hauled on drags or "lizards," as they were called, and the women brought the sand on pack horses from North River, several miles distant. The church was used as a fort during the Indian wars, and was called Fort Defiance.

Dr. Craig married the daughter of George Russell, to whom were born nine children. An entry in Dr. Craig's diary of 1742 records the baptism of Robert Young, and notes that the child was born with teeth. Dr. Craig died in 1774. A marble slab in the church yard covers his tomb.

---

7 John A. Brackenridge was born in 1800 and attended the College of New Jersey, forerunner of Princeton University.

8 In 1872, Judge Handy was elected to the judgeship of the Court of Common Pleas for Warrick, Vanderburgh, Gibson, and Posey Counties and four years later was elected judge of the Second Judicial District, composed of Warrick, Spencer, Perry, and Crawford Counties. In 1854, he married Amanda E. Muir, daughter of one of the earliest physicians of Boonville. See *History of Warrick, Spencer, and Perry Counties, Indiana* (Chicago: Goodspeed Bros., 1885).

Mary Craig married Captain Chas. Baskin, a Revolutionary hero, who lost his sight on account of wounds received at the Battle of Guilford Court House in 1781. Their daughter, Isabella Helina Baskin, married William Graham, of Scottish descent, and probably of the same Netherby clan that Scott mentions in his story of "Young Lochinvar."

> There was mounting 'mong Graemes of the Netherby Clan;
> Forsters, Fenwicks and Musgraves, they rode and they ran:
> There was racing and chasing on Cannobie Lea,
> But the lost bride of Netherby ne'er did they see.

William Graham fought for his country in the War of 1812, moved his family to Lexington, Ky., and finally, after liberating his slaves, settled on the free soil of Indiana.

The Grahams of Spencer, Warrick, Vanderburgh and the state of Minnesota are descended from this same Graham family, who, listening to the call of the West, left their Virginia home and founded new homes in Kentucky, and later in Indiana.

Mary Craig Graham, the oldest child, married James McCullough, a native of Belfast, Ireland, who had come to America at the age of four. He served in the second war against England, and died in Boonville in 1859, at the age of one hundred five.

(Note—It may be of interest to state that after the death of his wife, Mary Graham, in 1824, he remained a widower for eleven years, and at the age of eighty married Elizabeth Massie, by whom he had three children, the late James H. McCulla, and two daughters. He lived to see the son cast his first presidential vote.)

Of the eleven children my mother was the youngest. The third daughter, Isabella Helena, became the wife of John A. Brackenridge.

So three miles west of Boonville, only separated by the Newburgh road, the Handys and the Brackenridges reared their families. We may think it was a monotonous life, but it was not.

There were no Victrolas, but Mrs. Handy had brought her piano from Washington, and Uncle Johnny Hargrave fiddled for every gathering. Accordions were much in vogue and everybody sang.

There were no baseball diamonds, and no expensive uniforms, yet there was no lack of ball-playing.

Jumping, running and swimming were enjoyed as much then as now when they are dignified by the name of athletics.

If there were no clubs, there were log-rollings, quilting parties, spelling-matches, singing-schools, apple-parings, candy-pulls and stump-speeches.

The coming of the circuit rider was gladly welcomed, and camp-meetings were hailed with delight.

At stated times training-days were held, when all able bodied men gathered at the county seat and received military training.

There was no ice-cream, but plenty of cider and gingerbread and sometimes a little pure whiskey at 25c per gallon.

Neighbors were neighborly then. If one family killed a beef, a sheep or a hog, each neighbor in the vicinity had a share.

Both men and women were expert riders, and horses were taught to carry double. My mother, the young sister of Mrs. Brackenridge, was a fearless rider. Horses ran at large quite often, and on her way to school, if she could manage to catch one of them, she would lead him to a stump, jump on him and gallop to school with neither saddle nor briddle. She guided him by slaps on the head, according to the way she wanted him to go.

To this home occasionally came young Lincoln, who with his great love for learning thought it no hardship to walk from his cabin-home in Spencer County to Boonville that he might hear the pleadings of John A. Brackenridge, the most noted lawyer of this section at that time. Law books were loaned to him, and a friendship established which was never broken.[9]

Retaining his farm, Mr. Brackenridge moved his family to Boonville, where he conducted a general merchandise store in addition to his law

---

9 As noted earlier, this legend primarily relies on the statement of S. T. Johnson, who asserts Lincoln attended a murder trial argued by Brackenridge in 1828—but Johnson was not born until the year after Lincoln left Indiana. Furthermore, Warren disputes that Lincoln went to Brackenridge's Boonville home to read books because Brackenridge did not own a home near Boonville until after 1830. See Louis A. Warren, *Lincoln's Youth: Indiana Years 1816–1830* (Indianapolis: Indiana Historical Society, 1960), 198–199. Before the old Brackenridge homestead near Boonville was demolished in 1908, Brackenridge's children erected a marker stating, "Where Lincoln studied law as a boy." Sibley, *George W. Brackenridge*, 21.

practice. As clients were not numerous and fees not large the family of four sons and three daughters probably required a larger income.

When evening came the children gathered around the table to read and study. One of the chief pleasures was the debate, held by the boys, and presided over by the father. All were fond of books, and the classic selections in McGuffey's and Goodrich's readers were not only read but absorbed. This was a happy home, the center of culture and hospitality.

Sometime in the thirties, a brother, Thomas J. Brackenridge, came down the well-traveled road from Maryland to Indiana, where he married in 1840 the beautiful daughter of Thos. F. Johnson, a former member of the Robert Owen community, New Harmony, Ind. Seven sons were born of this marriage. None survive, or left descendants.

In politics, Mr. Brackenridge was a Whig, and in 1844 was an elector for Henry Clay. Abraham Lincoln, then living in Illinois, was also an elector and came to Indiana to consult with Uncle John. I have heard my mother sing snatches of a campaign song of that time.

> "When you see the Polk stalk rising,
> Look out for Clay and the Frelinghuysen,"

are two lines that I remember. Of course, Frelinghuysen was the name of the vice-presidential nominee of the Whigs, and Polk was the Democratic nominee for the presidency.[10]

The oldest boys, Thomas and George, were students at Hanover College and later at Indiana University. After Texas was admitted into the Union, Mr. Brackenridge must have had a vision of great possibilities for his family in the Lone Star State, and in 1853 left Indiana for Texas.

Dr. Robert J. Brackenridge of Austin, the youngest son, wrote to me a few years ago the following account of the trip:

> "We went on a flat boat from Newburgh down the Ohio. On board were father, mother, Thomas, James, Lillie, Lenora, myself and James H. Bates of Troy, Indiana. One cow, two dogs, apples, flour, corn and oats.
> "We floated down the Ohio and the Mississippi and landed at Lake Providence, Ark. Took two wagons and went overland to Texas. Camped

---

10 No contemporary sources document any Lincoln and Brackenridge meeting at this time. Yet, as two electors, it seems reasonable to assume they could have reconnected and interacted during Lincoln's return visit in 1844. Lincoln stayed in Jonesboro, west of Gentryville, in the residence of Col. William Jones.

out. Weeks and weeks on the way. Crossed the Red River into Texas and had my first view of prairies. I was delighted and turned somersaults for joy. We reached our home, a new house on the prairie; it was after sundown, and I heard the quack of the wild ducks, and was delirious with joy at the thought of shooting them."

The father engaged in general merchandising in Smith County, sent his boys north to college—and then the war between the North and the South put an end to these times. Thomas, James and Robert espoused the cause of the South, while George and his father were ardent Unionists, and George hastened to Washington to offer his services to President Lincoln.

My aunt Florinda Day, who lived with them, was heart and soul with the North, but was forced to conceal much of her zeal. She was noted for her forceful prayers at the weekly prayer-meetings. Not daring to pray openly for the Union soldiers, she prayed for the Confederates and then she prayed—for their enemies.

The president assigned George to a position in the Treasury Department, where he remained three years. After New Orleans had been captured, Lincoln sent the young man to that city to take charge of the commissary stores, where he remained until peace was restored. During his tenure of office in New Orleans, he was summoned by the president to Washington and entrusted with a message to Benito Juarez, president of Mexico. The message Mr. Brackenridge carried to Mexico was to the effect that the United States government would in adherence to the Monroe Doctrine support any movement for the overthrow of Maximilian.

During the War, John A. Brackenridge kept his store, but having no confidence in the success of the Confederacy, he refused to accept Confederate money for merchandise, and sold goods in exchange for cotton, which he stored to the amount of thousands of bales. At the close of the war, the value of this cotton had so increased that at his death, which occurred soon after, he left his family wealthy.[11]

11 John Brackenridge's son George erected a monument in the family cemetery and wrote of his father: "As a lawyer he inspired Lincoln who heard him in court when a boy. When a Henry Clay Elector, Lincoln came by his request to speak in his district. His last public speech was made against secession. His last case in court was defense of Negro slaves accused of killing their master." See Sibley, *George W. Brackenridge*, 21.

Thomas and James became successful lawyers in Austin, the capital. Robert was a much loved physician of the same city. Lenora (Mrs. Matthews) was a prominent club woman in San Marco, noted for her interest in the things which are for the betterment of the world. Her last work was the establishment of a Red Cross chapter in San Marco just before her death in 1918.

George W. Brackenridge, who died in December, 1920, was not only San Antonio's greatest philanthropist, but a notable citizen of Texas, because of his wealth, his prominent support of prohibition, woman suffrage, higher education, good government and equal opportunity to all classes. He established the San Antonio National Bank in 1866, of which he was president until 1912. He was a member of the League to Enforce Peace, which met in Washington in 1916.

His gifts, which totaled many millions of dollars, were shown in one of three directions: education, parks and the betterment of the Negro race.[12]

Believing that women should have equal educational advantages with men, he built Brackenridge Hall at the University of Texas to be occupied by young women students. He erected a similar hall at the medical college of the State University at Galveston.

He gave $50,000 for a building at Columbia University, New York City, to make possible the study of medicine by women on an equal footing with men.

He built three of the Public School buildings in San Antonio, gave funds for the establishment of Domestic Science, Manual Training, Linotype School, and built and endowed a Negro College at Seguin, Texas.

But the pride of Mr. Brackenridge's heart was the University of Texas. On the very day of his death he was giving thought to a plan for making the university one of the most beautiful, structurally, as well as one of the greatest educational institutions in the United States.

---

12 Although not included here, George Brackenridge appears to have been instrumental, through the *San Antonio Express*, in which he held stock, in establishing a fund of $100,000 to pay rewards for information leading to the conviction and punishment of persons participating in any mob lynching a prisoner, either white or black, anywhere in the United States. See "Memoirs" in *The New England Historical and Genealogical Register*, vols. 76–77 (Boston: New England Historic Genealogical Society, 1922), xliv–xlv.

To his native town, Boonville, Ind., he gave the site for Brackenridge Park, and four hundred volumes to the Public Library.

Of that family only one survives. Mary Eleanor Brackenridge, eighty-four years of age, a director in the San Antonio National Bank, the "Mother of Clubs for Texas Women," a leader in all good works.

Mrs. Minnie Fisher Cunningham, the state president of the League of Women Voters, ended a recent address with the following words:

> "But there is one among us who worked on the walls, and who has seen the consummation of her vision, and to her I bring the Olive Crown of Victory, to her I pay the honor of the work well done—Miss Brackenridge."

ELDORA MINOR RALEIGH (1852–1930) resided in Newburgh, Indiana. Her mother was sister-in-law to John Brackenridge, an Indiana attorney well known for his oratory and alleged influence on young Abraham Lincoln. Raleigh was a longtime teacher in Evansville and a local history student. She was admitted to the Warrick County bar in 1921 and became a leader in the local women's rights movement. Raleigh was the first woman to serve on the Newburgh Town Board.

24

★ ★ ★

John Pitcher

ALICE L. HARPER HANBY*

Holding a number of titles—lawyer, sheriff, judge, state representative, and state senator, among others—John Pitcher is often remembered mainly as the man who lent law books to Abraham Lincoln and helped inspire Lincoln's legal career. Pitcher also mentored Alvin Hovey, later governor of Indiana. This essay offers an enlightening portrait of Pitcher while arguing for Pitcher's influence on Lincoln. Hanby, however, asks why Pitcher rarely boasted of that influence later.

IT IS KNOWN TO MOST OF YOU HERE THIS AFTERNOON, THAT we Hoosiers of the Southwestern Historical Society have instituted an 'Inquiry' as to the influences here in Indiana that had to do with the making of Abraham Lincoln, and at the same time to disprove that charge of "Illiteracy"—the coiled snake of thousands of publications. Hoosier pride is in rebellion, and we have set ourselves the task, not only to prove such claims as may be made for certain Indiana men as to the making of Lincoln, but to disprove what so long has been accepted for the truth by hundreds of biographers. This in my opinion is the chief value of this 'Inquiry', and I shall give a few moments to this view.

While I am fully conscious that a score or more could handle the subject better and from different viewpoints, I, too, agree that the time has come to rally to the contention that not only was Lincoln's character

* Hanby first presented this paper to the Southwestern Indiana Historical Society on 31 January 1922 and published it in October 1922 in *Indiana Historical Commission Bulletin* 16, *Proceedings of the Southwestern Indiana Historical Society*, 60–66.

determined by his fourteen years of Spencer County experience, but that he went forth to Illinois in the Spring of 1830, almost, if not entirely equipped mentally for the great future that lay before him.

Most writers tell us that Abraham Lincoln's life, to all intents and purposes, began if not from the moment he first placed foot on Illinois soil, then, at least, from March 1, 1831, when freed from parental control, Lincoln "set out" to shift for himself. Lincoln was twenty-two at that date, and a dozen or more eminent biographers would have us believe that Lincoln, under the magic of a new environment sprang miraculously from the "cradle of ignorance" (southern Indiana in general, and Spencer County in particular) to the full stature of intellectual ability almost overnight!

But did he?

We admit that Lincoln developed rapidly after that date, but he was only building the super-structure upon foundations laid during those fourteen years spent in Spencer County, Indiana.

But the "End of the Rainbow" was not set for southern Indiana. It had moved beyond the Wabash, and there circumstances swiftly shaped to a course, calculated not only to call into action the native capabilities of the man, but to make immediately available what education Lincoln already possessed—his Indiana-acquired education. Whatever the opportunity in Illinois, there was no time in which to have acquired such education as Lincoln demonstrated was his in that first six months following his removal to New Salem.

Take Lincoln's quick rise to power. He held office after office immediately following his departure from Indiana, and note the one important fact of his extreme youth when attaining such office. In 1830 Lincoln was barely twenty-one, yet after a few months he was appointed Postmaster at New Salem.[1] Why? Because Lincoln was the one and only man in that community best fitted for the place—and this due to the education he had received in Indiana!

One might say that Lincoln's political life began almost in boyhood, for at the age of twenty-five we find him in the Illinois state legislature;

---

1 The Lincolns left Indiana in early March 1830 when Abraham Lincoln was twenty-one years old. He became postmaster of New Salem, Illinois, on 7 May 1833, at twenty-four and served until the office closed on 30 May 1836.

re-elected at the age of twenty-seven; re-elected a second time at the age
of twenty-nine; (at which age the Whigs put him in the Speaker's chair)
elected again in 1840—and in 1842, at the age of thirty-three, Lincoln
was the recognized leader of his party in the State of Illinois.[2] All this in
twelve years—a pretty good showing for a Hoosier illiterate!

Truly Lincoln was a Hoosier product, but one that did not spring spon-
taneously from Spencer County soil. Lincoln once said, "I was born in
Kentucky, 'raised' in Indiana, and lived in Illinois," from which one
might infer that "raised" was a term inclusive of all he had in the way
of education—and Lincoln had education. He did not go forth from
Spencer County an illiterate. Yet all the schooling Lincoln ever received
totaled only a scant twelve months. But he had "education"—self-taught
in the School of Men, and books, with the assistance of men and books.
But what were those books? And who were those men?

Somewhere in Spencer County Lincoln acquired the fundamentals of
English law. He was never known to be a deep student of law in Illinois,
yet David Davis of the U. S. Supreme Court said, after the assassination,
that "Lincoln possessed all the elements that constitute a great lawyer,"
and Davis knew whereof he spoke, for he, himself rode the circuit with
Lincoln some twenty years or more.

As a matter of fact, Lincoln did devote two years (1834–1836) to the
study of law before being admitted to the bar of Sangamon County, but
he did this without special instruction, and at home—bringing to the
task his Indiana-trained mind and his Indiana experience of courts,
lawyers, and law books.

And somewhere in Spencer and adjoining counties, Lincoln had acquired a literary style that smacks somewhat as to form, of Burke, Junius,
Bolingbroke, and other masters of English political prose, as well as of
our own American state papers, and early political controversies. It is
not known that these authors were in John Pitcher's library[a]—the books
were somewhere—and Lincoln read them.

Lincoln certainly did not acquire this mastery of English in Illinois, for
we find him just six months after locating at New Salem (one may well say

2 Lincoln was elected to the Illinois House of Representatives in 1834, 1836, and 1838, but lost his
bid for Speaker of the Illinois House of Representatives in December 1838.

just six months after leaving Indiana!)—on March 9, 1832, to be exact; we find him addressing a letter to the voters of Sangamon County—and that letter a model of English composition, with Lincoln, the author, just twenty-three years old!—and for study purposes just six months away from Spencer County, Indiana![3]

Now the question is, could Lincoln have acquired a literary style equal to that of the average college bred man of the period in that short space of time? Most assuredly not. Yet to account for which both style and composition, certain writers tell us that Lincoln studied Kirkham's *Grammar* in the interval, in that six month's interval! Well, it's asking too much of us Hoosiers to believe that neither Spencer, nor Warrick, nor Perry Counties could boast a single copy of somebody's *Grammar*, somewhere—and, admitting that one copy existed, then beyond a doubt Lincoln found that copy, and studied it thoroughly and well, as he did all text-books.

But Lincoln's literary style was not the product of *Grammar*, but of long and varied reading, in Indiana.

Lincoln an illiterate? No!

When during his first term as Representative in the Illinois legislature, aged twenty-five, he was looked upon not as an ignorant backwoods member, but as one of great ability and of whose future much was to be expected; all of which, with the implied study and training Lincoln supposedly had acquired in about two and one-half years in Sangamon County!

If Spencer County, Indiana, was the cradle of ignorance Sangamon County, Illinois, was more densely ignorant, for there Lincoln was considered a very learned man even as early as the first years of his stay at New Salem. There is no denying but that Lincoln climbed the rungs with flying feet, but nevertheless he served his novitiate right here in old southern Indiana.

And there were law books too, elsewhere than in Pitcher's office. It's probable that Lincoln read all that he could lay his hands on, and there were other books. In those days, the educated classes, especially

---

3 This date is actually two years after leaving Indiana. The author does not account for the family's residence near Decatur, Illinois, for a year. Lincoln does not get to New Salem until July 1831 after making another flatboat trip to New Orleans.

that of the law, brought their books with them into the wilderness; all educated people brought their books. Spencer County was nowise different from other counties in Indiana, and we contend that Lincoln did attend school—a magnificent school of perhaps fifty miles radius from that rude log cabin home in the Little Pigeon neighborhood—a school that embraced a goodly section of Spencer and adjoining counties. A section almost, if not entirely, inhabited by Hoosiers, and almost, if not entirely, surrounded by Hoosiers. And in this school of magnificent distances and magnificent opportunities there were also some very magnificent teachers who taught by precept and example, and by the loan of books.

And in this connection, there is one fact that none can dispute. Whether or not Lincoln studied law in Pitcher's office at Rockport, Pitcher did loan him books, moreover law books.[4] [b] This fact is known, more or less completely to many in Posey County. I know it myself, as I was shown the so-called Lincoln Books—the two volumes of Blackstone in which Lincoln had written his name. I saw them in the early nineties or late eighties, or earlier, I cannot fix the exact date. Possibly it was during a period of temporary illness, but it is very likely that it was during the few years or months immediately preceding Judge Pitcher's death in 1892. He died at the age of ninety-seven, yet at that time I mention there was no perceptible feebleness in either voice, manner, or mentality.

The Pitchers were old friends, and my calls there were always of a social nature, but on this particular occasion I went expressly to see him, and to take a look at those books.

The first was a volume of Blackstone in which, on a fly leaf, was inscribed the name, 'A. Lincoln', in old time goose quill writing. Both books were given me for examination, but as Kate had said with reference to the first that "the other was just like it", I didn't look at the

---

4 O. C. Terry wrote to Jesse Weik in July 1888 following an interview by Terry with Judge Pitcher (Pitcher was about ninety-four years old at the time). Terry quotes Pitcher saying, "Abe wanted to read law with me, but his father was too poor to spare him away from the farm and mill." When asked about the mill, Pitcher replied, "Tom Lincoln built a horse mill for grinding corn. It would not be called a mill now, but it answered them, and the people were glad to have it. I have ate many corn dodgers made from the meal from that old mill. It would make good chicken feed now, but we were glad to get it then. Abe use to bring me my meal regularly." See O. C. Terry to Jesse Weik, July 1888, John E. Iglehart Collection, Indiana Historical Society, M 0153, Box 2, Folder 18.

second volume very long or very closely. An instant later and Judge Pitcher had risen to greet me. For the moment he stood, a somewhat majestic figure in the dim light, yet he was not tall, scarcely taller than the average. As I shook hands with him, I said with perhaps a touch of reproach, "And you advised Lincoln not to study law! Why?" He answered quite promptly, "Yes. He was nothing but a long, lean, gawky country joke. In fact, I didn't think he had it in him." This last was spoken hurriedly, yet with such emphasis as to leave a keen sense of Pitcher's opinion of Lincoln—in those days. Also, that last sentence sounded to me almost a defense of such opinion. However, before I could venture a reply, Pitcher changed to personal matters, and no more was said on the subject of Lincoln. Nor did I ever see him again where such conversation was possible.

It is of interest perhaps to state that the Lincoln books were sold after Judge Pitcher's death, August 1, 1892—one or both going by purchase to Leroy M. Wade, as I have reason to believe.[c]

In the light of the present inquiry, the value of the foregoing lies in the fact that the incident given proves conclusively: First, that Lincoln was no illiterate; second, that John Pitcher loaned Lincoln his law books; moreover, it reveals the fact that Pitcher misjudged Lincoln to an extent almost inconceivable, and so pronounced was this misjudgment that it would seem almost sufficient of itself to reopen the question of Lincoln's ever having studied law in Pitcher's office.

When we consider Pitcher's poor opinion of Lincoln's ability, and his openly expressed contempt for Lincoln's circumstances fully fifty odd years perhaps subsequent to the Rockport period, together with such other evidence as might be advanced, one may well doubt if Lincoln ever did study law in Pitcher's office—in the common acceptance of the term.

Granting, then, that Lincoln may have studied law in Pitcher's office on some terms or other for a longer or shorter period, one must also allow the contention that during such time or times, Lincoln was subject to influences that had to do not only with the molding of character and the acquisition of knowledge, legal or otherwise, but which must have given the political bias that proved the cornerstone of Lincoln's rise to power. 'Black Republicanism' was only Whigism carried to a logical conclusion.[5] Pitcher at that time was an Old Line Whig, and later Lincoln became an Old Line Whig.

In the end, Pitcher became a Democrat, Lincoln a Black Republican, but up to the parting of the ways Pitcher's conservative views may have tempered Lincoln's more radical bent. Pitcher was a Union man before, and also after the Civil War, and was early an opponent to the extension of slavery into free territory, as was Lincoln. Both believed in collective vision, and followed it. What was guaranteed by the Federal Constitution neither would have tampered with, and neither, not even Lincoln, recognized the deeper issues involved, issues that doomed the protected institution of slavery. Pitcher was a Northern aristocrat, and a Democrat at a time when an opponent of slavery found his true place in the Republican ranks. Lincoln, almost throughout his whole career, was governed by the false thesis that slavery should be preserved *where it was* because of Constitutional provision—Pitcher's teaching left its impress[ion]![6] He it was that must have instilled that reverence for the Federal Constitution that blinded Lincoln all his days—so much then for Lincoln's party policies as may have been influenced by John Pitcher.

If Lincoln chose John Pitcher as his model in the matter of the law, he had, no doubt, ample opportunity for the study, in private, in debate, at the bar, on the stump (probably), in familiar intercourse, alone or with others, *Lincoln had the chance.*

The Lincoln books in Pitcher's possession would seem to point unerringly to at least one source of Lincoln's legal equipment. Moreover, Lincoln's superior merit as a lawyer was Pitcher's own, that quick seizing of salient points, and centering the attack where none but 'big guns' are of any avail. Both Lincoln and Pitcher had logic, practically invincible. Lincoln had humor as a rival to Pitcher's withering sarcasm. If Lincoln could convulse his listeners with his funny stories—sugar coating his logic to gain his point, Pitcher's powerful, impassioned

5 Although nowadays the phrase "Black Republican" refers to any Republican who is black, during the Civil War era, the phrase was a slur directed at white Republican politicians, especially allies of Abraham Lincoln. Most Southerners believed "Black Republicans" advocated abolition and black equality even though Lincoln and his party primarily sought to restrict expansion of slavery in the territories.

6 Here Hanby editorializes about matters still debated among Constitutional lawyers. Her position on Lincoln's constitutional approach likely would draw criticism even today.

eloquence could melt into tears an entire courtroom, judge, jury and audience.

Where Lincoln led, Pitcher could never have followed as a man and a patriot, but where Pitcher led as a lawyer, Lincoln was a close second, and although he never adopted Pitcher's bitter invective or his occasional whirlwind oratory, Lincoln became all that Pitcher could have wished for as a lawyer.

Again, if Lincoln needed the attrition of a mind as rare as his own, he found it in Pitcher. Pitcher's mind was as polished steel, and with an edge like a knife, and as wonderful in many ways as Lincoln's, although it lacked in prophetic vision. That, Lincoln had, to an extent. Both minds were essentially legal, but so different in character were the two men, that while the radical Lincoln "believed in the logic of events, and had the patience to await their development," Conservative Pitcher, had he had the initiative, would have molded the future to his own notion at the flip of a finger.

Pitcher could not do otherwise than tread the "beaten path," but Lincoln, though never a reformer had the power to sense a coming change before it showed above the horizon. The road was blazed in advance for Lincoln, who dared to take it, let it lead where it may. On Pitcher's road, loomed the Federal Constitution which blocked the way and which there was no getting around!

It is known of Pitcher that he was an artist in words, exquisitely picturing whatever struck his fancy. If he told of a summer evening, under the spell of his genius, one could see the lurid coloring of a Turneresque landscape fading into more delicate tints and melting into twilight, with a beauty unparalleled. His storms meant the crash of thunder, the swaying of trees, the riven bolts of lightning to hold us spellbound—as in the courtroom, his denunciation froze the blood. On the other hand, Lincoln moved by the solemnity of the occasion could rise to heights rarely attained, a truly heroic figure worthy of the immortal utterances of Gettysburg! The attraction of opposites is something that cannot be measured, and Pitcher's unusual personality, education, station, distinguished ancestry, etc., could scarcely have failed to impress Lincoln. It would, indeed, be strange had it been otherwise. Pitcher was an exceedingly well-read man and a fine conversationalist, and when in the mood could be a very affable companion. He was also of a certain philosophical turn that undoubtedly would have appealed to a mind such as Lincoln's.

Nor was Pitcher lacking in kindness; whatever his opinion of Lincoln in the Rockport days, *he did loan him his books.* And possibly, the strongest evidence in support of the claim that Lincoln studied law in Pitcher's office is Pitcher's action in the case of Alvin P. Hovey, who as a lad was as poor as Lincoln, and apparently of no greater promise; yet to whom Pitcher gave the best that was in him, interest, sympathy, encouragement, instruction, all of which speaks volumes for Pitcher's goodness of heart. Hence, in ways we know not of, as in ways we do, John Pitcher doubtless played a large part in the life of Lincoln. His may have been the masterhand.

Who can say that Lincoln did not find in Pitcher the spur to his ambitions? One may well claim that one of the great factors in shaping Lincoln's career was the man that determined Lincoln to become a lawyer, and incidentally a lawmaker. Depend upon it, the man that advised Lincoln *not to study law* was the very man that determined him to do that very thing, plus other things that Pitcher never dreamed Lincoln would attempt. Lincoln became a lawyer, not because of Stuart's persuasions but in defiance of Pitcher's dictum. To most, this assertion may seem far-fetched and impossible of proof, but the inference is backed by well known facts. On whatever terms Lincoln studied in Pitcher's office, he did not remain there. He was not admitted to the bar from Pitcher's office. (Nor from any other, which bears, also, against Brackenridge.) Lincoln left Spencer County to some extent unqualified for such a step.

In looking for reasons, one is not far afield in saying that there had been a break between Lincoln and Pitcher.[d] When and why is pure speculation, but not so the results. A break with a man of Pitcher's temper meant one of two things—either an utter crushing out of all ambition, or the bringing to the surface the latent strength of a nature that nothing can crush. Lincoln was of this fiber—and he wasn't crushed. But the gall sank deep—so deeply as to determine Lincoln to become what Pitcher no doubt said was preposterous. What a weaker man would have withered and died under, the lash of Pitcher's tongue, in Lincoln it only sprang into fuller being. And Lincoln carried with him into Illinois no mere budding ambitions, but ambitions full-grown and awaiting their chance.

Conditions in Spencer County made it absolutely imperative to re-move to a field more promising, and once in that new environment, he began immediately his efforts to bring about a realization of his ambi-tions. He was as we have seen, a candidate for the Illinois legislature at the age of twenty-three. Here was his foot on the first rung, with Spencer County clay still clinging to his very boot heels!

Again, the break was not the fault of Lincoln. If he were studying in Pitcher's office with a view to entering the profession, he would never have thrown away so golden an opportunity as admission to the bar as Pitcher's protégé. It is likely he would never have left Indiana, either. What we Hoosiers are most concerned in, is that from our standpoint, Lincoln's ambitions were Indiana-born and that the first as well as the final stroke on the Anvil of Fate was from the hand of John Pitcher—who "builded better than he knew!"

Before quitting the subject one must mention the fact—and briefly, that there were lawyers in Spencer County vicinity that may have in-spired Lincoln. Supporting the claim made for John A. Brackenridge is Lincoln's own testimony (valuable as far as it goes). Whereas, John Pitcher's influence is only inferred; inferred as has been shown from strong circumstantial evidence.

However, the present inquiry may end as to individual claims, it will beyond doubt settle some very important questions; it will determine the debt Lincoln owes his Hoosier environment, and the world's debt to those generous hearted lenders of books in Indiana! Too, it will silence forever that cry of illiteracy which we hate and which we know to be false.

And if, in addition, it were proven that Judge Pitcher was paramount in the making of Lincoln, as he was in the making of Alvin P. Hovey then, old Posey County will surely lock horns with Spencer County over her claim to the one man that guided two lives—one, to honors, the other to greatness!

The next paper on the program is on the Lincoln Inquiry also, by Mrs. Eldora Minor Raleigh of Newburgh, whose mother was a sister of

Mrs. John A. Brackenridge, the man to whom Lincoln avowedly recognized the obligation of the high ideals in his youth in oratory.

HANBY'S NOTES

a.   Besides his law book, Judge Pitcher had an extensive private library, bringing it from Rockport to Mt. Vernon, much of which he must have brought with him from the East. Many of these books were leather-backed, and covered the period of Junius and Bolingbroke. Those knowing Judge Pitcher's taste in literature, to say nothing of Pitcher's own peculiar characteristics, would have small doubt as to these authors being on his shelves, at Rockport.

b.   This assertion of Pitcher's relations to Lincoln is "susceptible" of direct proof. And, by courtesy of Mrs. Katie Whitworth Schultz (daughter of Kate Pitcher Whitworth) we will quote from a letter (unknown to the writer prior to January 31, 1922) written to Judge Pitcher by his son—General Tom Pitcher, who once during Grant's Administration found himself on an Excursion-train out from Washington.

Among the excursionists were President Grant and members of his cabinet and other notables, one being Joseph F. McDonald, Senator from Indiana. The train was crowded, even the smoking-car being given over to the ladies, so later, Gen. Tom Pitcher sat down on an express-box in the baggage-car, wedged in between President Grant and Senator McDonald—to enjoy a smoke.

Gen. Pitcher writes: "During the conversation McDonald said, 'Mr. President, do you know that Gen. Pitcher's father loaned Mr. Lincoln the first law-books he ever read?'" Whereupon, Grant turned to me and said, "Why don't you get your father to write out his early recollections of Mr. Lincoln—everyone else is doing so."

Now as it happened, Gen. Pitcher had long wished his father to do this very thing and the letter we quote begins with the request that Judge Pitcher write for him, his "early recollections of Lincoln at Rockport," and in a postscript adds "Now amuse yourself writing a Life of A. Lincoln." It is not known what reply was made to this request.

c.   Of greater interest is the "fact" that the "Lincoln Books," as seen by the writer, never did go into Mr. Wade's possession. Present knowledge on the subject goes to show that one was sold out of the family, the other beyond doubt, was sent to Gen. Tom Pitcher. That Gen. Tom Pitcher received one of the two volumes is corroborated by a statement made by Col. Wm. L. Pitcher in a letter dated May 1, 1922. He writes: "I recall such a book while my father was alive. This book I think was destroyed by fire when my brother's house was burned some years since. I remember my father saying that my grandfather once loaned to Mr. Abraham Lincoln, who studied law in his office. I never heard of the story of the law book being dropped in the ditch."

Thus, is submitted evidence that would seem to verify not only one but two of the Pitcher traditions as regards Lincoln. The volume now in possession of

Attorney Leroy M. Wade may once have been the property of Judge Pitcher, and if so, it may have been loaned by Pitcher to Lincoln. However, we doubt if anyone at present writing is prepared to prove or disprove the authenticity of Mr. Wade's volume. But assuredly, it is not one of the "Lincoln Books."

    d.   As evidence of that early break, Pitcher never claimed Lincoln. In many patriotic addresses made in Posey County, Judge Pitcher spoke with pride and feeling of "his two boys"—boys whose feet he had set on the upward path, meaning his own son, General Tom Pitcher, and Alvin P. Hovey, who became Governor of Indiana—never a word as to Lincoln. Much could be advanced to show that Pitcher's chagrin was lifelong.

ALICE L. HARPER HANBY (1852–1933) lived in Posey County and worked as a writer specializing in children's literature. She was active in the Posey County Historical Society and authored a history of the county.

25

★ ★ ★

Judge John Pitcher

JOHN E. COX*

In this presentation, Rev. John E. Cox recounts a secondhand story of Judge John Pitcher, one of the region's prominent citizens who undoubtedly influenced Abraham Lincoln and helped shape his view of the law. Rev. Cox leads us to believe Judge Pitcher was proud of his association with Lincoln. This perspective differs, however, from that of Mrs. Hanby, whose companion portrait in this book hints that Judge Pitcher may have broken with Lincoln.

I AM A NATIVE OF ROBB TOWNSHIP, POSEY COUNTY, INDIANA. My father was a Justice of the Peace, and so I heard many lawsuits in my father's court. Of course there were usually opposing lawyers, who made earnest pleas. These lawyer battles were the red-letter events in our community. But when it became known that the noted Mt. Vernon lawyer, Judge John Pitcher, would appear in a certain trial, there was great excitement in our community and all the male population was there.

Judge Pitcher, I suppose, was about 70 years old at this time. His hair was considerably tinged with gray. He was a little stooped in posture, but was a distinguished-looking man. He took no part in the trial proceedings, but when it came his time to address the jury, he showed that he knew all about the ease. He made no attempt to orate. He did deal in sarcasm or innuendo. He cast no reflections on the witnesses. At times he

* John E. Cox first presented this paper to the Southwestern Indiana Historical Society on 28 February 1923 and later published it in *Indiana Historical Commission Bulletin* 18, *Proceedings of the Southwestern Indiana Historical Society* (October 1923): 93–94.

showed wit and humor. He stated his case simply and clearly. He talked to the jury familiarly in a conversational tone. He quoted law applying to the case; he quoted court decisions and once or twice he quoted the Bible. The address was short, pointed, effective. The jury evidently under the spell of this remarkable speech, decided the case in favor of the Judge's client.

When Judge Pitcher was about 85 years of age, I lived in Mt. Vernon. He had learned some way that I had recently been discharged from the regular army, and that I had belonged to regiment of which his son, Colonel Thomas Pitcher, was commander, so he came to visit me often, to talk of his son, whom he adored. The Judge and the Colonel resembled each other very much. Colonel Pitcher showed his father's dignity, his judicial powers and his intellectual attainments and endowments, as evidenced by the fact that for years he was superintendent of the West Point Military Academy. Judge Pitcher once told me that he had given two sons to his government.

When the Judge learned that I was a theological student, he proceeded to give me some fatherly advice. "Of course," he said, "your principal textbook will be the Bible; but you should also read and study the best romance literature, in order to develop your imagination. I gave this advice to the Pentecost boys, and you know that they became noted preachers."

Then he continued: "Speaking of the Bible: I have studied it all my life and have found it a great help in my legal addresses, I have always urged young lawyers to study the Bible along with their law books."

He delighted to talk of his boyhood days when he was an associate of Abraham Lincoln, and it is the regret of my life that I did not make a note of all his remarks. I remember just one little scrap of our conversation. I think it was during his last visit that I asked what influences in his opinion, had most to do in shaping the character of Abraham Lincoln. I will never forget his answer:

"First, he had a good mother. Second, he had a good step-mother. Both women were above the average of their day and times, in character and intelligence. And both instilled into the mind of the boy an ambition to gain knowledge and make a man of himself."

The mental picture of this grand old man as he tottered from my home for the last time, will never be effaced as long as memory lasts.

JOHN E. COX (1850–1932) was a Posey County, Indiana, native who served as a Baptist minister for more than forty years in southwestern Indiana. In 1872, he joined the US Army and served in the Indian Wars in the west. Cox was stationed in the Dakota Territory about a hundred miles from Little Big Horn in 1876.

PART 5

THE INDIANA LINCOLN INQUIRY

26

★ ★ ★

The Environments of Abraham Lincoln in Indiana: The Best Witnesses

ANNA C. O'FLYNN*

Ida Tarbell credited A. Hoosier for the material she used about Lincoln in Indiana in her *McClure's Magazine* articles and later in her book *The Early Life of Abraham Lincoln*. A. Hoosier was actually Anna C. O'Flynn, an educator from Vincennes, Indiana.[1] In this essay, O'Flynn recounts how she obtained the information sent to Tarbell.

MR. PRESIDENT AND DEAR FRIENDS, [D]ON'T YOU FEEL SORRY for me to follow such a legal and logical mind as Judge Iglehart with his array of evidence? I never was a witness before and I am shaking now because I hate to even say one word.

When Mr. De la Hunt said: Miss O'Flynn, will you talk to us sometime in southern Indiana, I was flattered for I thought they would let me talk on Old Vincennes, but when Judge Iglehart said, "Miss O'Flynn, we want you to tell us about what you learned in southern Indiana about Lincoln," why I was terribly frightened because I thought, "What can I say to those people who have lived where Abraham Lincoln lived in his formative years; what can I take to them that would be new, I, a teacher, a witness." I am accustomed to telling stories to the children. Don't you

* O'Flynn delivered this paper on 17 November 1925. A copy is part of the *Southwestern Indiana Historical Society Annuals* 4: 71–86, at Evansville-Vanderburgh Public Library.

1 For more information on the O'Flynn-Tarbell connection, see William E. Bartelt, *There I Grew Up: Remembering Abraham Lincoln's Indiana Youth* (Indianapolis: Indiana Historical Society, 2008), 188–190.

imagine when you read a story of mine that it isn't positive history for it is, just as much as if it wasn't story form.

I will begin at the beginning of how I wrote *Lincoln's Boyhood in Indiana*. One evening Captain John Burke, deputy revenue collector for southern Indiana, and his wife were spending the evening in our home. He said, "Miss O'Flynn, I saw something today that would greatly please you. The grave of Abraham Lincoln's mother." Everyone knows what admiration I have for Lincoln, and of course I asked a great many questions. One was, "Did you bring a photograph with you?" He answered, "There are none." "Then have some taken and sell them on the train." He responded, "I will." Our best photographer, Mr. Elmer Shores, since dead, and Captain Burke went out and took a picture of everything in Spencer County and around Lincoln City that seemed to suggest boyhood. I think they took one hundred and two pictures. They were a big contribution to Ida M. Tarbell's *History of Lincoln in Indiana*. We had hoped to write a story from the pictures, but as we got into the pictures we thought we must have some historical data. I went down to Evansville one evening to interview Captain J. W. Wartman[2] who had a cabinet that Abraham Lincoln made for his step-mother. There under his wonderful magnetism I got so enthusiastic I couldn't wait for school to close to go down into southern Indiana and get some more inspiration. I made a pilgrimage with a friend of mine. When we arrived there was a soldier's meeting at Ferdinand. I thought *there* is where we will find everything we want. Dear me! They were so busy with their own affairs they didn't have time to look at me. "Over there is a man that is just full of information." We went over there. Another said, "Yonder is a woman who knew the Lincolns." We went over yonder. We had headquarters at Lincoln City, and we had a two-seated wagonette, with double brakes. You know that one just holds their breath while riding down the hills of Spencer County. I feared we would be in Eternity before we found all we wanted. Well, we went all over the country and talked to the people that had talked to Lincoln, or whose mothers and fathers had talked to Lincoln. They were charming people. They were hospitable, they were strong and

---

2 Captain J. W. Wartman's (1832–1917) daughter, Sarah, donated the cabinet to the Evansville Museum of Arts, History, and Science in 1927.

sturdy and healthy, and they were kind and thoughtful, and to me it was an ideal summer vacation.

We went back home; we wrote a story. Captain Burke said, "Send that to Saint Nicholas." "No," I replied, "that is not a Saint Nicholas story." (In those days it dealt with weird stories.) "I don't want to send it there." "Oh, yes, you must, for we have raised our children on Saint Nicholas, and we want this story in Saint Nicholas." Well, this doubting Thomas sent it, and the doubting proved true. The manuscript came back. I sent the manuscript to the Inter-Ocean, the greatest middle West newspaper of the day. In three days it was back again, but oh, joy: the editor said, "Send this to McClure. They are hunting articles like this. It is so good." I was very glad. I sent it to McClure; it never came back. Then McClure asked, "Are you a relation of Lincoln's?" "Have you any other information concerning Lincoln in Indiana?" "This is such a fine article." Well, again I felt happy. I answered telling them I was not a relation but I offered to go down in Spencer County and obtain all the information possible.

We went down to Spencer County to get facts about Lincoln's boyhood. We had found Lincoln in Vincennes, but he was a man when there. I wanted his boyhood for my scholars. I wanted them to get the inspiration he got, to be as considerate as he, as persevering as he. Honorable Carl Schultz said, "The Story of Abraham Lincoln's Boyhood in Indiana in the McClure Magazine is the most sympathetic article that has ever been written about this great hero."

A speaker in the State Historical Convention in Indianapolis last winter critici[z]ed nearly every Life of Lincoln that has been published. When he finished I thanked him for not critici[z]ing Ida M. Tarbell's Life of Lincoln, as I had furnished her the Indiana story, and Marse Henry Watterson, Editor of the Louisville Courier Journal, wrote the Kentucky history; Lawrence Graham, a fine young lawyer of Illinois furnished the material for his state.

You want to hear about the people with whom I talked and the stories they told to me. Mrs. Nancy Taylor Volke gave me her brother's address, saying that Green B. Taylor[3] would give me the facts concerning Abraham Lincoln working for her father and running the ferry boat. Here

3 Green B. Taylor was born in 1818 and died in 1899.

was where Abraham earned his first dollar by taking two men out to
a steamboat. I wrote to Captain Green B. Taylor, of South Dakota, received an answer and his photograph. He told me that the two boys were
shelling corn to take to the mill. Abe got so much more done than he
did that he got mad and threw a corn cob and hit Abe over the eye. The
scar remained on Lincoln's face until death. Abe reached over, grabbed
Green, and spanked him good and plenty. Green ran screaming to his
mother. She inquired into the facts and sympathized with Abe, washed
his wound and tied up his head. She gave Green another spanking.

I interviewed Mrs. Crawford who had a wardrobe made by Thomas
Lincoln, Abraham's father. This was a fine piece of work proving that
Thomas Lincoln was a skillful carpenter. The wardrobe was of black walnut inlaid in white oak. Around the panels were small diamond shaped
bits of white oak forming a wreath. In the center of the panels were the
letters, "J. C." for Josiah Crawford on one door and "E. C." for Elizabeth
Crawford on the other.[4]

It was Josiah Crawford's "Life of Washington" that Abe borrowed. It
got wet and Abe shucked corn to pay for it. Ah, the Crawfords were a
mine of stories which I have not time to repeat.

Locating the grave of Mrs. Lincoln was a hard problem. Mr. Bruner[5]
said he thought he could locate his mother's grave. They were side by side.
Lincoln sawed down a tree, whip-sawed the boards and made his wife's
coffin. That was not poor carpentry! Thomas Lincoln was a fine work-
man. When one sees these pieces of his workmanship you will decide
that he did excellent work.

I signed my name "A. C. O'Flynn" to my letters to Spencer County
people. When I went to see General Veatch[6] in Rockport, he said, "Are

4 In the question-and-answer time following the presentation, O'Flynn said she visited Spencer
County in 1895 and 1896. Elizabeth Crawford died on 17 September 1887. In the A. Hoosier file of
Tarbell papers at Allegheny College is a document by O'Flynn stating she obtained information
from Ruth Crawford Jennings Huff (1827-1906), the daughter of Elizabeth Crawford. The furniture
described here appears to be the Crawford cupboard at Lincoln Pioneer Village, not a wardrobe.
Mrs. Huff also owned a corner cupboard, now at Greenfield Village. See *Lincoln Lore*, Number
1476, February 1961.

5 She refers to Rev. Allen Brooner (1813-1902); his mother died at the same time as Nancy Hanks
Lincoln.

6 General James C. Veatch (1819–1895) was a prominent Rockport citizen, serving as
adjutant-general of Indiana and collector of internal revenue for the first district of Indiana. See
The Rockport Journal, 27 December 1895.

you a woman?" "I thought you were a boy, or man." His wife said, "If he had known you were a lady he would have been writing long letters to you." General Veatch warned me not to go down to Lincoln Station and get a drink, as that is what most people who have a half hour do. "They go into a saloon. They gather anything they can from any toper that is in the saloon, and they give it out as true. I greatly regret it, for stories have gone out that have not a grain of truth in them."

There is one monument to Lincoln that can't be duplicated. It is a cedar tree planted by James Gentry after Lincoln's family had gone to Illinois. He said to his brother, "I am going to stick this down and when Abe comes back it will be a big tree." It was.

I interviewed Mr. Lamar.[7] He said the first time he saw young Lincoln was when as a little boy he was riding to the mill on a horse behind his father. Lincoln was letting the horse rest from plowing, and was reading a book. Lamar's father said, "Son, look at that boy. He will make a mark in the world. He either works or reads. He never wastes a minute!" You know that was a big story for me to tell my scholars. "*He never lost a minute.*" So I think they profited by it for I never had a boy that went to the Reformatory, nor a girl to go astray. Thank God!

I went to every city, village, or hamlet in the vicinity of Lincoln City. I interviewed people in each one of these places, then back to headquarters with my friend. There was a very fine young man who owned the livery barn. I hear he is now a millionaire. His name is Sidney Romaine.[8] He was very courteous and never complained of the long waits while we interviewed the people who knew Abraham Lincoln as a boy. We met people that didn't seem inclined to talk to newspaper writers. This caused us to get the name of the leading person in each neighborhood. When at home we wrote to that person to get the news from those who knew any facts. In this way we got a very good reliable history of his boyhood. You can well imagine the first place we went when we returned from Ferdinand. It was to see Lincoln's mother's grave.

---

7 The man of the story is identified as John Lamar (1822–1903) in Ida M. Tarbell's article "Abraham Lincoln," *McClure's Magazine* 6, no.1 (December 1895): 7. Tarbell got the story from A. Hoosier.

8 The name was probably Romine. We know nothing else about this man.

I presume you all know the story of the little marble marker that stands on the hill where rests the body of Mrs. Nancy Hanks Lincoln. This is General Veatch's story. A newspaper man whose nom de plume was "Babbe" wrote twelve verses about the deserted grave. This Stone poem was erected by a friend of her son, and is all there is to lead to the identification of the patriotic citizen. General Veatch and some other people of the neighborhood put up the iron fence and saw that the grave was kept up.

After talking with General Veatch I wrote to Mr. Studebaker of South Bend. I will quote the answer to my letter of inquiry:

> **Mr. A. C. O'Flynn, 310**
> **Church St.,Vincennes, Indiana.**
>
> Dear Sir:
>
> Yours of the 16th is at hand and duly noted.
>
> The monument erected over the grave of Mrs. Nancy Hanks Lincoln was put up by Mr. P. E. Studebaker, the second Vice President and Treasurer of this Company.
>
> The circumstances leading up to the action on his part were substantially as follows:
>
> Picking up his South Bend paper one evening he saw an item stating that the grave was without a headstone. He thereupon wrote the editor, suggesting a movement for the performance of the work by the public through a fund. The late Schuyler Colfax happened to be present when the editor opened the letter, and on being made acquainted with the contents of the letter he urged that Mr. Studebaker undertake the work without waiting the chance of enlisting the assistance of the public. The matter being presented to Mr. Studebaker with arguments in its favor by Mr. Colfax, the stone was erected accordingly.
>
> Quite a good many papers have made mention of it. Harper's Weekly, among others, when the subject was fresh some years ago.
>
> > *Yours Very truly,*
> > *Studebaker Bros. Mfg. Co.*
> > *D. S. Marsh.*

I will tell you a story relating to Vincennes. I have many photographs, but you will not have time to see them. We have Colonel Allen and his home where Lincoln stayed when in Vincennes. It is still a historical spot. It is now the home of Gardner's Undertaking Establishment. The Gardners are historical undertakers of four generations. Lincoln got his first five hundred dollar lawsuit through Colonel Allen, and Colonel Allen then gave him the B. & O. attorneyship. Allen was the first President of the B. & O. road. Lincoln came to Vincennes and as he was going away he cut off a lock of his hair, saying, "Here, Colonel, take this and keep it because you may never get to talk to me so long again, and you will always think of me when you see this." Mr. Allen wore it in his watch as long as he lived. When he died his son threw it in the fire not knowing its value.

When Lincoln was President living in the White House Colonel Allen went to Washington City and took his family with him. His little daughter rode around on one of the White House horses and when she got down she was holding her hand closed. Her father asked, "What have you in your hand, Grace?" She answered, "Mr. Lincoln told me not to show you until we are in our rooms." It was a five dollar gold piece. Colonel Allen had it put on a necklace for her. When in New York he had her portrait painted. This portrait is in Vincennes. The gold piece is now in Lincoln University where Rev. Wesley Hill guards it.

When speaking in favor of Henry Clay Lincoln came to Vincennes in 1844. He made a speech at Bruceville the same evening that one of the brilliant young attorneys of Vincennes was the Democratic attraction. He was dressed in the latest style and was an orator. I think he must have been a fine one from all reports. He talked on the Democratic side and Lincoln's Whig friends were very uneasy. They said, "Let's go over to the schoolhouse. Over they went, calling all to follow to the little old brick schoolhouse. Abe made a speech that carried conviction, you may be sure. That night he stayed at the Bruce's home. Mr. Bruce said, "Lincoln, that old box up on that pole has a rooster in it, and that rooster gets out every morning and proclaims a Democratic victory." "Don't worry about that; if my speech was any good it will not be there tomorrow morning." In the morning when they pulled the string the rooster didn't come out and the feathers flew away in every direction. Then a coon came out on the board where the rooster had previously proclaimed his victory. The people thought that Abe Lincoln had put that coon in the box to devour the Democratic rooster. This joke made him many friends.

When Lincoln was nominated for President in the Chicago Convention, Colonel Allen was there. He had said before going, "Now boys, I will be ready to give you the signal. I am going to nominate Abe Lincoln and he will win, and you be ready with the bonfires." The young railsplitter did win. It wasn't long until that good news reached Vincennes, and Vincennes sent it on to Bruceville. Bruceville celebrated with all sorts of noise, bonfires, and public speakings. This was the first celebration in honor of Lincoln as a candidate for president. An account of the booming cannon, bon-fires and speaking are in the old Vincennes papers on file in our Vincennes Courthouse.

Someone said that the records of the Thomas Lincoln farm were lost. I have a copy of the transfer of the land. Captain John Burke who was greatly interested in my National School project went to the Courthouse. He there met the County Recorder who gave him access to the books and greatly assisted in getting the transfers.

Now following this lead you will find it on down until Oskins sold it to Harry Davis of Cincinnati. Well, you know a great big idea so gigantic that it is not yet finished took possession of my mind when I read the records. I wanted a school on this farm where every child of any genius could be educated just as we educate our sailors at Annapolis, and our soldiers at West Point. I wrote to many, many prominent people of our U. S. A. telling them of the project. We got a very hearty response from some. I wrote to John Shillito Co. of Cincinnati who had purchased the farm. They said, "We are very willing to sell the original tract excepting the right of the railroad and the place where the homestead stood." The men who examined the records did not find where Oskins sold to James Gentry. That is the only break. Mr. Incoe and Mr. Watson McCoy assisted Captain Burke. I have it all in legal form if it is not now in your Courthouse.

Abraham Lincoln made three speeches in Spencer County. Some people doubt it, but these facts were told by Mr. Bruner, Mr. James Gentry, and Mr. Redmond Grigsby. They remember the speeches. One speech was made out at the Carter School where the Buffalo road crosses. Lincoln stood on the schoolhouse steps with his back to the schoolhouse and talked to all the people from the surrounding country. Many of them knew him when a boy. We were told by the old settlers that the second speech was made down in front of the harness shop one hundred fifty feet south of Jones store (locating it very closely). This time Abe talked to the neighbors and the people of the vicinity right near, or in Gentryville. His big speech was at the Rockport Courthouse. I obtained a picture of that old courthouse, altho[ugh] it had been burned. I have it.

I am writing the women of Indiana that if any of them have a picture and will lend it to me I will be so glad to insert it in this historical gallery that we are striving to arrange.

Questions

Q. By Mr. Fortune: In what year did you interview Spencer County people?

A. 1895 and 1896.

Q. By Mr. Embree: How long were you down there?

A. Well, once for a few days and another time about four weeks in all.

Q. By Mr. Embree: Can you tell why Thomas Lincoln's grave is not marked?

A. Oh, he did not die here in Indiana. The father died in Illinois.

Q. By Mr. Barker: What year was it he made the speech at the Jones stores?

A. 1844. There was one man that said he was sure that Lincoln was making speeches in 1840, but he didn't remember. I wrote to nearly everybody in the United States that knew Lincoln when a boy. I think I had over two hundred letters. One said that Lincoln made a very strong speech in Lawrenceville, Illinois, 1840. We have records in Vincennes that he spoke in 1844. The account appeared in papers that we have preserved. They have a file at our courthouse and you can find it. It will tell you about the aristocratic young man, standing up in his handsome carriage making a rhetorical address, and the Whigs and Democrats had a fight that night. They fought with hickory hoop poles. They were going to make barrel hoops and the poles were handy for the boys to pick up.

Q. By Mrs. Ehrman: Would you describe these men and women that you interviewed, Miss O'Flynn, their personal appearance and their opportunities for education?

A. They were like the men that we have here. Their faces were different. Some people are ugly, you know. I found the mind and soul were what I wanted. Their faces and their clothing were as varied as you find in any gathering today. Did you ever go to a country fair, or did you ever go to one of these little affairs where you get out and meet everybody? I found the aristocrat, the intelligent, and I found the unlearned. Why not? Aren't they everywhere? I found those people were all mighty fine. I didn't interview any common people in Spencer County. I wish I could even tell you in appreciative words how nice they were to us, and how kind they always were. So if a historian wants to go down in Spencer County today, if he will follow Colonel Veatch's advice, he will stay away from the saloons and the riffraff and go to the best people, then he will get what he came for. I don't think that it is very wise for one who is hunting something for an article for newspapers to hunt the sensationalist. I don't believe in the murders of today being on the front page in inch type. I think we ought to give good deeds the big print. When I was trying to start that school I thought we are too civilized to ever have another war. Now, the practical business men of today have turned my Lincoln school into the Lincoln Highway, and I hope in the future that the Lincoln Highway will take the bodies of the children and put them in some Hall of Learning, that *Mind* school will be somewhere on that road, Lincoln Highway. I have faith in that Hall of learning. It won't be Annapolis, nor a West Point. I know many of you were soldiers and I have some of that blood in me, but I don't believe in wars. We can arbitrate. I notice on the Lincoln Highway the rich and the poor, the unlearned and the learned, in their automobiles. And in some future day that Highway will lead to the Hall of Learning where everybody can have the best that will help him to love our Nation, and cherish his neighbors. This is what we are praying for.

Q. By Mr. William Fortune: Could you give the name of the person furnishing the Taylor story? Did you get the Taylor story directly from him?

A. Yes, I think I have his letter. You know he is in South Dakota. He gave me that story himself. His sister gave me his address.

Q. Is she living in Evansville?

A. No, I went out in Troy.

Q. Is there anything else?

A. Well, when we were taking pictures, Mr. Redmond Grigsby held his head different ways. He would not let me have his pictures. Afterwards his niece wrote, "You just use Uncle Redmond's picture. It is just a little modesty in him not wanting it published." I didn't get that letter until too late to have it in *McClure's* magazine. The picture he took of the valley stretched away out was such an inspiration to me. I said, "No wonder Abraham Lincoln had broad visions; it looked to me like it was miles across the Buckthorn valley in that one picture. Everything was an inspiration.

Questions by Mr. Iglehart

Q. By Mr. Iglehart: I want to ask you a question. I haven't heard what you said as I am quite deaf. Is there any part of your investigation or your notes which you haven't given us for any reason that you desire not to give it to us?

A. Oh, no. You see they didn't use all my articles. Miss Tarbell did what you call "edit" the work, but I wrote a boyhood of Lincoln in Indiana for the *Indianapolis Star*. That was about two or three years ago.

Q. Are you willing when it comes to filling out your paper to add anything that inquiries by us may suggest?

A. I would be willing to do that. Anyone that wants any information that I have I will gladly give it.

Q. By Mr. William Fortune: Could you give the names of others of the people whom you interviewed besides Lamar and Mrs. Crawford?

A. I think I have them written down. I might count hundreds of good people to whom we talked. To others we wrote letters. I saw many who gave me something, and the others I saw didn't give me anything. Many a time I went home without anything at all, but still uplifted because we had met people who had nothing to say, yet were kind to us and were interested in my work. You know that meant much to us. I would have to tax my memory to give you all the names, but here is a partial list: General Veatch, Captain Green B. Taylor, Mrs. Emma Bullock, Mrs. Mary Adams, Mrs. Ruth Huff, Mrs. Jones, Mrs. Turnham, Hon. H. B. Brooner, Capt. LaMar, Capt. C. T. Doxey, Hon. Alfred McCoy, Mr. N. S. Roberts, Capt. P. A. Bruce, Capt. Wartman, Capt. Burke, Capt. F. J. Charlton, Capt. George Riley, Ed Roy I. Purcell, Ed. Thomas Adams, Hon. H. W. McCoy, Mr. Studebaker, Hon. Schuyler Colfax, Hon. Wm. English, Capt. Wm. Jones, and his son, Attorney Wm. Jones, Mr. Raymond [Redmond] Grigsby, Mrs. James Gentry, Mr. Bruner, Mrs. Nancy Taylor Volke, Mr. W. M. Daniel, S. H. Burton, Mr. Frank. Gahon, Miss Mary Inco.

Others there are who gave me inspiration and encouragement. But we are forgetting something wonderful. When he came to Vincennes we had a printing press. Of course Abe Lincoln found that printing press and watched it. It was the first newspaper in the northwestern territory in 1804, established by the grandfather of a young lady that came here with me. Abraham Lincoln looked and looked at that wonderful printing press. He did not go around aimlessly, here and there, you know. He went where there was something he could learn, something could give him some information that would improve his mind.

There were many other good people who gave me encouragement and have a warm spot in my heart-picture of Jasper [Dubois] and Spencer Counties, with their picturesque hill roads, its monks, its shrines, its churches. The memory seems a bit of another land sacred to our hero boy, Abraham Lincoln, and God.

ANNA C. O'FLYNN (1854–1938) was a schoolteacher in Vincennes, Indiana, for more than fifty years. In the late 1890s, she visited Spencer County to talk with residents about Lincoln's youth. Ida Tarbell used much of O'Flynn's material, referring to her as "A. Hoosier."

27

★ ★ ★

The Lincolns in Spencer County

IDA D. ARMSTRONG*

Ida D. Armstrong relates stories from many Spencer County citizens about Lincoln, the most important her account of her father marking Nancy Hanks Lincoln's grave in 1874. Born in 1837 in Meade County, Kentucky, Joseph D. Armstrong moved to Spencer County in 1857 and worked in William Thompson's store in Gentryville. In August 1861, he enlisted in the 42nd Indiana Volunteer Infantry Regiment serving as orderly sergeant until discharged in October 1862 due to a disability. A Democrat, he held appointed and elected positions.[1] He died in 1906.

TO WRITE A LINCOLN STORY TODAY, WITH ANY PART OF IT unpublished and authentic, is, you will admit, almost unbelievable, yet the writer of this article has the temerity to present it, making the claim that a small portion of it has never been published, is authentic, therefore true.

The history of the Lincoln family in Spencer County is familiar to everyone and this is only a little sketch of a few items connected with the Lincolns while in the county that may be of interest.

To begin with, Spencer County is proud of the fact that Abraham Lincoln spent the formative years of his life in this county, coming here in his eighth year, with his parents, from Kentucky.

---

* Armstrong delivered the paper on 28 February 1923 and published it in *Indiana Historical Commissions Bulletin* 18, *Proceedings of the Southwestern Indiana Historical Society* (October 1923): 54–62.

1 *An Illustrated Historical Atlas of Spencer County, Indiana* (Chicago: D. J. Lake, 1879), 22.

Lincoln in writing his own autobiography, in December, 1859, published in 1881, by W. H. DuPuy, A.M., D.D., who for 16 years was associate editor of the *Christian Advocate*, said as an introductory: "I was born February 12, 1809, in Hardin county, Kentucky. My parents were both born in Virginia of undistinguished families, second families perhaps I should say. My mother, who died in my tenth year, was of family of the name of Hanks."[2]

Referring to their arrival in what is now Spencer County, he said:

We reached our new home about the time the state came into the Union. It was a wild region, with many bears and other wild animals still in the woods. There I grew up. There were some schools, so-called, but no qualifications were ever required of a teacher beyond "readin', writin', and cipherin'" to the rule of three. If a straggler, supposed to understand Latin, happened to sojourn in the neighborhood he was looked upon as a wizard. There was absolutely nothing to excite ambition for an education. Of course, when [I] came of age, I did not know much. Still somehow, I could read, write and cipher to the rule of three, but that was all I have not been to school since. The little advance I now have upon this store of education I have picked up from time to time under the pressure of necessity. I was raised to farm work, at which I continued till I was twenty-two. At twenty-one I came to Illinois and passed the first year in Macon county, then I got to New Salem at that time in Sangamon (now in Menard) county where I remained a year as a sort of clerk in a store. Then came the Black Hawk War, and I was elected a captain of volunteers, a success which gave me more pleasure than anything I have had since.

I went into the campaign, was nominated, ran for the legislature the same year (1832) and was beaten, the only time I ever have been beaten by the people. The next and three succeeding biennial elections I was elected to the legislature. I was not a candidate afterward. During the legislative period I had studied law and removed to Springfield to practice it. In 1846 I was elected to the lower house of Congress, was not a candidate for re-election.

From 1849 to 1854, both inclusive, I practiced law more assiduously than ever before. Always a Whig in politics and generally on the Whig electoral ticket, making active canvasses. I was losing interest in politics when the repeal of the Missouri Compromise aroused me again. What I have done since then is pretty well known.

If any personal description of me is thought desirable, it may be said, I am in height, six feet four inches, nearly; lean in flesh, weighing on an average, one hundred eighty pounds, no other marks or brands recollected.

2 For the autobiography referred to, see Abraham Lincoln to Jesse W. Fell, "Enclosing Autobiography," 20 December 1859, Roy P. Basler et al., eds., *The Collected Works of Abraham Lincoln*, 9 vols. (New Brunswick, NJ: Rutgers University Press, 1953–1955), 3:511–512.

This is a whimsical and meager account of his early life.

The act creating Spencer County provided that ten percent of the pro-
ceeds of the sale of town lots should be used to establish a library. After
1820 several hundred volumes were on the library shelves but the name
of Lincoln never appeared on the records at any time as a borrower of
books.

Many stories have been told of Lincoln's borrowing a book from Josiah
Crawford, which book was damaged while in Lincoln's possession. It has
been told that Lincoln made a cabinet for pay, etc., etc. However, the following is the true account of it:

Lincoln borrowed from Josiah Crawford, grandfather of William F.
Adams, now living in Rockport, Weems' *Life of Washington*. This book
was taken to the Lincoln cabin and read many times. Lincoln placed the
book between logs in the cabin, and rain ruined the book. Lincoln went
to Crawford and said, "I got the book damaged, how much was it worth?"
Crawford replied, "Well Abe, you come over and pull fodder a couple of
days and we will call our accounts even." This Lincoln did.

William F. Adams' grandfather has told him the above story repeatedly
and I give Mr. Adams as authority.

It was while Sarah Lincoln was working in Josiah Crawford's home
that Aaron Grigsby courted her. Abe also worked at divers[e] times for
Mr. Crawford.

Josiah Crawford gave to his grandson, William F. Adams, of Rockport, Indiana, a school reader, *The Kentucky Preceptor*,[3] used by Lincoln.
Adams sold the book in 1865, to William H. Herndon, the law-partner
and biographer of Lincoln. The blank spaces in the book were filled with
Lincoln's writing.

Many have the impression that Thomas Lincoln and family at one
time lived on Anderson Creek, when he kept a ferry and Abe was the
ferryman. This is not true. The Lincolns never lived on Anderson Creek
and so never kept a ferry, but they came directly to the homestead near
what is now Lincoln City, about the year 1816 where they remained until
1830. However, in 1825 Lincoln was employed by James Taylor to manage a ferry at $6.00 a month. The ferry plied between the banks of the

3 This book is in the collection of Indiana University's Lilly Library, Bloomington, Indiana.

Ohio, also Anderson Creek. This perhaps gave rise to the belief that the Lincolns lived on Anderson Creek. In 1828 Lincoln went, as what was then called a "bow hand" on a flat boat, laden with country produce, to New Orleans.

Lincoln went to "A B C Schools" in Spencer County, kept successively by Andrew Crawford, a man by the name of Swaney, and Azel W. Dorsey. Lincoln told John G. Nicolay immediately after his first election, when giving a sketch of his boyhood days to be used in a biography, that he remembered these three teachers and no others.[4] He also stated that "what he had in the way of education was picked up after he was 23."

While in Spencer County, he roamed the hills and dells, studying the birds, the bees and the flowers; living close to nature, which undoubtedly helped to develop the wonderful human qualities so much admired and eulogized. All through boyhood and youth, Lincoln was in the habit of saying, and perhaps believing, that he would be President of the United States someday.

Lincoln never studied law while in Spencer County and was never a student in Judge Pitcher's office, as the Judge, like many others of that day, only saw an awkward, idle boy, full of pranks, equally ready for a fight, a joke, a sympathetic tear, as occasion demanded, never once catching a vision of the wonderful character developing in this sad-faced boy; and so refused to have Lincoln even as an office boy, and after he was elected President, Judge Pitcher steadfastly refused to acknowledge that Lincoln could even remotely be considered presidential timber.

In 1844 when Lincoln was a candidate for presidential elector and was making stump speeches for Henry Clay, he came to Spencer County, making one speech in the old courthouse, another at Gentryville in a blacksmith shop and another at a schoolhouse in Carter Township near what is now Lincoln City. While in Rockport, he stayed all night in what is known as the old Sargent house, an old-fashioned brick house perched high on a bluff at the head of Main Street. The door entering the room in which he slept has been an item of great interest to visitors in Rockport. On the door is an old-fashioned door latch, the lock of which is four and

---

4 Abraham Lincoln and Roy P. Basler. 1953. *The Collected Works of Abraham Lincoln* (New Brunswick, N.J.: Rutgers University Press) 4:61–63.

one-half by six inches, with a small brass doorknob which, when turned, raises the latch. Lincoln undoubtedly used this door latch while occupying the room. Mrs. Mary E. Frank now owns the house and has been offered a vast sum for this door latch.[5]

Lincoln wrote a good deal of doggerel and some poetry, some of it coarse and common, some of it charming as the following opening stanza of a little poem he wrote, just after having visited the graves of his mother and sister in Spencer County in 1844, and inclosed in a letter to a friend, explaining when they were written and their inspiration:

> My childhood's home I see again,
>   And sadden with the view;
> And still as memory crowds my brain,
>   There's pleasure in it, too.
>
> O Memory! Thou midway world,
>   'Twixt earth and paradise,
> Where things decayed and loved ones lost,
>   In dreamy shadows rise.
>
> And, freed from all that's earthly, vile,
>   Seem hallowed, pure and bright,
> Like scenes in some enchanted isle,
>   All bathed in liquid light.

In presenting two small Lincoln stories for the first time, I am reminded of the man who published a number of Lincoln stories a few years ago, and when asked why he hadn't published them before, replied, "Well, to tell you the truth, I never thought of them before." However, the stories I am presenting are true.

During the winter of 1887–8 my sister, Kate Evelyn Armstrong, taught in the public schools at Lincoln City. A Mrs. Oskins who enjoyed smoking a cob pipe, frequently came to the home where my sister boarded and often spoke of having known Abe Lincoln. On one occasion, Mrs. Oskins said, "Well Abe used to go with me and Lord knows I never would 'a' sacked him, if I'd knowed he was goin' to be President someday. But law! he was so ornery and shiftless, I wouldn't keep company with him."

---

5 The building no longer survives, but a historical marker stands near where this structure was located.

During the same winter, when my sister Kate was visiting in the home of Mrs. Mat Jones, an old lady named Lukins, who also loved a cob pipe, was sitting in a chair tipped against the wall, talking to my sister and spoke of knowing Abe Lincoln. During the course of the conversation, Mrs. Lukins removed her pipe from her mouth and said, "I could a' been Abe Lincoln's wife, if I'd wanted to, yes sirree, I could a' been the first lady of the land." Mrs. Jones said, "Now, Sarah, what are you talking about, you know you couldn't." "I could, too," said Mrs. Lukins. On being pressed further she said, "Well, Abe tuk me home from church oncet."[6]

In speaking of Thomas Lincoln, Redmond Grigsby, Sr., said, "Thomas Lincoln was a very kind-hearted man and cabinet-maker by trade." By way of diversion, I might say, however, that if Thomas Lincoln had made all of the cabinets attributed to him while living in Spencer County, he would have had superhuman ability. Abe Lincoln was not a cabinet maker.

In the relic room of the Spencer County Courthouse, is perhaps the only cupboard that Spencer County can authentically claim as having been made by Thomas Lincoln during his residence in the county, the lumber for which was whipsawed by Abe Lincoln. The cupboard has this note pasted on it: "This cupboard was made for Elizabeth Crawford by Thomas Lincoln and son Abraham, while they lived near Lincoln City, Spencer County, Indiana. Mrs. Ben Meace, granddaughter of Elizabeth Crawford fell heir to it and later transferred it to C. F. Brown [the present owner] of Rockport, Ind. (I will stop here to say that to C. F. Brown is due credit for the preservation of this cupboard, for at the time Mr. Brown came into possession of it, it had been sadly neglected, was not held in high regard by its owners and was on the rapid road to destruction.)

To proceed:

"In 1904, July 17th, Redmond Grigsby, Sr., brother-in-law of Sarah Lincoln Grigsby, identified it as the handiwork of Thomas Lincoln, father of Abraham Lincoln."

6 For list of women who said they had relationships with Lincoln, see Louis A. Warren, *Lincoln's Youth, Indiana Years, Seven to Twenty-one, 1816–1830* (New York: Apple-Century-Crofts, 1959), 155–158. No Mrs. Oskins appears in the list.

William F. Adams, grandson of Elizabeth Crawford, identified the cabinet as the original Lincoln cupboard made for his grandmother.

It is handmade and very roughly made; small pegs are used for nails; it has a great deal of carving and inlaid work on it. The letters E. C. are inlaid on the upper left door.

This cupboard was on display at a reception given to the Southwestern Indiana Historical Society by Mr. and Mrs. A. J. Cook at the meeting in Rockport on October 11, 1921, together with a number of Lincoln relics; for instance, a handmade, two-brick brick mold, (small pegs are used in this, also, instead of nails), and it was used by Abraham Lincoln when building a chimney on the first church built near Gentryville.[7]

The mold was given to my father, Joseph D. Armstrong, by the son of the man who helped Lincoln build this chimney. The pity of it is that the record of this mold was burned when my father's office burned, and while I have heard my father tell of its coming into his possession, and know positively it was the one used by Lincoln, I have forgotten the name of the man who gave it to my father. A Chicago paper had an account of this mold a number of years ago, but carelessly that paper was destroyed.

In 1860 when Nathaniel Grigsby[8] was in Springfield, Illinois, he had an interview with Abraham Lincoln in which Lincoln stated he intended to return to Spencer County and see the people whom he once knew, and felt it a sacred duty to erect a suitable monument at his mother's grave. This he never did. Nancy Hanks Lincoln's grave became over-run with weeds and briars. In the year 1874 my father, Joseph D. Armstrong, was in the woods surrounding Mrs. Lincoln's grave. Noting the neglected, lonely spot and knowing that hunters were trampling it under foot, that there was not the slightest regard paid to it, and realizing that soon there would be no way of locating this sacred ground unless it was in some manner cared for and marked, my father returned to Rockport and purchased a small marble slab, two feet high with a foot marker. The words "Nancy Hanks Lincoln" was the only inscription on the slab. A few of the business men of Rockport at that time contributed a small amount to help place the markers. My father had the grave cleaned and the markers

7 The cabinet and brick mold are both in Lincoln Pioneer Village, Rockport, Indiana.
8 See "The Grigsbys" by Mrs. Calder D. Ehrmann in this volume for a letter Lincoln wrote Nathaniel Grigsby (1811–1890) in 1860.

placed.[9] A few years later one of the Studebakers (Clement, Sr. Ed.)[10] was in Lincoln City waiting between trains and noted the modest slab at this hallowed grave and conceived the idea of a larger tombstone and so wrote to the postmaster at Rockport, Luman S. Gilkey, sending money for this purpose. Alfred H. Yates of Rockport, pioneer marble man, donated the work on the monument. The marble came from Italy through W. H. Sarvis, pioneer marble man of Cincinnati, who also contributed to this cause. Mr. Yates' work and donation on this monument amounted to more than the amount of money sent by the Studebakers. Mr. Yates went to Lincoln City and superintended the placing of it on the grave. The Southern Railway, through the courtesy of their superintendent, provided free transportation for its shipment and for all who desired to attend the ceremonies in 1879 when the monument was erected. F. W. Wibking, of Gentryville, had two teams at the station to haul the monument to the grave. General James C. Veatch, of Rockport, took small subscriptions from a number of the hundred people present, of not more than a dollar each, to procure funds to place an iron fence around the grave. In speaking of the event, one of Rockport's newspapers said: "Mr. Alfred H. Yates has just finished the stone that is to mark the grave of [the mother of] our martyred President—Lincoln. It will be put up tomorrow. H. C. Branham, Supt. of the C. R. & S. W. Ry., with characteristic liberality, has tendered free transportation for the monument and to all those who desire to go out on the morning train to see it set up. It is a plain slab, very heavy, and beautifully finished by Mr. Alfred H. Yates, whose excellent taste and artistic skill are admirably displayed in the work. There will be a number of prominent persons here from Evansville and other points, Douglas the photographer of Evansville, General Veatch and others. While it is not intended that any special display shall be made, the event will doubtless be an interesting one." So I feel that to two Spencer County men, great credit is due, to my father, Joseph D. Armstrong, who was the first person in the United States to pay tribute at the neglected grave of Nancy Hanks Lincoln, and to Alfred H. Yates, now 81 years old, for his large share in the Studebaker monument and

9 See *Lincoln Lore*, no. 218, 12 June 1933.
10 The editor's addition is incorrect; Peter E. Studebaker erected the stone.

who goes each year to Lincoln City to clean and care for the grave. The slab erected by my father was laid on the grave after the larger monument was erected and was literally broken to pieces and carried away by sightseers, during the next few years.

My father came to Spencer County in 1857 and in 1858 drew a picture of the Lincoln cabin, with its famous tree which tradition tells us was planted by Abraham Lincoln. James Atlas Jones, of Rockport, who worked for Atwell Morgan in 1861 at the time Morgan owned this farm, John Meir, Joseph Gentry, John L. Main, all of Lincoln City, also Alfred H. Yates, of Rockport, all agree that this is an exact drawing of the cabin as it was at that time. Mr. Yates, who came to Rockport in '56, remembers well the old log cabin where the Lincolns dwelt and the log church where they worshipped.

The church, which stood one mile west of what is now Lincoln City, was built of logs with a stick and mud chimney. It was a long, narrow building one and a half stories high, having a very, very large fireplace on one side of the building, with a pulpit made of roughly hewn boards. It had a window (with no glass but heavy wooden shutters, immediately behind it) at one end of the structure, and a ladder leading to the upper story where the people who came great distances might stay overnight. Split logs, with wooden pegs for legs, and a puncheon floor, were also features of this church, the logs of which were sold and used in the building of a barn. My grandfather, Rev. James Fair Armstrong, preached in this quaint old church many times.

In closing I will just repeat that Spencer County is proud of the fact that Lincoln spent his boyhood days within its confines and

> When in 1830 he ceased to be a Spencer County resident
> Who could prophesy that in the future he would
> Become the nation's idol, its President,
> So great and so good.

IDA D. ARMSTRONG (Moore) (1880–1933) was the daughter of Rockport businessman Joseph D. Armstrong, who, in 1874, erected a two-foot tall marker on Nancy Hanks Lincoln's grave. By 1879, when the current marker was erected on the grave, the small marker had disappeared.

28

★ ★ ★

The Artist's Ideal of Lincoln

GEORGE H. HONIG*

George Honig (1874–1962), a prolific sculptor and artist, possessed a lifelong interest in Abraham Lincoln. He grew up near Lincoln's boyhood home; and although a generation separated their time in the region, Honig nevertheless spoke of Lincoln "in the present tense and in the manner of an eye-witness observer."[1] For thirty-three years, he worked to build southern Indiana into a "historical mecca around Abraham Lincoln."[2] Even though Honig never achieved that lofty goal, he did help preserve the story of Lincoln's Indiana boyhood. This presentation demonstrates Honig's artistic reverence for Lincoln.

> Chisel his face with care, O, Sculptor.
> And carve each feature well
> For his was the face of a Martyr,
> A Martyr we love so well.
> *Alda McCoy Honig*

WE ARE ALL SCULPTORS, MOULDING AND CARVING CHARACTER on our countenance. Character building is the process through which we carve a great and lasting piece of work. When we cast our eyes upon the multitude we are convinced the world is filled with many, very many, poor artists: it is indeed refreshing to note an example of the power of expression and beauty of soul in such a face as Abraham Lincoln.

* George Honig presented this paper on 14 October 1924 and published it in *Indiana History Bulletin* 3, extra no. 1, *Proceedings of the Southwestern Indiana Historical Society during Its Sixth Year* (December 1925): 51–53.

1 Keith A. Erekson, *Everybody's History: Indiana's Lincoln Inquiry and the Quest to Reclaim a President's Past* (Amherst: University of Massachusetts Press, 2012), 149.

2 "George Honig, 87, Ex-Sculptor, Dies," *Evansville Courier*, 5 May 1962.

Let us all remember that we are sculptors and artists, and must manifest the same spirit of endeavor, inspiration and above all the same kind of sincerity which was the consuming desire of this beloved and immortal man, who once stood upon this soil. It is indeed Holy Ground.

Here in this neighborhood, at the age of seven years, Abraham Lincoln began his Spencer County career and for fourteen years, in this community, he acquired the artist habit of observing and studying and chiseling these sincere traits of character into every muscle and every feature of his wonderful countenance. Here in the savage wilds of Pigeon Creek young Lincoln grew up long, lank and swarthy, six feet four inches tall, strong as a giant, with a heart full of courage, ready and eager to fight it out with Destiny.

What does the face of Lincoln reveal? In studying the photographs we find features that reveal courage, fortitude, sacrifice, sympathy and love. His face is that of a strong man who knew the forest and was hardened to the storms.

He knew nature because he had lived close to its heart. No doubt in this vicinity the hardships of a pioneer life developed a rugged country boy, face tanned by the wind, muscles strengthened by hard labor, and a heart full of sunshine and cheerfulness; it gave him a wealth of love for all mankind. He was not the man who makes the most out of life, but the man who gave the most to life.

I am sure that you can feel the touch of a mother's hand as she laid it on young Abe's head and whispered the last message from loving lips: "Be good to your father and sister—be kind to one another—and worship God." Nancy Hanks Lincoln whispered those words, and now she rests on yonder knoll where the sunlight pours its golden wreaths upon her grave. We sense all of this, when we examine the photographs of Lincoln, and know what was in his heart when in after years he bowed his head and called her "My angel mother."

There is something intensely human about old photographs. In them still lives one who is absent. The expression on the face, the light in the eye, the kindness and forgiveness of the mouth; one can almost feel the heart beat beneath it; the man comes back.

The first photograph, youthful, expresses hope and courage; in it you can see the storms gathering about his life. You can understand from these pictures that Lincoln knew what it meant to start life at the bottom and work to the top. "He met misfortune face to face and overcame it with the might of manhood."

His psychological insight into human nature, his philosophical grasp on life and its opportunities, his appeal to the American heart and conscience, the Lincoln of everyday life, these inspire one with new courage and ambition.

You may read the hundreds of books on the story of Lincoln, but not until you look upon his portraits will you understand the real character of the man. Upon this face is written the history of a nation and the hopes of a people—the face of Democracy.

Richard Watson Gilder, the poet, says:

> This bronze doth keep the very form and mold
> Of our great Martyr's face—yes, this is he;
> That brow of all wisdom, all benignity;
> That human, humorous mouth;
> Those cheeks that hold,
> Like some harsh landscape, all the summer's gold;
> The spirit fit for sorrow, as the sea
> For storms to beat on; the lone agony
> These silent, patient lips too well foretold.
> Yes, this is he who ruled a world of men
> As might some prophet of the elder day.
> Brooding above the tempest and the fray,
> With deep-eyed thought and more than mortal ken,
> A power was his beyond the touch of art
> On armed strength—his pure and mighty heart.

GEORGE H. HONIG (1874–1962), a Spencer County native, was a student of Lincoln's Indiana history all his life. He was a well-known Evansville artist and sculptor whose work is still evident around the city. Honig was very active in the Lincoln Inquiry project and the creation of Lincoln Pioneer Village in Rockport.

29

★ ★ ★

What Indiana Did for Lincoln

BESS V. EHRMANN*

Bess V. Ehrmann devoted much of her life to garnering recognition for Spencer County's role in the Lincoln story; she was instrumental in the creation of the Lincoln Pioneer Village in Rockport, Indiana, and served as president of Southwestern Historical Indiana Society (SWIHS), an unusual role for a woman at the time. In this address to the SWIHS, Ehrmann defends their methods and findings against competing historians and corrects what she views as errors in public perceptions of Lincoln's Indiana life.

THE SUBJECT OF LINCOLN'S GREATNESS IS A NEVER ENDING source of inquiry and investigation. Hundreds of books have been written about this greatest American, some dealing with his political career, some with his life as a whole, some with his peculiar melancholy but more on his ancestry and possible influences of hereditary.

Writers for years have been trying to solve the mystery of the man's greatness. Born in poverty with but little schooling and living in a pioneer age when life was so full of hardship, *where* did Lincoln get his ambition to make something more than the ordinary of his life?

Read most any of the histories of Lincoln's life and you learn that he was born of humble parentage in Hodgenville, Kentucky, and at about the age of seven years he migrated with his family to Indiana. There after living fourteen years he moves on with his family to Illinois, and soon we find that he is making a name for himself.

* A copy of this presentation is in *Southwestern Indiana Historical Society Annals* 3: 113–135, at the Evansville-Vanderburgh Public Library in Evansville, Indiana.

Historians begin to inquire *where* and *when* did Lincoln absorb so much knowledge, where [did he get] his ambition for worthwhile things and most writers suggest that all these things came to him after reaching Illinois, because surely it was not in Indiana he acquired them, that state which was made the laughing stock of the world by certain novels dealing with the uncouth illiterate pioneers in the Hoosier state, people who are even yet spoken of as the "scum of the earth" by some. Now it has ever been an established fact that Lincoln read everything he could get to read and yet there must have been something else somehow, somewhere to inspire him. For Lincoln undoubtedly arrived in Illinois in 1830 almost if not entirely equipped for the great work before him.

Many historians writing of his life have spent a few days or a few hours in Spencer County, and then speak with authority on those early people. How impossible it is to always judge people's ancestry, breeding, and mental qualities by mere physical appearance or manner of dress, and so it is small wonder that people from a distance coming to a small country town and seeing its inhabitants for a few hours more or less are unable to speak correctly of its people. It is the desire of the Southwestern Indiana Historical Society to stamp out the blot of this supposed illiteracy of southern Indiana's early settlers and to describe fairly the better class of people whom the early travelers seldom saw and did not know. People who have lived here always, and their ancestors before them for several generations, know the Indiana pioneer type.

What then is the missing and unwritten chapter in his life? It has remained for an Indiana man of good pioneer stock to discover this missing history. In 1920 Mr. John E. Iglehart of Evansville, Indiana, with the active aid and co-operation of a select body of men and women whom he has described as belonging to the social and intellectual aristocracy of Indiana, most of whom trace a lineage back to the beginning of the State and a number to the early history of the Territory of Indiana, founded the Southwestern Indiana Historical Society composed of the nine counties of Knox, Warrick, Spencer, Vanderburgh, Perry, Dubois, Pike, Posey, and Gibson.

Soon after this organization was perfected, knowing that Lincoln was the society's greatest asset, and wishing to learn everything possible concerning Lincoln's life of fourteen years in Spencer County,

Mr. Iglehart started what was called "The Lincoln Inquiry." The purpose
of this Inquiry was to collect from many new sources information concerning Lincoln's life from 1816 to 1830, and in his opinion this missing
chapter in Lincoln's life would never be written until the life of the people
in the section of the state where Lincoln found his environment was
written, that the former was a corollary to the latter. His environments in
southwestern Indiana for at least the radius of fifty miles did not necessarily recognize county lines in social, business, and political life, and in
fact previous to 1814 there were no county lines in southwestern Indiana
other than those of Knox County, which originally covered a large part
of the old Northwest Territory.[1]

After the "Inquiry" was started and people in southern Indiana began
to write the biographies of their pioneer ancestors and bring forth letters,
documents, pictures, and old newspapers of that early time, it was discovered that there would be a wealth of history valuable to Indiana and
to the life of Lincoln. The Lincoln neighbors then form the background
for the boy Abe Lincoln who worked, played, and studied from the age
of seven to twenty-one years — the formative years of any life we will
admit, so it must have been with him, and then the field extended fairly
to the circle including the nine counties of this Society, with Harrison
County added (the location of the two early capitols of Indiana Territory and the first capitol of the State till 1825),[2] which circle is described
within the fifty mile radius from his Spencer County residence mentioned by Lincoln.[3]

1 When created in 1790, Knox County extended to Canada and encompassed all of Indiana,
western Ohio, western Michigan, a strip of Wisconsin along Lake Michigan, and eastern Illinois.
See *History of Knox and Daviess Counties* (Chicago: Goodspeed Publishing, 1886), 166ff. When
Congress formed Illinois Territory in 1809, portions of Knox County beyond the Wabash River
became part of Illinois. In the southern part of Knox County, as settlements increased, citizens
wanted new county organizations. Thus, in 1813, the large area south of the Wabash River was divided into two new counties, Gibson and Warrick. In 1818, Spencer County was formed from parts
of Warrick County and Perry County. See *History of Warrick, Spencer and Perry Counties* (Chicago:
Goodspeed Publishing, 1885), 35ff.

2 The capital of Indiana was moved to Indianapolis in 1825.

3 As Ehrmann elaborates later, the fifty-mile radius features prominently in the Lincoln Inquiry
because Lincoln told his adviser Leonard Swett that "he had got hold of and read every book he
ever heard of in that country for a circuit of about fifty miles." Leonard H. Swett, "Mr. Lincoln's
Story of His Own Life," in *Reminiscences of Abraham Lincoln by Distinguished Men of His Time*, ed.
Allen Thorndike Rice (New York: North American Publishing, 1886), 459.

In the vast literature on Lincoln's life and character given by Sand-burgh [sic] at more than 2700 volumes, as compiled by competent in-vestigators, the missing chapter in nearly all involves the knowledge and description of Lincoln's environments in Indiana, with the effort by historical writers to make an inadequate supply of unreliable state-ments of early travelers, and conclusions drawn from them, and Lincoln's poverty and humble home life supply the defect.[4] Ida Tarbell says our work has remedied this defect and for the first time historians are able to chart Abraham Lincoln.[5] While therefore the facts now submitted to the world in one sense may seem to deal with local conditions, both the actual environments of Lincoln in his Indiana life and the best evidence on that subject now obtainable from the children and grandchildren of Lincoln's associates here with the capable and industrious efforts in gathering together by us for the use of historians facts scattered over a wide field, neglected by or unknown to most of these writers, those few sympathetic historians who have so far furnished the best and fairest history of that Indiana life, including Tarbell and Sandburgh [sic], treat our work here outlined not local but of vital importance in interpreting the opportunities, life, and character of the man for which till now no adequate explanation has been found, and I need not emphasize its su-preme importance in the record of Lincoln's life.

Who were these pioneer neighbors of Lincoln? Where did they come from, what [was] their education, their home life and their ambitions, or were they the body of the people as pictured in those early novels of Indiana life?

It is the descendants of those early people who live near the scenes of Lincoln's early life and within a reasonable radius of such locality who are best able to interpret its environment. They know the character and life of the people in the same locality now, and have an accurate, definite

4 Ehrmann refers to the work of Carl Sandburg. His book *Abraham Lincoln: The Prairie Years and the War Years* is among the best-selling, most widely read, and most influential books about Lincoln. The two volumes of *The Prairie Years* appeared in 1926; and the four volumes of *The War Years* in 1939. The books have been through many editions, including versions of a one-volume edition Sandburg prepared in 1954. According to historian Merrill Peterson, more Americans have learned about Lincoln from Sandburg than from any other source. See Merrill D. Peterson, *Lincoln in American Memory* (New York: Oxford University Press, 1994), 389.

5 See Ida M. Tarbell, *In the Footsteps of the Lincolns* (New York: Harper and Brothers, 1924), 150.

understanding of their ancestors in Abraham Lincoln's time. They are intimately acquainted with the descendants of Lincoln's boyhood friends, have heard the stories of his life as related by their elders, and therefore ought to be in a position to write more understandingly of those early days and those pioneer people.

It took Mr. John Iglehart to realize that the missing chapter in Lincoln's life could never be written by outsiders, writers who would perhaps spend a few days or weeks in investigation in Spencer County, but it must be written by the children and grandchildren of those people who knew Lincoln's neighbors intimately, or who knew the type of men to which Lincoln as a frontiersman and a descendant of the backwoodsmen of the Alleghenies and the men of the Western Waters belonged and who appreciated more intimately than was possible for persons not so situated, the environments, opportunities and characteristics of the men of the type of which Abraham Lincoln was a true representative. There was a common type of pioneer in the zone north of the Ohio River who came from the South, to obtain free land as did Thomas Lincoln, and who found the chance of equal opportunity which could not exist in slave territory where society boasted and was dominated by an aristocracy founded on the cornerstone of human slavery.

Having been born in Spencer County and lived here practically all my life and being of the third generation on my grandfather's side and the fourth on my grandmother's, to live here, I have known the children and grandchildren of many of those pioneer people who were friends and neighbors of the Lincolns. These people can produce heirlooms of silver, china, linen, letters, books, and personally give evidence of culture that certainly prove their ancestors of good stock and breeding and not uncouth illiterates.

My mother told me much of the lives and histories of Spencer County pioneers as her father, Thomas Pindal Britton, came to Indiana from Virginia in 1827 and settled in Rockport which is seventeen miles from Lincoln City where the Lincoln family lived. My grandfather was a college man and unusually well-educated for that time and did much in helping to settle Spencer County.[6]

6 For more on Britton, see Bess V. Ehrmann, "Thomas Pindal Britton," *Indiana History Bulletin* 5, extra no. 1, *Proceedings of the Southwestern Indiana Historical Society during Its Eighth Year* (March 1928): 63–68.

History tells us that the Gentrys, Grigsbys, Jones[es], Hessons, Craw-fords, Oskins, and Hevverns [*sic*] were the nearest neighbors of the Lincolns. I have known the descendants of all these families, some of whom still live in Spencer County, all honest, up-right, honorable citizens.

Then in Boonville and Rockport were prominent lawyers, judges, ministers, many of whom the Lincolns undoubtedly knew and some of who, such as Pitcher and Breckenridge [*sic*] must have influenced the young Abraham.

Lincoln said to Leonard Swett that he had got hold of and read through every book he had ever heard of for a circuit of fifty miles from where he lived, and the owners of those books must have come in for their share of interest to this boy.[7]

Daniel Grass and his son were both men of good minds and breeding, and Abraham Lincoln stayed in the Grass home at one time.

John Pitcher was one of the most brilliant lawyers in the State of Indiana. He lived in Rockport when the Lincolns lived in Spencer County, and was postmaster from 1827 to 1832, and it has always been known that Lincoln borrowed books from Pitcher. There is one woman still living, Mrs. Hanby of Mt. Vernon, who heard Pitcher say that Lincoln had read some of his books.[8] It has been recorded by historians that Lincoln went often to the store of Wm. Jones in Gentryville and read a Louisville, Kentucky, paper that Mr. Jones received.

I have gone through many files of old Rockport, Indiana, newspapers and they tell much of the social, literary and business affairs of Spencer County and although published 18 years after the Lincolns left Indiana they show the type of people (for they were the same) who lived near the Lincolns all those formative years of Abe's life.

In these papers are mentioned banquets, balls, dinner parties, and musical affairs. There were long lists of books that could be ordered by mail and magazines advertised for sale. News from all over the world was printed and a reader of those early papers would have a general fund of information if they read nothing else. Such was the newspaper of Rockport, a town seventeen miles from where the Lincolns lived, a few years

7 See supra note 3.
8 See chapter 24, "John Pitcher" by Alice L. Harper Hanby.

after the Lincolns moved to Illinois. Judging from these papers that I
have read I know the *Louisville Journal*, which Lincoln read, would be a
still greater source of education to a constant reader.

In Boonville was John A. Breckenridge [*sic*], noted lawyer, and it has
been shown that Lincoln walked to Boonville to hear Breckenridge [*sic*]
in his law cases, and to borrow his books.ª 9

The Gentrys were very superior people, and Lincoln worked for them,
and was in their home a great part of his youth. He could not help but
be inspired and helped by the Gentry family, their standards of living,
their home comforts and their conversation. It was with Allen Gentry in
1828 that Abraham Lincoln made his first flat-boat trip to New Orleans.

The Gentrys lived in Gentryville and brought their produce from there
in wagons, their hogs they herded and drove overland, and butchered
them on a farm near Rockport owned by James Gentry. Then at the
lower landing in Rockport the flat-boat was loaded for its southern trip.

Near the old landing was the home of Alfred Grass, son of Daniel
Grass, Spencer County's first landowner and a cultured man.[10] Here
Lincoln [stayed] for the week or two loading the boat and preparing for
the southern trip.

In the Grass family is the story of how Lincoln pored over the books
that were in their home. Dr. John Grass of Denver, son of Alfred Grass,
speaking of those days said: "Lincoln would sit in the evening near the
table with the rest of the family until the tallow dip had burned out then
he would lie down on his back with his head toward the open fire place,
so as to get the light upon the page of his book, and there he would often
read until after midnight." Dr. Grass said his mother said it seemed to
her that he would bake the top of his head or wear himself out for want
of rest, but he was always up in the morning ready for his work.[11]

---

9 The name is properly spelled *Brackenridge*. As discussed in the annotations of a separate chap-
ter on Brackenridge, Louis A. Warren disputes the Boonville connection. See Louis A. Warren,
Lincoln's Youth: Indiana Years 1816–1830 (Indianapolis: Indiana Historical Society), 198–199.
Lincoln's contact with Brackenridge was more likely in Rockport than Boonville.

10 Daniel Grass made the first legal land entry at the federal office in May 1807.

11 The legendary image of Abe reading by firelight may have originated in the Grass home in
Rockport. Most other accounts of Lincoln reading place him outdoors. When he was nineteen,
Lincoln stayed in the Grass home for a week or two while loading a flatboat in preparation for his
trip to New Orleans.

As I have stated before, the Grasses were educated and well to do. Living here also in Rockport at that time were a number of educated and cultured people, a few of whom were: Judge John Graham, John Morgan, A. W. Dorsey, Samuel Hall, William Berry, John Proctor, John Pitcher, Thomas Britton, Alexander Britton, and John Greathouse. Out from Rockport but within a short distance of where the Lincolns lived were many families of refinement and culture and Lincoln's social affiliations were not alone in Spencer County but in Dubois County around the neighborhood of Enlow Hill, as George R. Wilson has described it, also in Warrick County there was Ratliff Boone [sic], Congressman during six years of Lincoln's time, and the people described by Mrs. Eldora M. Raleigh in a recent paper.

All these families Lincoln could have known and as he was of an inquiring nature we can be assured he learned all there was to learn from those he came in contact with.

We Spencer County people feel that the flat-boat trip to New Orleans that Lincoln took with Allen Gentry in 1828 when he was nineteen years old and had a man's stature and vision, had much to do with his inspirations and ambitions of later years because on this trip he saw slaves whipped and sold and said to his friend—"If ever I get a chance to hit this evil, I'll hit it hard."[12]

---

12 The original quotation is actually, "By God boys; let's get away from this thing. If ever I get a chance to hit that thing I'll hit it hard." It originates in William Herndon's interview of John Hanks, Lincoln's first cousin, once removed (his mother's cousin), and the line is of dubious value. Some regard Herndon more of an abolitionist than Lincoln; if so, Herndon may have sought sources that confirmed his own views. Moreover, while Herndon was compiling the Hanks interview, prominent abolitionist William Lloyd Garrison visited Springfield and stayed at Herndon's house; he may have biased Herndon's perspective even more. Further weakening the credibility of the quotation is that in an earlier interview with Hanks on 13 June 1865, when New Orleans was mentioned, Hanks described the trip but never mentioned Lincoln's outrage at slavery. Other interviewees of Herndon mention Lincoln's trips to New Orleans but do not discuss Lincoln's views about slavery. See Herndon's Informants: Letters, Interviews, and Statements about Abraham Lincoln, ed. Douglas L. Wilson and Rodney O. Davis (Urbana: University of Illinois Press, 1998), 44, 72–73, 114, 259, 381, 429. Hanks's later testimony about Lincoln's outrage appears on pages 457–458. In Recollected Words of Abraham Lincoln: Compiled and Edited by Don E. and Virginia Fehrenbacher (Stanford: Stanford University Press, 1996), 198, the editors rate Lincoln's statement arising from this situation as E—the lowest possible credibility mark they give. Herndon does say, however, that Lincoln spoke to him about the ugliness of a slave auction. See Michael Burlingame, The Inner World of Abraham Lincoln (Urbana: University of Illinois Press, 1994), 22–23; David Donald, Lincoln's Herndon (New York: Da Capo, 1988), 99–104.

Without attempting to go more fully into details, these suggestions illustrate the field in which the Southwestern Indiana Historical Society has been working for seven years under a common purpose, continuously producing and publishing to the world evidence of the opportunities existing in southwestern Indiana within a reasonable range of Lincoln's observations, investigations and inquiries, and particularly in Spencer and Warrick Counties. Some of our active workers have produced valuable research work in this direction before the organization of this Society, and the work is continuing by men and women of ability, education, and culture, who have been to the manor born, who are in sympathy with the people and the life existing within the environments mentioned, and who know that the fiction published in an early day does not correctly describe the people, their life and habits as they are actually known to have existed, as the evidence already produced shown.

Out of the mass of material which has been produced, and is now being produced by the members of this Society, may be mentioned several comprehensive papers referring to work done in whole or in part, in our field of work. Attention has been called by Ida Tarbell in her last book on Lincoln, in which she deals with awakening of Abraham Lincoln during his life in Indiana, and she gives particular emphasis to the work of this Society in general, and in particular to the first British Settlement in Indiana, located within the fifty mile radius of the farm on which Lincoln lived.[b] An article by Judge Roscoe Kiper on the "Boyhood of Abraham Lincoln,"[c] and the "History of Lincoln in Indiana" by Dr. J. Edward Murr,[d] as well as number of other papers, which are described in a comprehensive review of the work of the members of this Society by the writer, elsewhere referred to. Included in this list also is an address on the subject of the Environments of Lincoln in Indiana,[e] in which the pioneer type of the DeBrulers of Spencer County, of good ancestry and culture is discussed, relating to one of the distinguished families of Indiana, which grew up under conditions to those which produced Abraham Lincoln. This article shows what Lincoln's environments in Spencer County and within the fifty mile radius mentioned were, and what his opportunities were, and later work since that paper was read February 1925 makes still clearer the claim that we have accounted for the man Lincoln at 21 years of age in Illinois, by opportunities for development in association with men of all classes, including the highest, and access to the standard works of standard libraries while he lived in Spencer County, Indiana. This article contains a number of references to kindred bulletin publications in which further detail references are accessible to persons interested in this subject.

Enough has been produced and proper references furnished to all fair minded inquirers to satisfy them of the falsity, unfairness and misleading character of the old literature mentioned and of the truth of facts which show a condition of society under which a man of Lincoln's type, ambition and curiosity, could develop and did develop as Lincoln did.

That such people and such opportunities were known to and influenced Abraham Lincoln, should cease to be a matter of surprise to any thoughtful inquirer as has already ceased with many, that he had the reserve store of knowledge of books and men and a perfect acquaintance with human nature in pioneer life from the viewpoint of a master mind which account for the man as the world now known him when he left Indiana at the age of 21 for his home in Illinois.

The leading living historian on research for facts relating to Lincoln's early life, Miss Ida Tarbell, personally worked in the Spencer County field and interviewed men and women who knew Lincoln, and within the environments of the 50 mile radius mentioned by Abraham Lincoln, as well as in a wider field in work conducted and directed by her. This work was begun by *McClure's Magazine* in 1895, when under the direction of S. S. McClure and Miss Tarbell herself, also Miss Anna C. O'Flynn of Vincennes, a competent investigator was employed to work in Spencer County, one who had already collected a large number of photographs and had written a manuscript of unpublished life of Lincoln in Indiana. All such fresh new material was taken over by Ida Tarbell as editor of *McClure's* life of Lincoln mentioned, and the work followed later by her individually, and the *McClure's* life of Lincoln then resulted, and other books later were published by Tarbell. I know of no investigation in which so much time and labor and expense were expended in that work, while there were yet many such survivors living of the individuals who formed the environments of Abraham Lincoln while he lived in Indiana. The field was then fresh, among people now dead, and while Tarbell in such history used the work of others available, no such real investigation had up to that time to my knowledge been made, nor any as free from bias, and from that day to this Ida Tarbell has been an interested observer, and has missed no opportunity to keep in touch with the work of investigators. From the organization of this Society she has been in the fullest sympathy with our work, has recognized its value beyond all other historians or critics outside of our territory. From time to time expressions by her have been quoted and published in addresses made before this Society, and her judgment of the character and value of our work is based upon a personal knowledge of what we have done and a personal acquaintance with our leading workers who have received from her great encouragement. Miss Tarbell's attitude toward this work has always been in a broad minded spirit, free from all rivalry, and any desire to conceal the results of work from the public, so common generally on the part of book writers and students, and her judgment as to the character and value of our work is entitled to the greatest weight. I quote by permission from two recent letters written by Miss Tarbell to Mr. John E. Iglehart, one relating to a recent published address by him, elsewhere referred to, and one in response to an elaborate summary contained in a letter by him to her of recent date. After reading Mr. Iglehart's published address mentioned, Miss Tarbell, December 19, 1926, writes:

> Thank you for sending me this latest pamphlet of the Indiana Historical Society, 'The Environment of Abraham Lincoln in Indiana.' It is a genuine contribution to the subject.
>
> It places and gives an importance to the subject which it seems to me never to have had before. I think it will force future biographers to concede that there were big and inspiring influences exerted directly or indirectly on Lincoln in the period that he lived in Indiana.
>
> Up to now there seems to have been an unwillingness to concede that anything elevating touched him. The whole emphasis has been on the sordid and vulgar which, as nearly as I can make out, is incident to life everywhere. Wealth certainly never conquers it—sometimes seems to accentuate it. Academic education does not prevent it—simply gives it new forms. Nothing but character, high notions of life, really overcome sordidness and vulgarity. Is this not true? There was abundance of character and high notions of life in the atmosphere of Southwestern Indiana when young Lincoln

lived there, and you cannot make me believe that he did not respond to what was in the air.

Afterwards having read Mr. Iglehart's letter to her mentioned, she writes, December 30, 1926:

> It was not until yesterday that I found an opportunity to read your interest-ing review of the work which has been done in the last few years by the Southwestern Indiana Historical Society. It is an admirable statement, rounding up the activities as no one but yourself could do it, and pointing out at the same time the important relation these activities have upon the fourteen years that Abraham Lincoln spent in Southwestern Indiana.
>
> I told you before how essential to our full understanding of Lincoln I felt the work that you are doing to be. I have been long convinced that we Lincoln biographers have failed to chart the all-important intellectual and ethical influences which filled the air of your part of the world in its pioneer period. You are making it possible for us to do this charting. The really important thing about the life of Abraham Lincoln between 1816 and 1830 is what the serious people in that fifty mile radius which he covered were thinking and saying. We know that it was to the superior people in that neighborhood, the Judges Pitcher and Breckenridge [sic], that he looked. His mind was always occupied with what the superior in his environment thought and to capture these thoughts and aspirations of this time in this neighborhood, is altogether the most important Lincoln quest in rela-tion to Southwestern Indiana and, under your leadership I feel that the Southwestern Indiana Historical Society is doing thoroughly a fine and useful piece of investigation.

Some of the most valuable work of this Society both completed and partially completed work has not been published, and the Society is en-tering upon the new year's work with renewed energy, enthusiasm and hope, for there is yet a rich field along the line of previous work.[f]

Indiana has the right to claim a large share in the making of the man, Abraham Lincoln. It was on Indiana soil he lived those fourteen forma-tive years and it was those pioneer neighbors who undoubtedly helped to inspire him intellectually.

Biographers, excepting Ida Tarbell and Carl Sandburgh [sic], have passed over those fourteen years that Lincoln lived in Indiana and yet they were the years that formed his character, gave him his inspiration for knowledge, gave him his physical strength and his knowledge of pio-neer life. Years that counted in the making of America's greatest man.

In a recent magazine⁸ under the title "Books About Washington",
Dr. Albert Bushnell Hart, Professor Emeritus of Government, Harvard
University, reviews the recent books of Charles Moore, W. E. Woodward,
and Rupert Hughes, and referring especially to Woodward's George
Washington, "The Image and The Man", he says: "Woodward contributes
a valuable account of territorial and social conditions which surround
the young Washington. He has been the first biographer to seize upon
the frontier and the wilderness as educators of a future president." If a
distinction is to be made between a biographer and a historian, this statement may perhaps be literally true, but the interpretation of the frontier
and wilderness life as educators of a future president is by no means new,
and in fact Mr. Hart has been criticized in the literature of this Society
for ignoring the leading authority among historians upon the subject of
the frontier under circumstances when Mr. Iglehart thought it would be
expected that he would feel under obligation to deal with that subject, in
a fair introduction of the man, but wholly disregarded it.ʰ

Dr. Hart as the editor of "The American Nation, a History", vol. 14,
Rise of the New West, 1819–1829, by Frederick Jackson Turner, published
in 1906, the period covered in this book of Turner, 1819 to 1829, which covers the mature life of Lincoln from the time he was 10 till he was 20 years
old when he lived in Spencer County, Indiana, writes the introduction.

In Dr. Turner's Chapter V on Western colonization, he deals with the
subject of the American spirit and Western democracy, which he says
came stark and strong and full of life from the American forest, p. 69,
citing essays published by him.ⁱ In this chapter is a colored gap showing
the population in Indiana and Illinois in what Turner calls the transitional zone north of the Ohio River, populated by Southern pioneers
in the Northwest in 1820 and 1830, in which Abraham Lincoln lived
both in Indiana and Illinois the full period of his life after he was seven
years old. Chapter VI on Western development, like most of his papers
in this book, is pregnant with new truths of this character. These two
chapters on Western colonization and Western development deal in the
fullest manner with the movement of the frontier and the social and
economical development of the West under the frontier movement,
and in illustrating the wave of population out of Kentucky he deals with
the Lincoln family, tracing Abraham Lincoln into Indiana and to Illinois

in the transitional zone north of the river and the moving of Jefferson Davis "with the stream of southward movers to Louisiana and to Mississippi". In a number of his papers he makes Lincoln the product of the wilderness life on the frontier. Dr. Turner's great workʲ is now generally recognized as the first true interpretation of the frontier in American History, and these essays in various forms deal with the movement in almost every conceivable form in the emigration of the backwoodsmen of the Alleghanies [sic] and the Men of the Western Waters, from whom Abraham Lincoln is directly traced as a typical frontiersman,ᵏ and in this Dr. Turner calls attention to the effect of the frontier upon Thomas Jefferson, Andrew Jackson and Abraham Lincoln, and traces the great evolution of American democracy, the democracy of the world which came into full fruition in the states of the old Northwest Territory north of the Ohio River and west of the Alleghanies [sic], materially modifying the democracy of the Atlantic Coast States as it existed at the time of the Revolution. It will appear from the article already referred to by Ida Tarbell in her letter of December 19, 1926,[l] that Mr. Iglehart has been persistently presenting this doctrine as dealing with the effect of the frontier and the wilderness as an educator of Abraham Lincoln, and that Frederick J. Turner, who is the recognized head of the doctrine among historians has featured Abraham Lincoln as the product of the frontier and wilderness life, and that Mr. Iglehart as early as 1919 in his first historical publication quotes Turner fully on this subject, and has in all of his addresses and papers delivered and made before this Society continued to call attention to the fact that Abraham Lincoln is the product of frontier life, and that the formative period of Lincoln's life existed while he lived in Spencer County in the transitional zone mentioned, a fact which must be taken into account in no small degree in the interpretation by this Society of the acts of Abraham Lincoln during his life in Indiana and during the active part he took in the slavery question, and later his acts as president. Among others who have referred to the effect of the frontier as an educator upon future presidents may be mentioned a paper of Dr. David Muzzey, Head of the History Department of Columbia University, in an article published in the New York Times Magazine July 4, 1926,ᵐ which contains a very able sketch of Thomas Jefferson as the embodiment of the wilderness and pioneer movement and ideals of his time in the making of the nation. Turner says that Jefferson was not the Moses of American democracy, but the John the Baptist before the coming of Andrew Jackson, but he shows that the American spirit came in the transitional zone north of the Ohio River upon free soil and under free institutions as the agricultural democracy, while the democracy of Andrew Jackson was a militant one, which sought unsuccessfully to exist consistently with the southern ideal of an aristocracy founded upon human slavery as its cornerstone, the end coming in the Civil War.

The address referred to by Ida Tarbell in her letter of December 19th traces the effect of the frontier life on the characteristics of the Western mind, producing a militant individualism and other traits in the Western pioneer of the time and place of Lincoln's environments, not so well developed elsewhere, shadowed by Milburn when he says: "There is hardly a more striking commentary upon, or interpretation of, the pristine radical element of Anglo-Saxon character in the whole range of the records of our race, than is to be found in the history of its occupancy of Kentucky and the Northwest Territory."[n]

In an address before our Society at Boonville last year Mr. Iglehart gave these views in substance, quoting Milburn as the chief explanation why the southern half of Indiana had furnished practically all of the literature which the state of Indiana had produced, which he said Meredith Nicholson had stated as a fact in his "Hoosiers", but for which Mr. Nicholson had not been able to give a reason. Mr. Nicholson's father and grandfather were born in Kentucky.

A careful consideration of these facts ought to establish our claim that the descendants of the frontiersmen in the transitional zone mentioned—the workers in this Society—are the logical interpreters of the life of Abraham Lincoln after he left the state of Kentucky as Ida Tarbell has so well shown.

In my judgment the time has come when the attention of the world should be directed to this *new literature*, as Mr. Iglehart describes it. Already the attention of a number of other leading American historians, including professors writing history and teaching it in our great American universities has been called to this work, and a unanimous expression of approval in enthusiastic terms has been given to the importance and character of it.

EHRMANN'S NOTES

a.   Paper by Mrs. Eldora Miner Raleigh. "Lincoln in Indiana," *Indiana Magazine of History*, by Dr. J. Edward Murr, cited elsewhere.

b.   "In the Footsteps of the Lincolns" by Ida Tarbell (1[9]24), Chapter. 12, p. 150. Two new histories on Lincoln, one by Dr. Barton, "The Life of Abraham Lincoln", vol. 1, p. 116, and one by Mr. Louis Warren, "The Ancestry of Lincoln", p. 60, each quote from a paper written for the Southwestern Indiana Historical Society by Miss Ida Armstrong of Spencer County, and read by her before this Society. This shows the value of the work being produced by it.

c.   Proceedings of the 4th Annual Conference of Indiana History 1922, Indiana History Bulletin, No. 17, p. 50.

d.   Indiana Magazine of History, Vol. 13, p. 307. Id. Vol. 14, p. 13, Id. p. 148.

e.   "The Environments of Lincoln in Indiana", Indiana Historical Society Reports Vol. 8, No. 3, yet unbound, p. 147, by John E. Iglehart.

f.   In the Indiana Magazine of History, Vol. XXI, No. 1, appeared a poem upon Abraham Lincoln, the Indiana Pioneers, by Indiana's distinguished poetess, Albion Fellows Bacon, also an article called "The Lincoln Inquiry", which contained a list of 34 papers published by members of this Society, most of them under the auspices of this Society, and although the list was by no means complete at the date of its reading, Oct 14th, 1924, and a large amount of material has been added since that date, the paper was prepared by the author under an assignment to the task for one reason among others given at the time, that she had been born and reared and always lived in Rockport, in Spencer County, and had a knowledge of the matters involved in such investigation, especially in Spencer County. In that paper the author states the fair inferences and conclusion arrived at by Mr. Iglehart from the work of the Society up to that time in the interpretation of Lincoln's environments before he reached full manhood, which conclusion is substantially that reached by Ida Tarbell in her subsequent letters above quoted, and he calls attention to the fact that no other adequate explanation has ever been given or attempted.

g.   Current History, Jan. 1927.

h.   The Environment of Abraham Lincoln in Indiana by John E. Iglehart, Indiana Historical Society publications, Vol. 8, No. 3, p. 149, n.4.

i.   Contributions of the West to American democracy in Atlantic Monthly, vol. 91, p. 83, The Frontier in American History, p. 243, and The Middle West, International Monthly, vol. 4, p. 794, Frontier in American History, 126.

j.   The Significance of the Frontier in American History was a paper read at the meeting of the American Historical Association in Chicago, July 12, 1893, which first appeared in the proceedings of the State Historical Society of Wisconsin, December 14, 1893, and which was in 1920 issued as Chapter 1 in a collection of 13 essays and addresses under the title of "The Frontier in American History", all of which chapters center to the same common theme.

k.   See Ida Tarbell's last book, "In the Footsteps of the Lincolns", in which seven generations of the Lincoln family are traced from Massachusetts through New Jersey, Pennsylvania, Virginia, and Kentucky, and thence to Indiana.

l.   Environment of Abraham Lincoln in Indiana, p. 148, The Frontier, and notes.

m.   "Jefferson's Great Work Still Goes On", by David Saville Muzzey, N.Y. Times Magazine, July 4, 1926, p. 6.

n.   Milburn, Pioneer Preachers and People of the Mississippi Valley, 255.

BESS V. EHRMANN (1879–1963) was a Rockport, Indiana, native who dreamed that Spencer County would receive deserved recognition in the Lincoln story. She wrote a number of books including *Missing Chapter in the Life of Abraham Lincoln*. Ehrmann was instrumental in creating Lincoln Pioneer Village in Rockport, served as president of the Southwestern Indiana Historical Society, and was curator of the Spencer County Historical Society.

30

★ ★ ★

Correspondence between Lincoln Historians and This Society

JOHN E. IGLEHART*

Mr. Iglehart outlines a broad mission of the Indiana Lincoln Inquiry and the Southwestern Indiana Historical Society while assessing the region's influence on Lincoln and the inquiry's influence on Lincoln scholarship.

AT THE REQUEST OF YOUR SECRETARY AND OF THE EXECUTIVE Committee of this Society, I was prepared to present to the members of the Chamber of Commerce, former Senator Albert J. Beveridge, who, I personally know, desired to be present as an interested spectator at this annual session of our Society. He is unable to be present, and at the request of the same officials, I will occupy the time with a presentation to you of some interesting problems which confront us in our work, including some correspondence scheduled in today's program, in all of which Senator Beveridge has a strong personal interest. I regret very much that he is not here.[1]

* Mr. Iglehart offered this presentation on 28 February 1923 as guest at a luncheon meeting of the Evansville Chamber of Commerce. The presentation appeared in the *Indiana Historical Commission Bulletin* 18 (October 1923): 63–68.

1 Albert J. Beveridge (1862–1927), US senator from Indiana, was an intellectual leader of the Progressive Era. As his political career waned, Beveridge dedicated his efforts to history, particularly to biographies of Chief Justice John Marshall (which won a Pulitzer Prize for biography in 1920) and Abraham Lincoln. In January 1923, when Beveridge wrote to Iglehart that the Lincoln Inquiry's work was "of vital interest to me at present," Iglehart invited him to attend the society's next meeting in Evansville. After Beveridge agreed, Iglehart persuaded him to give an extemporaneous talk at this Evansville Chamber of Commerce meeting. Three days before, however, Beveridge came down with flu and was forbidden to travel. Albert J. Beveridge to Iglehart, 16 January, 14 and 27 February 1923, box 1, folder 5, John E. Iglehart Papers, 1853–1953, Indiana Historical Society, Indianapolis, Indiana.

Upon the publication of Bulletin 16 of the Indiana Historical Commission, which contained a transcript of the *Proceedings* of the annual
meeting in 1922 of this Society with all of the papers read and addresses
delivered at that meeting, a critical review of the work of that Society
relating especially to the "Lincoln Inquiry," was published editorially
in the *Indianapolis Star*, the first notice of which came to me in a letter
from Senator Beveridge enclosing the editorial clipping. In that letter
he expressed a deep interest in our work and desired to become more
intimately acquainted with it, and stated at some length his plans, which
had already been publicly announced, to devote whatever time was necessary to prepare and publish an authoritative life of Abraham Lincoln.
This review summarizes the work of this Society already done, and in
contemplation in the "Lincoln Inquiry," more accurately than I could do
it otherwise, and for that reason I quote from it.

> "The printed *Proceedings* of the Southwestern Indiana Historical Society,
> just received at the office of the Historical Commission, indicate that this
> society, composed of the eight 'Pocket' counties, not only has a rich field
> for work, but is diligently engaged in working it. Among the tasks imposed
> by the president, Judge John E. Iglehart, upon the several counties is the
> writing of biographies of the early settlers—the Indian fighters and the
> commonwealth builders. The subjects chosen indicate that the president has
> what Thayer characterizes as the art of biography—the ability to select from
> a mass of material, much of which is mere uninteresting detail, that which is
> of public interest.
>
> "Among the subjects treated by this Society, the most interesting to the
> general public is what is known as 'The Lincoln Inquiry.' Until very recently
> the years spent by Abraham Lincoln in Indiana have been practically
> ignored by his biographers. It is said on good authority that Herndon spent
> only four days in Indiana, and Ida Tarbell only one day, personally inquiring
> among Lincoln's neighbors. Lord Charnwood takes the year 1830, when
> Lincoln was in his twenty-second year, and when he moved to Illinois, as
> the starting point for estimating the influences of the times, chiefly political,
> upon Lincoln's nature and mind. This, no doubt, because Charnwood had
> no record of Lincoln in Indiana to which he could refer. He should, however,
> have begun with the earliest period at which the mind of Lincoln was able to
> comprehend the issues of the time, the Missouri compromise of 1820—the
> struggles in 1823 of the slave interests to amend the constitution of Illinois by
> popular vote to establish slavery there.
>
> "It is known that Lincoln was a familiar visitor at the home of John A.
> Breckenridge [*sic*] of Warrick County, and that Mr. Breckenridge [*sic*],
> an eminent lawyer, lent him law books, and that the two formed a close
> friendship. It is known, too, that Lincoln read law in the office of Judge John

Pitcher at Rockport, one of the great men of Indiana. Since one of Lincoln's most striking characteristics was an intense thirst for knowledge, it is impossible that he could have been associated with Judge Pitcher and not have discussed with him the most important events of the day. In the society of these men and with their books Lincoln's character was, without doubt, largely formed, and his nature and intellectual life molded in a marked degree.

"Since American democracy was not of New England or of Atlantic Coast civilization, but was born in the northwest territory, the history of pioneer Indiana assumes a new importance; particularly because of its effect on Lincoln. Unfortunately, the history of pioneer southern Indiana has not been written in full. Judge Iglehart is convinced, however, that there is in local histories and in families much material which will throw light on Lincoln's early life. Judge Iglehart is himself engaged in writing the life of Judge Pitcher; the life of John A. Breckenridge [sic] is also to be written. The purpose of 'The Lincoln Inquiry' is to collect from many new sources information concerning Lincoln from 1816 to 1830. Judge Iglehart considers it 'one of the chief assets of the society.' If it is carried on with the energy which has characterized the other work of the Society, it also will be one of the chief assets of the state."[a]

I should here correct a statement made in this newspaper criticism based on an inaccurate statement made in one of my addresses, printed in Bulletin 16, that Abraham Lincoln studied law in John Pitcher's law office.

He knew John Pitcher who was at that time the leading man in Spencer County and one of the able, indeed one of the great trial lawyers of Indiana. He was on terms of familiar acquaintance with Pitcher, had access to his library and borrowed one or more of his law textbooks to read, but never studied law in Pitcher's office.[b] Miss Ida M. Tarbell has probably made more exhaustive investigation in regard to Lincoln in Indiana than any other person who has published a biography of him, and is said by some competent judges to have written the best history of Lincoln in Indiana published up to this time. I have always regarded her work as the fairest to the people of the State of Indiana. Her book on the *Footsteps of Abraham Lincoln*, now in press, has brought her closely in touch with the work of this Society, of which she is certainly a competent judge and mention of which occurs in that book.

Upon the next meeting of the Executive Committee of this Society following, I was directed to invite Senator Beveridge to attend this annual meeting. In response to the invitation he expressed great pleasure, and gave the most positive assurance that he would be present if it were possible. In this I know he was sincere, for although he is a man who has many more invitations to deliver public addresses than he can fill, he is deeply interested in our work. In his letter of acceptance to me he said that he did not wish to make a speech, that he preferred to come as a visitor, that he was deeply interested in our work, that he was engaged in the preparation of the life of Abraham Lincoln, which would probably be a great work of his life, and under the circumstances (which I have not now time to state) he said he wanted to come here and study our methods. We all regret the inability of Senator Beveridge to leave home this very inclement weather, which has been prohibited by his physician, but we will have the chance to see him yet. For my part, I hail his entrance into the historical field! It has been lonesome down here not to have some man of vision from the outside who was able to sit with us and aid us in this work. Our work is pioneer work. It has never been done, as we are doing it, in the State of Indiana before. It is of local interest; it is of state interest; it is of national interest. Our work is greater than we know, and I shall welcome the coming of Senator Beveridge at some other meeting, that may be held in some other city in the near future.

I am glad of the opportunity to be able to present to a representative body of the city of Evansville and the large number of members of this Society some of the work and purposes of this Society which are thus brought prominently before you. The Southwestern Indiana Historical Society includes within its territory the eight counties of Posey, Gibson, Vanderburgh, Warrick, Spencer, Perry, Pike, and Dubois. An organization of this kind has been found to be more effective for investigation of pioneer life in early Indiana than the organization of county societies; for one reason, among others, that pioneer life in Indiana was well advanced before these eight counties were formed, and while they were yet part of old Knox County in Indiana Territory. Even after statehood, for a number of years all of these counties were included in the same congressional district, and most of them in the same judicial circuit for the purposes of election or appointment of judge and prosecuting attorney.[2] Practically

2 When created in 1790, Knox County extended to Canada and encompassed all of Indiana, western Ohio, western Michigan, a strip of Wisconsin along Lake Michigan, and eastern Illinois. See *History of Knox and Daviess Counties* (Chicago: Goodspeed Publishing, 1886), 166ff. In 1813, the large area south of the Wabash River was divided into two new counties, Gibson and Warrick. In 1818, Spencer County was formed from parts of Warrick County and Perry County. See *History of Warrick, Spencer and Perry Counties* (Chicago: Goodspeed Publishing, 1885), 35ff.

from its beginning in 1818 the village of Evansville gave promise of being the metropolis of southwestern Indiana, and drew to it in a sense a number of the leading men of southwestern Indiana, who from time to time lived in more than one county, and whose history cannot be found in the local history of any single county.

Since the organization of this Society we have held our meetings in most of the counties. I have traveled the circuit as a member of the Southern Indiana Bar in all of the counties except Dubois, most of them for fully fifty years, and am acquainted with the old families, and know the people of this section. I have presided at all of the meetings of this Society which have been held to this time, and I can truthfully say that in the various counties which compose this Society the meetings of this Society have attracted great interest in each community. The representative people of all of these communities have taken an active interest in the entertainment of the members at these meetings, and have aided materially in the progress of our work.

The meetings of this Society have been in all of these counties a centripetal point for the social and intellectual culture of this section. Vanderburgh County has been the last to organize, but it has been organized very effectively.[3] Mrs. George S. Clifford, chairman of the Executive Committee of our Vanderburgh County Museum and Historical Society, with the aid of her able assistants, recently gave a card party in the Coliseum which was attended by about five hundred of the leading women of the city, representative of our best people. At that meeting something over 270 additional members joined our Vanderburgh County Society, which had already been organized and with many other things had taken over the fine museum of Indian relics presented to it by Mr. Sebastian Henrich.

I am glad to have the opportunity to see present so many leading men in the city of Evansville, and to assure you that the movement represented in this Society is one well worthy of your attention and interest. I believe that the time will come when in this great city of southwestern Indiana, the centripetal point of intellectual and social culture will be, as it has been in every other county in the Society, in the meetings and work of our Historical Society.

3 Vanderburgh County was formed on 7 January 1818 from partitions of Gibson, Posey, and Warrick Counties and named for Captain Henry Vanderburgh, a Revolutionary War veteran and judge for the Indiana Territory.

Relating to my own interest in this historical work, and explaining how it happened that late in life out of the active field of professional and business life, I have been thrown to the surface, so to speak, in historical work, I wish to emphasize what I have on more than one occasion stated in historical articles published by me. The field of our work is almost wholly new. The history of southern Indiana began in the southern third of the state in that territory nearest the Ohio River and its tributaries, and as late as the period of 1819 to 1829, (the limit fixed by Frederick J. Turner as the period embracing "The Rise of the New West,") altogether the dominating part of the population of Indiana was in the southern portion.

Why the history of that part of the state has been neglected I have not time to state. Probably in part because the history of the rest of the state is, compared to the southern part, new, and co-existent with the period of newspaper publications which are preserved, and from which historical data may easily be obtained sufficient to furnish clear statements of the history of the early period; but the history of the people of southern Indiana has never been written, and many of the facts of interest in that particular have perished. The chief purpose of this Society, so far as I am able to express it, is to preserve and so far as possible put into print for permanent preservation, the history of the people of, and the development of the southern portion of the state in its beginnings.

For this reason we have resisted the efforts to impose upon this Society by the State Historical Commission any labor in connection with county societies, which are so efficiently organized; additional work, much of which relates to the present condition and future growth of our life in the various counties. There is no existing history of southwestern Indiana worth mentioning for real historical purposes. This is not the fault of our able historians, such as Dillon,[4] Esarey,[5] and Dunn.[6]

4 John B. Dillon (1808–1879) is considered "the father of Indiana history." After beginning in the newspaper industry, he eventually turned to history. His first and most frequently cited work remains *The History of Indiana*, published in 1843, and revised, extended, and republished in 1859. In 1845, Dillon became Indiana State Librarian. For a biographical sketch of Dillon, see John Coburn, "Life and Services of John B. Dillon," and Horace P. Biddle, "Notes on John B. Dillon," in *Indiana Historical Society Publications* (Indianapolis, Indiana, 1895), II (1895), 39–62.

5 Logan Esarey (1873–1942) served as superintendent of the Perry County school system and as principal of Vincennes High School before becoming dean of Winona College. After earning a

There are three sources of literature describing early Indiana, and the chief source of our history, including the three sources mentioned, may be said to be misleading, and do injustice to the better class of people; rather to represent the bottom layer of social life only.

The first of this literature which I mention is a book entitled *The New Purchase* by Baynard Rush Hall, a recent edition of which has been published by the Princeton University Press, entitled "The Indiana Centennial Edition," edited by Dr. James A. Woodburn of Indiana University, issued 1916.[7] The book never had much circulation for which fact "explanations" are given. The editor in his introduction gives a history of the first and second edition, and even quotes the Indianapolis *Sentinel* at the time of the publication of the second edition that "the original design of the work was principally to hold up to public indignation and ridicule the late Rev. Dr. Wylie, president of the University, with whom the author had a disagreement, which led to his leaving the college, and also the late Governor Whitcomb, General Lowe, and others."

Not only is this newspaper criticism true, but the work breathes a contempt for western character in the people with whom he was thrown, and shows that the author was for some reason unable to adjust himself to pioneer life and to become a part of it. He represented rather the sentiment of New England, and several Atlantic Coast states in addition, which looked with an unfriendly eye upon the growth of the West.[8] The eastern states opposed the addition of new states to the Union, and there existed a fear of the development of an agricultural

---

PhD in 1913, he joined the faculty at Indiana University as professor of history and was regarded as an authority on Indiana history. His published works include *History of Indiana*, *Courts and Lawyers of Indiana*, *Letters and Papers of William Henry Harrison*, *Messages of Indiana Governors*, and *The Indiana Home*.

6 Jacob Piatt Dunn (1855–1924) was a prominent journalist, lawyer, historian, and political figure. His historical writings include *Massacres of the Mountains: A History of the Indian Wars of the Far West* (1886), *Indiana, a Redemption from Slavery* (1888), *True Indian Stories* (1908), *Greater Indianapolis* (2 vols., 1910), and *Indiana and Indianans* (5 vols., 1919).

7 Hall came from Philadelphia to Indiana to teach at the seminary (a forerunner of Indiana University). The school passed him over as president, commencing a feud with school officials. Hall returned East and wrote *The New Purchase*, offering plenty of critical observations about Indiana.

8 Hall described most Hoosiers as illiterate. Allegedly he brought the first piano to Bloomington, and he saw himself as the first Indiana resident who understood classical Greek.

democracy on account of which theological students like Hall came West in part to preserve the religious and intellectual *status quo* of these older states. Such a thing was impossible and therefore Hall failed. Hall was wrecked on the shoals which even today confront every eastern man who for the first time comes West as a minister or teacher among western people—shoals which a tactless and narrow-minded man cannot successfully navigate. It cannot be denied that his viewpoint of the people is that of a leading actor in the play of early Indiana life where he failed to succeed and he makes no effort to disguise his bitterness as a bad loser.

I desire to say from this platform that the people of Indiana are tired of a third effort to perpetuate this book which never had real public recognition—the editor says "its sales were disappointing",—and for the printing of which no reasonable excuse ever existed. It was libelous in the extreme, full of express malice against leading men more successful than Hall was, who, upon the facts shown in the book, could do nothing less than discharge him as teacher.

It was cowardly libel as the author concealed his name and identity, so that in a prosecution for criminal libel he could not be identified, and the editor of the third edition had much difficulty in making a "key" now that Hall and his victims are all dead, giving their names.

The editor reports much indignation when the book was first published, as the public soon identified the victims of Hall's malice.

The doctrine of financial responsibility for breach of obligations in civil and commercial life involving libel, negligence of carriers, etc., has resulted in later times in the better protection of personal and private rights and safety than theological training or moral urge.

Recently an Indiana publisher issued a novel, wholly innocent of any malicious intent, but one of the characters lampooned by the author was identified (by a jury in New York City, where the publisher was served in a suit for libel) as the judge of a *nisi prius* court, and the author a disappointed suitor in that court, who gratified his malice in the book. The jury rendered a verdict of about $35,000 damages against the publisher.

In the *New Purchase* in all of its editions, there was no innocence of knowledge, by anyone who read the book, of the malice of the author, which is open and expressed.

The editor of the "Indiana Centennial Edition" of the book at the close of his introduction expresses a doubt as to the propriety of publishing an "account of an unseemly quarrel", yet "the publishers and editors of the present edition are convinced that they should allow" its publication, etc., and it "is therefore reprinted, college quarrel, personalities and all, without change or expurgation".

I hope that Princeton University Press managers are satisfied and will give us no more of this kind of missionary literature.

The second item of literature of this class I mention as Eggleston's *Hoosier Schoolmaster,* and in a less degree several others of his novels describing pioneer life and vocabulary. The *Hoosier Schoolmaster* is a dialect novel of low life. It was hurriedly written to furnish copy for a New York periodical, of which Eggleston had been chosen editor. The extraordinary history of this book furnished by the author in the second or "library" edition is well worth reading, as containing a view of western life not so well found elsewhere. Eggleston did not intend to create the impression in his book that the low life described by him represented the average, or the better class of people, but it was so misinterpreted, practically universally so outside of the state, and has always done the reputation of the state great injury. The book has continued to be a good seller, and is so much in demand in the Indiana libraries today that it is generally "out" when inquired for.

Relating to the position which this class of literature holds as descriptive of the people of early Indiana, it may be said that in the history of the better class of early Indiana people all such books are irrelevant and should be excluded from consideration.

The third source of material in which an attempt has been made to furnish some description of the people of southern Indiana is found in the numerous volumes dealing with the early history of Abraham Lincoln, who lived in Spencer County from the time he was nine years of age.[9] [c] When this Society was organized, in an inaugural address, I said that "The Lincoln Inquiry" was one of the chief assets of this Society, but that we should not permit it to overshadow the other very important lines of our work. Two years later

---

9 Abraham Lincoln actually lived in Spencer County from the time he was seven years of age.

in an annual address to this Society, I said on that subject, that on that point I had changed my mind. That I had come to the conclusion that the missing chapter in Lincoln's life in Indiana results in a substantial degree from the fact that there is a missing chapter—which fact we all recognize—in southern Indiana life, and when we have supplied the latter, which we hope to do, we will, I think, have furnished the facts from which the competent historian will in a measure supply the former.

Last year I received a letter from Miss Ida Tarbell, who was then preparing for the printer her manuscript on her newest work, *The Footsteps of Abraham Lincoln*, and in this letter she sought to obtain from me such information as I could give her for use in her work.

In response to Miss Tarbell's letter, I sent her by return mail copies of magazine articles, as well as printed addresses of this Society, giving my views as publicly expressed, and also some additional facts which were supplemented by me later in an interview with her when in New York during the holidays I met her.

I take this opportunity in stating the viewpoint which I gave to Miss Tarbell, to add some further suggestions relative to what seems to me to be the correct standpoint of the investigator after facts, relating to the history of Abraham Lincoln, while he lived in Indiana. Explaining my own relations to the work and to the people of southern Indiana, I said in substance that I was born in Warrick County in 1848, less than eleven years after the birth of Edward Eggleston, still the pioneer age in southern Indiana; that I was trained as a lawyer in the school in which John Pitcher was first a pupil, then a teacher; that my first schoolteacher was one of the Squeers type (lacking Squeers' criminal instincts and record) who reduced cruelty to children to an exact science. My grandfather sat upon the Board of Justices of Warrick County from 1825 till 1831, when the law abolished that form of county government. He lived about twenty miles from the Lincoln farm, and was much of the time in Boonville, to which place it seems during those years until 1830 Abraham Lincoln was much attracted as a spectator to court trials at Boonville and elsewhere.

I disclaimed interest in the knowledge of facts and documents of the kind about which Miss Tarbell inquired, but again stated that in my judgment the missing chapter in Lincoln's life would never be written until the missing chapter in the life of the people of southwestern Indiana had been written; that upon the latter work, which necessarily embraced in a substantial degree the former, our society was now engaged; and that there was no shortcut on getting into "The Lincoln Inquiry," but as our work progressed, light would be thrown upon it.

This seems to me to be the best solution at the present time to the inquiry about Abraham Lincoln's life in Indiana from 1816 to 1830. The facts and circumstances relevant to that inquiry can only be found and put together by the most painstaking and discriminating study of the environments existing in the whole of southwestern Indiana, certainly including the eight counties within this district, all of which, as I have stated, had but recently been created out of old Knox County. I believe when this work is done the application of the rules applying to circumstantial evidence will confirm my judgment as to the fact that Lincoln availed himself of all of the opportunities existing in pioneer life in this section when he lived in Indiana; but that the problem involved in such inquiry when first made after Lincoln's death was too complex for, and beyond the vision of the only witnesses who could testify, and who might have known the actual facts had they been able to appreciate them at the proper time, and been interrogated along these lines. I believe also that my conclusion is the correct explanation of the equipment of the man Lincoln as he is found in Illinois in 1830 and later. Such an interpretation would furnish the method of solving the problem underlying "The Lincoln Inquiry," none other having been furnished by the historians.

The evidence can be found when it is discriminatingly searched for. The movement of people and of trade north and south, as well as east and west in southwestern Indiana during the period mentioned, was what may be called "fluid" and not "frozen" to use a modern figure coined in the financial world. By this I mean that for the space of fifty miles or greater, in all directions, from the Lincoln farm, contact with the people was accessible to Lincoln. He was not confined to the meagre showing of facts which his biographers furnish, and it cannot be reasonably inferred because the people of those times are all dead, and left no record easily available, that therefore they did not exist and were not potential factors in the life of that period.

Lincoln himself in later years stated that he had read every book available within the radius of fifty miles of the farm upon which he lived, and this included well-known centers of culture with the best opportunities of the time for a man like Lincoln, so thirsty for knowledge, to learn and to know substantially what was worth knowing in that section at that time.

Vincennes was still the mother city of a large territory, including all this section, and was the residence of many of the leading politicians and lawyers, able men, who were well-known, and traveled on professional political business, as well as in trade. Men like Judge Isaac Blackford, General W. Johnson, and other prominent men, were speculators in land, which fact the various county records show. General W. Johnson lived in Evansville for about a year and acted as deputy clerk about 1820.

There was a stage line from Evansville to Vincennes, from 1824 continuously, making at least two trips each way a week, till railroads were built. Evansville was the receiving and discharging point for New Orleans, and the Ohio River traffic for Vincennes, and all intermediate territory, as well as a wider territory as newspaper advertisements of the time show.

New Harmony was during that time at its zenith, a point of world-wide importance, where resided men of national reputation, and where the intellectual standard, as appears in the magazine and newspaper literature then published in New Harmony, was high, judged by the highest standards of that period throughout the country. In 1827 Robert M. Evans lived in New Harmony. His brother, James Evans, was a wool carder at the same time, and earlier in Princeton, to which point history says Abraham Lincoln walked once each year to have his wool carded.

In 1822 a road was built from New Harmony to Boonville, built in Vanderburgh County in two sections, extending from the Warrick County line to the Posey County line, centering at Saundersville, the heart of the first British settlement in Indiana.

Corydon was the capital of the state till 1825, and long after that period the residence of prominent men, and travel was continuous between that point and Vincennes and Evansville by roads which went past the Lincoln farm.

The entire eight counties in the Society, including Lincoln's county of Spencer, were all in the same judicial circuit, for judges and prosecuting attorneys, and the lawyers, including leading men of the time, as commonwealth builders, followed the judge on the circuit on horseback. Judge James Hall during that period was circuit judge in southern Illinois where conditions were similar in this respect to conditions in southwestern Indiana, and he says that in this manner the judge, prosecuting attorney and lawyers who traveled together, spent nearly half of their time on horseback. The court seldom lasted over two or three days, unless some felony or tort case with many witnesses was to be tried.

It was on these occasions that Lincoln attended court at Boonville and Rockport. In February, 1823, Thomas J. Evans, formerly of Princeton, a brother of General Robert M. Evans and of James Evans, the wool carder, advertised in the Evansville *Gazette*, that he had moved to Rockport and would practice in all of the counties in southwestern Indiana.

The doctors had well organized societies, which held their annual meetings in Evansville and elsewhere, the members of which extended through the various counties, and the regulation of the practice of medicine by statute and by license from these societies was a matter of much public interest.

The Congressional district in Lincoln's time included southwestern Indiana, and excepting two years, from 1824 to 1838 and during all of Andrew Jackson's time, Ratliff Boon, who lived near Boonville, and within about twenty miles of Abraham Lincoln, was congressman for these counties, including Spencer County. He was elected on the Jackson ticket in 1828 when Lincoln, interested in the study of the law, was nineteen years of age, and (as he was at seventeen years of age) six feet two inches tall, or over. The *Congressional Record* shows that Ratliff Boon was a self-constituted floor leader of Jackson in the House of Representatives, and Jackson spoke of him as "faithful among the faithless". There is no doubt that Ratliff Boon and the Lincolns in Spencer County were well acquainted, while Boon was their congressman. When Lincoln left Indiana he was a voter, and there were a number of voters among his near relatives. Boon was an attractive and persuasive man as a campaigner, and was the political czar of southwestern Indiana, a strict party man, and the Lincolns lived on one of the main roads which Boon must and did travel in passing through Spencer County.

Herndon quotes one verse of a doggerel song that Lincoln sung at that time, as follows: "A stanza from a campaign song which Abe was in the habit of rendering, according to Mrs. Crawford, attests his earliest political predilections:

> Let auld acquaintance be forgot
> And never brought to mind,
> May Jackson be our president,
> And Adams left behind.

History records that the Lincolns followed the Boons west over the mountains, and I have made the statement in print that the Lincolns followed the Boons to Harrison County, Indiana, and that I believed that Thomas Lincoln followed Ratliff Boon to Indiana in 1816. Boon came in 1809, and there is as much evidence that Thomas Lincoln followed Ratliff Boon to Indiana in 1816 as for any other reason, for settling where he did. Lincoln settled within twenty miles of Boon, by no means a long distance in those days, and much closer than to his relatives, the Lincolns who followed the Boons in Harrison County.

The county records, the congressional records, the court records (particularly of the movements of the leading members of the bar, which appear in the order books of the courts in each of the counties), the minutes of the governor of the Territory and State of appointments to office, the early history of the churches, the history of New Harmony and of the first British settlement in Indiana, will furnish interesting facts in the line of these suggestions.

Individual families are known to have moved into and out of the Lincoln neighborhood. Some have left their descendants still living in the neighborhood, some have left their names in the names of creeks, townships, and villages.

There were during all that time newspapers published at Vincennes; most of the time at New Harmony; from 1821 to 1825 at Evansville, all of the time at Louisville, and history records that Lincoln read the Louisville newspaper, and the scant direct evidence furnished by the historians, records that Lincoln did read the newspapers.

Of course, in the absence of any record, it will be presumed that John Pitcher and John A. Breckenridge [sic] had the available literature of the time, books and newspapers, and history records that each of them furnished these to Abraham Lincoln.

Any man who knew John Pitcher as I knew him for several years before he finally retired from the practice of the law, would not have cared to ask him whether he took the Vincennes *Sun*, and other current literature available at that time.

The same family of Casselberrys have left their name in the name of a creek in Perry County, as well as a township in Posey County during this period.

The Harts were a great western pioneer family, the three brothers were partners with Richard Henderson in his great scheme of Richard Henderson and Company, and in the very beginning of Warrick County, the Hart family settled, while it still included Spencer County. Nathaniel Hart was the first county agent of Warrick County, and one of the leaders. The Hart families have always been prominent in Warrick County, and are to this date. Members of that family were early in Dubois County. The Harts were especially prominent in Kentucky, and one of the prominent members of that family from Posey County is a member of this Society. One Kentucky history mentions the claim of one of the Hart brothers, that he consulted with Daniel Boone in the beginning of Kentucky history, but that he was entitled to priority over Boone in his claim as pioneer in early Kentucky settlement.

John A. Graham was appointed (I think by Lincoln) Assistant Register of the United States treasury, and lived and died in Washington after 1870. The Graham family in those days lived both in Spencer and Warrick Counties, and they were people of culture. I remember very well about 1870 that my father after his visits to court in Washington City would report with much interest and pleasure his visit to John A. Graham, who was one of his boyhood friends.

Many other families which I have not time to mention may be traced during this period in this locality, where descendants are still living in this section. Miss Tarbell in her letter to me speaks of these including people in the English settlement as "many fine upstanding people".

That Lincoln knew many of these people, and knew about all worth knowing of them, I believe. I believe that in 1830 Abraham Lincoln knew pretty well all that was worth knowing in his locality which could be learned by reading the papers, intelligent inquiry, and personal acquaintance with the better class of people whose history has not been properly recorded as I have shown.

Every well written biography and sketch of pioneer conditions of early Indiana people and life ought to throw some light, however small, on "The Lincoln Inquiry."

The history of those families and others who were not remote neighbors of the Lincolns in Indiana will furnish the environment of Abraham Lincoln while he lived in Indiana.

These are some suggestions of lines of inquiry relating to the life of our people in which Abraham Lincoln and his opportunities figured. I have in magazine articles referred to other items of this class of evidence, but must leave its investigation to others.

I began this historical work too late in life to finish it as I would like to do.

Whatever vision of interpretation I may have into "The Lincoln Inquiry," which I have treated in my addresses as only one of the important lines of our work in historical research in southwestern Indiana, it has come to me in part at least from birth and early training under pioneer conditions—influences which I have described in addresses, the most important of which I have published in magazine articles; also in a long, active career as a trial lawyer, who has lived on the battle line, whose duty imposed judicial investigation of facts, and evidence, both direct and circumstantial, with a sense of responsibility for thoroughness and accuracy based on hard work without which a lawyer in such work must fail. In addition, I have had very active experience in the organization and work of this Society from its beginning, and work of similar nature while acting as chairman of the Centennial Historical Commission of the City of Evansville previous to the organization of this Society.

The continued opportunities during my entire professional life in Evansville and southwestern Indiana as remote successor in the law practice to Judge Battell, an original pioneer, John Ingle, Jr., Horatio Q. Wheeler, and as direct successor to my father, all pioneers, placed me in touch with the unfinished work of many of the original pioneers themselves, which I have finished in my own professional life. Many of the original pioneers I have known personally, as well as most of their children who have succeeded in life.

The preservation of the county records, including those of the clerk's office, contained pleadings (especially bills and answers in chancery suits, in their nature descriptive and often historical in narrative, with occasionally a deposition, always interesting), which have placed me in close touch with the master spirits of the early Indiana Bar, which was established chiefly in the southern portion of the state. They have left their impress for good on our early history, for the qualities of a lawyer necessary to the best work in pleading, have changed little in one hundred years.

All these have given me a knowledge of the times and people often accurate as to such as I have never known or seen, but as I have learned from corroborating circumstances.

It has been, and will be my purpose, to deliver over this trust to other capable and willing workers in their own fields as well, who will take it up where I may leave it unfinished.

In addition to a number of valuable papers, original research work by members of this Society, are at least two sources of record of facts worthy of mention. First, George R. Wilson, of Jasper and Indianapolis, author of a history of Dubois County, has compiled more than a dozen volumes (continually increasing) of unprinted manuscript references to sources of relevant facts relating to people, events and matters of public interest in early Indiana. These are his private property, but I have never failed to obtain interesting facts on inquiry from him, and have twice drafted him for important biographical sketches which he has made, furnishing important additions to early Indiana history.

The other is a series of historical articles published under the title of "The Pocket Periscope" on the editorial page of every Sunday morning for three years past in the Evansville *Courier*, the leading morning daily in this section. These articles are attractively written and have created a real interest among the readers of that paper in a large territory. Their permanent value to my mind is in the fact that their writer, Thomas James de la Hunt, of Cannelton, author of a history of Perry County, has collected from many sources, much of them unavailable in their original form, a very large amount of material which, if put together in a single volume with a proper index, would be of real value for present use by historical writers. Their contents would be suggestive to the members of this Society in our current work; and as such would make an excellent beginning in the systematic preservation in available form of much good material. It is the purpose of this Society, if practicable, to have these "Periscope" articles collected, edited and published in a single volume with a good index for use in this Society, and in the State of Indiana, for legitimate historical purposes. They would, I believe, stimulate interest throughout the state.

In response to my letter to Miss Tarbell, I received from her a letter which reads as follows:

> November 20, 1922
> Judge John E. Iglehart
> Evansville, Indiana.
>
> My Dear Judge Iglehart:
>
> I am under many obligations to you for the trouble you have taken in my behalf. Your letter is so full and so suggestive that I feel that it would be much wiser for me to study it and the documents you have sent me, before talking with you.
>
> I am glad that you take the view you do. It is mine. I do not believe that Lincoln can be understood without understanding better than I do, at least, Southwestern Indiana. What that country was, what its people thought and did, had, I am convinced, a deep influence on the young Lincoln. I feel that in my previous Lincoln work I have been too much interested in picking out the facts and incidents which could be directly connected with Lincoln, that I have not sufficiently studied his intellectual and moral and social environment, particularly in the years that he was in your part of the country. I am more and more convinced, too, that that environment was shot through with fine feeling and ideas. I shall be greatly interested in studying what you are doing.
>
> I have decided to go through to New York tonight, instead of going down to Evansville. I am much needed there, but later I hope I shall have a chance of talking with you. I fear I cannot go on to Evansville in January, but I shall depend upon you to let me know how I can get copies of all of your proceedings, and later I surely shall get to your part of the world.

I am much gratified by your point of view. I think it's the sound one, and it is bound to illuminate the life of Lincoln as well as to introduce us to many fine, upstanding people.

Very sincerely yours,
    (Signed) IDA M. TARBELL

In a letter dated December 4th Miss Tarbell says "I am much interested in the work in Southwestern Indiana. It seems to me of the most fundamental sort."

Among other letters which our program calls for are several from Rev. Dr. William E. Barton, author of several books on Abraham Lincoln. May 25, 1922, he writes and puts the following inquiries. The first and second questions I have answered in this address in a general way as far as I am able.

"What effect did Indiana have upon the career of Abraham Lincoln?"
"Was his life in any material respect influenced by reason of his 14 years in Indiana?"
"Would it have been as well for him if he had continued to live in Kentucky and gone from that state in 1830 to Illinois; or if in 1816 he had gone direct to Illinois from Kentucky?"

For want of time to answer them I did not do so at the time, but in the meeting of this Society at Boonville, last year, my remarks covered in part the third inquiry above mentioned, substantially as follows:

That the curse of the slave code in Kentucky affected the development of an ambitious and capable youth. Under that code, manual labor such as Lincoln was destined to endure was the badge of servitude. Social surroundings of the most humble character, out of which Lincoln arose from the bottom layer of the social world, furnished a bar to that patronage in public opinion and of leading men almost, if not entirely, necessary under southern ideals to great success in political life. Whether Lincoln, if reared in Kentucky as he was in Indiana, would have studied law as he did in Indiana or Illinois no one can say, but I seriously doubt it.

Conditions outlined in Turner's definition of the development of the chief characteristic of agricultural democracy, represented in the northwest by Lincoln as compared to the militant type represented by Jackson in the southwest,—the right and opportunity of the individual to rise to the full measure of his natural and acquired powers under conditions of social mobility—did not exist in Kentucky in Lincoln's time, before the Civil War.

If Lincoln had taken the pathway of the legal profession in Kentucky as he did in Illinois, the wonderful opportunity and progress opened to him in the latter state were impossible to him in Kentucky. No person familiar with Kentucky and Illinois history during that period can doubt it. It was the aggressive struggle for expansion and existence of the slave power, entrenched in free territory, which gave the one great opportunity of his life to Lincoln.

Free speech and a free press were denied under the slave code—a curse which the best and greatest representatives of the South in its literature since the Civil War now freely concede,—made a southern literature impossible, before the Civil War.

Had Lincoln chosen the legal profession in Kentucky, he would in my judgment have been merely a vigorous, able lawyer, and a dangerous opponent in a jury trial, such as our western life of that period (as exists today) produced in nearly every judicial circuit; the representative of a class of men who when they are right, and properly prepared in advance, cannot be overmatched in the battle for the truth.

As this Bulletin goes to press I have been permitted to read some of the advance pages of Miss Tarbell's latest book, *In the Footsteps of Abraham Lincoln*, now being published in the Los Angeles Sunday *Times*, in which an interesting reference is made to the work done by this Society, bearing upon the particular line of investigation which I am in this address outlining with still fuller detail.

In the chapter dealing with Lincoln's opportunities while living in Indiana she gives much emphasis to the method of investigation outlined by this Society.

> There has been in the last few years a considerable amount of solid work done on the character of the men and women who settled this corner of the state; particularly important from the Lincoln standpoint, is that of Judge John E. Iglehart, of Evansville, Ind., president of the Southwestern Indiana Historical Society. Judge Iglehart's work gives us a better basis for judging of the calibre of the men under whose indirect influence at least Lincoln certainly came at this time, than we have ever had before. He has developed,

with a wealth of detail, the character of the English settlement which started in 1817 north of Evansville and twenty-five or thirty miles west of where Lincoln lived—a settlement whose descendants are still among the leading people of the section.

These English settlers, as well as the Scotch and Scotch-Irish that came with or followed them, were intelligent, thoughtful people, many of them with property, who had left their homes because of the dark prospects in Europe. Their small properties, they complained, were 'wearing to pauperism'. Moreover, the interference with their social and religious affairs were so constant and humiliating that they were willing to undergo any hardships to get a better chance and greater freedom in the world. The experiences of these men at home, the ideas that they brought with them, the way they went to work to build up communities—all of these things must have been matters of discussion at Jones' grocery in Gentryville and everywhere else that Lincoln met with men. The English settlers brought books, many of them, as Judge Iglehart shows, and it is his opinion that many of these books found their way into young Abraham Lincoln's hands.

A reference to a straw—a scrap of evidence from that English settlement (whatever may be its value I shall not judge) may be pardoned if I am required to give personal testimony. In Herndon's *Lincoln* (1889), is a poem of eight stanzas of which he says Mrs. Crawford furnished him a manuscript copy, but which he says was composed by Abraham Lincoln previous to the marriage of his sister Sarah in 1826.

I quote them all in order that the question of the authorship of the poem may be tested in part by its "internal evidence", the method by which Gladstone solved to his own satisfaction the controversy as to the authorship of the Homeric poems.

When Adam was created
    He dwelt in Eden's shade,
As Moses has recorded,
    And soon a bride was made.

Ten thousand times ten thousand
    Of creatures swarmed around
Before a bride was formed,
    And yet no mate was found.

The Lord then was not willing
    That man should be alone,
But caused a sleep upon him,
    And from him took a bone.

And closed the flesh instead thereof,
    And then he took the same
And of it made a woman,
    And brought her to the man.

Then Adam he rejoiced
    To see his loving bride
A part of his own body,
    The produce of his side.

The woman was not taken
    From Adam's feet we see,
So he must not abuse her,
    That meaning seems to be.

The woman was not taken
    From Adam's head, we know,
To show she must not rule him—
    'Tis evidently so.

The woman she was taken
    From under Adam's arm,
So she must be protected
    From injuries and harm.[d]

Since my active interest in historical study which began in 1916 in centennial work, my attention was much aroused in studying this poem, and
I was astonished to read that it was claimed that Abraham Lincoln was
the author of the poem. Every verse and every line in it were familiar to
me, not from having seen it in print, (as I do not recall to have ever seen
it except in Herndon's book,) but from my earliest memory, I remember
hearing my mother recite the entire poem, so frequently that there is
even now at the age of nearly seventy-five not an unfamiliar line in the
poem. I have verified my own recollection by sending a copy of the entire poem to three persons, one 80 years old, who corroborate fully my
memory as to this fact, all of whom were in their youth members of my
own family, and heard what I heard.

At the last meeting of the executive committee of this Society, I handed
to Mrs. Albion Fellows Bacon, (my cousin, who as a young girl was much
in my mother's company,) the first volume of Herndon's book open at
page 49 upon which this poem is printed in full; and, without other
statement or any leading question, for the first time I ever mentioned

the subject to her I asked her in the presence of several persons if she remembered ever having heard that poem. After looking at it, without a moment's hesitation she said, "From your mother."

Ten years ago I could have easily produced a dozen reliable witnesses to the same point, and I have no doubt I could now find others if it were necessary.

My mother was born in 1817 in Somerham, Huntingdonshire, England, and in her fifth year came with her widowed mother to her mother's brother, John Ingle, living on a farm near Saundersville, the "Capital" of the English settlement referred to by Miss Tarbell. Soon afterwards her mother married Mark Wheeler and removed to the Wheeler settlement not far from what is now known as the Hilliard settlement.

I have shown that this settlement during the third decade of the last century contained more than 100 families, and while the Saundersville, Wheeler and Hilliard neighborhoods embraced the larger portion of these settlers, they were scattered and owned farms from across the Posey County line on the west, some distance to the east into Warrick County toward the Lincoln farm, nearer to it than the main settlement.

In this family were a large number of children of previous marriages, who had all been born in England, some of them in London where Mark Wheeler was a tradesman, some of whom were older than my mother, and she learned in her childhood and youth to recite from memory the English nursery rhymes and humorous English poetry as well as beautiful poems of Burns, Moore and Campbell, set to music, and as long as she lived, she could repeat them with much vivacity which always entertained and often amused her family and friends.[e]

Among these the poem which I remember as well as, if not better than any other, is the poem which Herndon says was composed by Abraham Lincoln.

I have always until I read this claim believed that this poem was English in its origin, and after a careful reading of Herndon's statement, I do not see any occasion to change my mind.

Full credence is given by Herndon to the statements of Mrs. Crawford, wife of Josiah Crawford, "Blue Nose" Crawford who is mentioned by him as furnishing the "few specimens of Abe's early literary efforts and much of the matter that follows in this chapter". (Ch. III.) She was an old woman whose memory was subject to the infirmities of age and the only facts she produces beyond her memory of their recitation are copies of manuscript poems preserved by her.

That Lincoln recited these poems may be conceded and this would corroborate the memory of this old woman, about all I think that should be claimed, considering the faultiness of memory in old age as to events occurring in youth; but that Lincoln wrote the poem under consideration involves evidence which Herndon does not produce.

As to the internal evidence the author of the poem mentioned wrote with a facile pen and shows some imagination and the poem contains a moral from first to last scarcely to be expected from a backwoodsman of the West living under the most primitive conditions of culture. The poem came to me in a collection of English nursery rhymes and nonsensical humor which, though crude in literary finish, had the touch of the old world civilization.

Lincoln was only seventeen years old in 1826 when his sister was married, when Mrs. Crawford says the Lincoln family sang this poem at the wedding.

Lincoln's mind was slow in developing a facile use of words in writing. Herndon elsewhere says: "Mr. Lincoln's mind was not a wide, deep, broad, generalizing, and comprehensive mind; nor versatile, quick, bounding here and there, as emergencies demanded it. His mind was deep, enduring, and strong, running in deep iron grooves, with flanges on its wheels. His mind was not keen, sharp, and subtle; it was deep, exact, and strong."

The poem copied half a dozen pages later in Volume I of Herndon, beginning with the line, "I will tell you a line about Joel and Mary," bears the internal evidence of the backwoods origin identifying also individuals by name, but the style of the two poems is very different. It seems to me that the evidence as to Lincoln's responsibility for this very coarse composition with little humor or imagination in the style is equally scant to justify the charge that Abraham Lincoln was the author of it.

I have no doubt that the poem of eight verses was recited by the young people in Mark Wheeler's family as English poetry. My mother lived in health until after Lincoln's death, and with her I traveled as a youth of sixteen from Evansville to Indianapolis to view the body of Lincoln in the state capitol where it lay in state on its way from Washington to Springfield, and I am sure that the authorship of this poem was not in her mind associated with Lincoln as the author.

If this scrap has any value, it seems to me to point to the fact that there was in some form in the twenties, a century or longer ago, a familiarity with the same current literature of this type in the Lincoln settlement and the British settlement both, and one probably obtained it from the other. Whether this poem is of English origin or not can be readily settled by proper inquiry. If it is English, the use of it by Herndon, the "authentic" historian of Lincoln, based on the testimony of one of his most "reliable" witnesses, illustrates the character and value of his history of Lincoln's life in Indiana.

In the line of Miss Tarbell's interpretation of the influence of the English settlement, I will add that when in 1823 my grandfather left Rough River in Ohio County, Kentucky, where my father was born in 1817, the English settlement was most flourishing, and probably well known in southern Indiana and in Kentucky. I do not believe that when he came to Indiana my grandfather settled by chance on the eastern edge of the English settlement.

All of his three sons, (the youngest born in Warrick County,) found their wives in the English settlement, and two out of his four daughters found their husbands there also, one of whom married John Erskine, a Scotch-Irishman and was the grandmother of Annie Fellows Johnston and Albion Fellows Bacon.

When this Society was organized, I said to my associates that if we carried out our plan as proposed, the American historians would have to come to us for the facts which we would develop. They have come sooner than I expected, particularly relating to "The Lincoln Inquiry," although the leading men in historical work and publications, in the State of Indiana also, are showing great interest in our progress and work. Upon this subject, the State Historical Commission in its announcement to Bulletin 16 uses the following language:

> Enrolled among its members are some of our ablest and most enthusiastic students and writers of Indiana history. The papers read at their regular meetings and the lines of historical investigation which are being pursued comprise one of the primary sources of our state's history.

This recognition of the character of our work and the character of our workers is a proper one, and of great satisfaction to us all.

There are present in this audience today men and women whom many of you know, worthy descendants in the third and fourth generation of pioneers of high character, who aided in founding this commonwealth. I make profert of them here today and say that their ancestors were as good a class of men and women as ever settled the beginnings of any American state.

The members of this Society present today embrace a good representation of the descendants of the pioneers who settled Indiana in its beginning, and who come of a class of people whose history has not been written, and who never had any resemblance whatever to the social class described by Rev. Baynard Hall, Edward Eggleston, and the Lincoln historians of whom I have spoken. The appeal of family pride and state pride has been one of the influences which has thrown me to the surface in historical work. The reasons why the Lincoln historians have not been able to refer to the better class of Indiana life, without which no adequate history of Abraham Lincoln in Indiana can be written, as I have clearly shown, is that no such history is available, and for the first time, this Society, which is dealing directly with the facts involved in such Lincoln inquiry, is producing the material which we hope before long will furnish the basis for the missing chapter in the life of Abraham Lincoln.

IGLEHART'S NOTES

   a.   *Indianapolis Star,* December 16, 1922.
   b.   As to the influence of Pitcher on young Lincoln, see *Indiana Magazine of History,* v. 17, p. 147.
   c.   Ed.: Ida Tarbell in her *Life of Lincoln* states that Lincoln came to Indiana in 1816 at the age of seven years.
   d.   Herndon's *Lincoln,* v. I, p. 49.
   e.   See *Indiana Magazine of History,* v. 15, p. 140, where the English Settlement is referred to on this subject.

JOHN E. IGLEHART (1848–1934) was admitted to the bar in 1869 and practiced law in Evansville. He was the founder of the Southwestern Indiana Historical Society and the Lincoln Inquiry.

LINCOLN AND SOUTHWESTERN INDIANA CHRONOLOGY

11 December 1816	Indiana became the nineteenth state. Around this time, the Lincoln family (Thomas, Nancy, Sarah, and Abraham) arrived to make their home in the new state.
12 February 1817	Abraham celebrated his eighth birthday. A few days earlier, he shot through a crack in the wall of the new cabin and killed a wild turkey. For the rest of his life, he never pulled the trigger of a gun on any larger game.
15 October 1817	Thomas Lincoln filed a land claim for his quarter section of land in the Vincennes land office. Around this time, Nancy Lincoln's aunt and uncle, Elizabeth and Thomas Sparrow, along with Dennis Hanks, settled on the Lincoln farm.
10 January 1818	The Indiana legislature created Spencer County out of Warrick and Perry counties. The Lincolns lived in Perry County up to this time.
September–October 1818	Thomas and Elizabeth Sparrow died from milk sickness.

5 October 1818	Milk sickness caused the death of Nancy Hanks Lincoln. She was buried in a coffin Thomas and Abraham made, on a hill south of the Lincoln cabin. Abraham probably attended Andrew Crawford's school later that year.
Fall 1819	A year following Nancy Lincoln's death, Thomas traveled to Kentucky to seek a new wife.
2 December 1819	Thomas and Sarah Bush Johnston were married in Elizabethtown, Kentucky. Soon Thomas, Sarah, and the Johnston children, Elizabeth, John D. and Matilda, made the trip to Spencer County and met Abraham and Sarah Lincoln.
10 March 1821	Plans were finalized for the Little Pigeon Baptist Church. Thomas Lincoln oversaw the construction.
14 June 1821	Dennis Hanks married Elizabeth Johnston.
7 June 1823	Thomas and Sarah Lincoln joined the Little Pigeon Baptist Church.
1824–1826	Around this time, Abraham attended Azel Dorsey's school. In this year, Abraham wrote in his ciphering book:

> *Abraham Lincoln is my name*
> *And with my pen I wrote the same*
> *I wrote in both hast and speed*
> *And left it here for fools to read*

Within the next couple of years, Abraham attended a school taught by James Swaney.

1825	For six to nine months during this year, Abraham worked for James Taylor at Troy on the Ohio River and operated a ferry for him across the Anderson River. While living in Troy, Lincoln came in contact with river travelers and read newspapers from up and down the river.
10 December 1825	The burial ground was laid off for the Little Pigeon Baptist Church.
8 April 1826	Abraham's sister, Sarah, joined the Little Pigeon Baptist Church.
14 September 1826	Abraham's stepsister married Squire Hall.
2 August 1826	Sarah Lincoln and Aaron Grigsby were married.
6 June 1827	Thomas Lincoln received a land patent from the US government for eighty acres. Earlier that year, he relinquished land in Spencer and Posey Counties to make this possible.
20 January 1828	Sarah Lincoln Grigsby died as a result of childbirth. She and her baby were buried in the Little Pigeon Baptist Cemetery.
April–June 1828	Abraham and Allen Gentry made a trip to New Orleans on a flatboat. They sold local produce along the way.
16 April 1829	Charles Grigsby married Matilda Hawkins and Reuben Grigsby Jr. married Elizabeth Ray. The events following these marriages led to Abraham writing *The Chronicles of Reuben*.
20 February 1830	Thomas and Sarah deeded the Spencer County farm to Charles Grigsby.

1 March 1830	After thirteen years and three months, the extended Lincoln family left Indiana for Illinois. There were thirteen members in the party.
October–November 1844	Abraham made his only return visit to Spencer County while campaigning for Whig presidential candidate Henry Clay. He also visited Vincennes, Bruceville, Washington, Rockport, and Boonville.
1846	Abraham shared with a fellow lawyer, Andrew Johnston, three poems he wrote about Indiana.
12–17 September 1865	William Herndon traveled to Spencer County to interview citizens who remembered Abraham's days in the county.
1879	Nancy Hanks Lincoln's grave site was identified and a headstone, paid for by Peter Studebaker, was placed on the grave. One-half acre of land around the grave was deeded to Spencer County.
1870s–1890s	Several curious individuals interviewed Spencer County residents to record the Indiana Lincoln history.
5 November 1900	Spencer County deeded sixteen acres around Nancy Hanks Lincoln's grave to the Nancy Hanks Lincoln Memorial Association.
8 October 1907	The Indiana General Assembly created the Board of Commissioners of the Nancy Hanks Lincoln Burial Grounds. This followed some twenty years of attempts to care for the grave area.

June 1916	A large monument was dedicated on Sarah Lincoln Grigsby's grave in the Little Pigeon Cemetery.
28 April 1917	A stone marker was erected by Spencer County on the Lincoln cabin site.
January 1920	Amateur historians founded the Southwestern Indiana Historical Society to correct the negative image of Indiana and claim the importance of Lincoln's Indiana formative years. They called this effort the Lincoln Inquiry.
1925	All authority for caring for the Nancy Lincoln grave was transferred to the Indiana Department of Conservation.
1926	Governor Ed Jackson issued invitations to 125 prominent citizens of Indiana to form the Indiana Lincoln Union. This group acquired part of the Lincoln farm, placed a cabin site memorial, and developed the Nancy Hanks Lincoln State Memorial over the next fifteen years.
1944	An impressive memorial building in the park was completed.
19 February 1962	President John F. Kennedy signed a bill making the state memorial Lincoln Boyhood National Memorial.

INDEX

Page numbers in italics refer to illustrations.

William E. "Bill" Bartelt is a Lincoln historian and retired educator. His books include *There I Grew Up*, which tells the history of Abraham Lincoln's Indiana years and helped inspire *The Better Angels*, a 2014 biographical drama-historical film about Lincoln's formative years. For many years, Bartelt worked as a ranger and historian at the Lincoln Boyhood National Memorial. He is a board member of the Abraham Lincoln Association and the Indiana Historical Society and received the Indiana Historical Society's Hoosier Historian award in 2003. Previously, Bartelt served as a member of the federal Abraham Lincoln Bicentennial Commission's Advisory and Education Committees and served as vice chair of the Indiana Abraham Lincoln Bicentennial Commission.

Joshua A. Claybourn is an attorney and author or editor of several books, including *Our American Story: The Search for a Shared National Narrative*. A widely published commentator on legal, political, and historical topics, Claybourn has also appeared as a guest on CNN, MSNBC, and NHK. He is a board member of the Abraham Lincoln Association.